Abraham

Friend of God, Father of Faith

Abraham

Friend of God, Father of Faith

Vinu V Das

Tabor Press

ISBN 978-1-997541-26-4

Table of Contents

Chapter 1 – Terah's Household: The Genealogical Tapestry

Every story finds its roots in the soil from which it springs, and Abraham's journey is no exception. Before the thunder of divine promises or the drama of faith-testing trials, there lay a family tapestry woven through generations—men and women whose lives, hopes, and struggles created the backdrop for God's unfolding plan. In this chapter, we peer beyond the familiar name of Abraham and delve into the household that shaped him: the patriarchs and matriarchs whose alliances, occupations, and worldviews formed the cultural and spiritual contours of his upbringing. Here we begin not with solitary heroism but with a network of relationships, responsibilities, and religious currents that prepared Abram to step into history as "the friend of God."

Set against the urban splendor of ancient Mesopotamia and the caravan crossroads of Haran, Terah's family navigated shifting economies, polytheistic devotion, and the weight of clan loyalty. Yet even amid idolatrous customs and the pragmatism of nomadic life, subtle threads of covenant faith ran like golden filaments through a larger fabric of tribal identity. As we trace the lineage from Shem down to Abram, we will uncover both the human strengths and foibles that echo in Abraham's own responses to the divine call. This genealogical tapestry—marked by births and deaths, marriages and migrations—reveals how God fashions instruments of promise out of ordinary family dynamics.

1.1 From Shem to Terah: The Post-Flood Lineage

1.1.1 Shem's Blessing and the Hebraic Stream

Shem, the second son of Noah, emerges from the deluge narrative as the bearer of divine blessing upon the human race. His name, meaning "name" or "renown," signifies a perpetuated reputation tied to covenant faithfulness (Gen 9:26–27). From Shem descended Arphaxad, whose own progeny would carry forward the memory of the true God in a world swarming with polytheism. The blessing pronounced upon Shem ("God shall dwell in the tents of Shem") laid the spiritual groundwork for Israel's identity as a people set apart. Hebrews would later look back to this line when defining the meaning of their name (Heb 11:9). As the narrative unfolds through Genesis 11:10–11, we trace a direct male line—Arphaxad, Shelah, Eber—each generation a fragile link preserving monotheistic devotion amid cultural drift. Eber's significance in the genealogy hints at the genesis of the term "Hebrew," reinforcing that this family, unlike its neighbors, answered to one God. Though scant personal details survive, the mere preservation of their names in Scripture underscores their role as covenant stewards. The narrative pauses at Peleg—"in his days the earth was divided" (Gen 10:25)—marking not only geographic separation of peoples but also a testing of faithful witness. Peleg's placement in the line anticipates forthcoming national distinctions, yet the blessing remains intact. The subsequent names—Reu, Serug, Nahor I—present a tapestry of lengthening lifespans and shifting cultural influences. Each patriarch bore responsibility for passing oral traditions of God's promises, though the details fade into the shadows of prehistory. By the time we arrive at Terah, eleven generations after Noah, the legacy of Shem's blessing has spanned centuries of social change. This lineage, preserved against the currents of time, forms the bedrock upon which Abraham's faith will stand.

1.1.2 Arphaxad, Selah, and Eber: The Etymology of "Hebrew"

Arphaxad's brief biblical mention belies his importance as the conduit of divine remembrance in a world increasingly enamored with idols. Although Gen 11:12–13 offers only his age at fatherhood and death, Jewish tradition credits him with establishing early tent-dwelling practices that foreshadow Abraham's pilgrim life. His son, Selah (Shelah), inherits not only the family name but also the role of oral transmitter, ensuring that narratives of Noah's covenant remained vibrant. With Eber comes a defining moment: his name becomes synonymous with those who "pass over" or "cross over"— the Hebrews—signifying a community distinct from Canaanite city-states. The etymological link between Eber and "Hebrew" highlights how identity in Scripture often emerges from ancestral milestones rather than mere geography. This terminological shift underlines a movement from tribal affiliation to a covenant people, anticipating Israel's later self-understanding. The text itself, though terse, suggests that Eber's household maintained a knowledge of Yahweh's deliverance, a treasure in an era of polytheistic proliferation. As Eber fathered Peleg, genealogical records briefly pause the naming of places, focusing instead on generational continuity. Yet the foundational role of Eber's faith heritage cannot be overstated; it set the stage for Abram's reception of a promise that would outlast physical borders. In every repetition of Eber's name, Scripture signals that covenant identity transcends time, a theme that will reemerge when Abraham stands apart from Ur of the Chaldeans.

1.1.3 Peleg's Division of the Nations and Its Impact

Peleg occupies a unique place in the genealogy: "for in his days the earth was divided" (Gen 10:25). While interpretations vary—some envisioning continental shifts, others tribal separations—the theological thrust is clear: divine sovereignty shapes human history at critical junctures. Peleg's generation witnessed the scattering at Babel (Gen 11:1–9), a cosmic caution against human pride and linguistic uniformity. Amid this fracturing of nations, the faithful line of Shem persisted, illustrating that God preserves covenant even when humanity splinters. The division under Peleg's watch highlights how cultural differentiation and divine purposes intersect; as tongues multiplied, the promise narrowed to a chosen family. Traditionally, Jewish commentators see Peleg as a pivot from global to particular focus, a transition mirrored later in Abraham's call to leave family for a divine mission. Moreover, Peleg's story alerts us that God's plan often unfolds amid human chaos, not despite it. His presence in the lineage reassures readers that covenant continuity is maintained through epochs of upheaval. By the time Terah appears, the expectation of a chosen progeny has crystallized, ready to assume its historic role. Peleg's legacy thus prefigures the narrowing arc from universal humanity to a people bearing God's name before the nations.

1.1.4 Reu, Serug, and Nahor I: Cultural Shifts toward Mesopotamian City-States

Following Peleg, Reu, Serug, and Nahor I preside over generations increasingly influenced by emerging city-state cultures in Mesopotamia. Though the biblical text offers little biographical detail (Gen 11:18–22), modern archaeology sheds light on urbanization trends that would have affected these patriarchs. Serug's era likely saw the rise of ziggurats and centralized governance, structures often dedicated to local pantheons. As leaders of a clan rooted in tent-dwelling tradition, they would have negotiated identity boundaries between nomadic faith and urban rituals. Nahor I, in particular, stands on the cusp of this cultural shift;

his name later resurfaces as that of Abraham's brother, evoking a thematic echo across centuries (Gen 22:20–24). This convergence suggests that the narrative intentionally foreshadows later family dynamics, binding the past to the promise. The lengthy lifespans recorded—well over nine hundred years in the earliest entries, declining gradually—reflect ancient worldview on human longevity before divine adjustment post-flood. Each patriarch, by maintaining generational records, acted as a custodian of covenant memory, safeguarding oral histories amid changing contexts. Their minimal narrative footprint in Scripture paradoxically amplifies their importance: they represent the "silent years" wherein faith incubates away from headline-grabbing miracles. By sustaining distinct lineage markers through eras of burgeoning local religions, these ancestors create a genealogical corridor leading directly to Terah. Their stewardship sets the stage for a family prepared to hear God's call, despite centuries of cultural entanglements.

Having traced the sacred thread from Noah's son Shem through successive generations, we now focus on Terah himself—patriarch of the clan and steward of its fraught intersection between inherited faith and prevailing idolatry.

1.2 Terah in Focus: Patriarch, Migrant, Idol-Maker?

1.2.1 Terah's Occupational Traditions in Jewish Midrash

Jewish Midrash and later Rabbinic literature portray Terah not merely as a patriarch but as an artisan of religious significance— reportedly an idol-maker by trade. These traditions, while extrabiblical, aim to dramatize the spiritual tensions within Abram's home. Terah's crafting of wooden and stone images illustrates a cultural milieu where idol worship served both economic and devotional functions. Each idol, sold or displayed, embodied a deity's power in the marketplace, reinforcing local religious identity. Terah's reputed role as temple craftsman suggests he had status and influence, shaping communal worship practices. Yet this prominence also positioned him in direct conflict with emerging monotheistic impulses, intensifying Abram's eventual rupture. The Midrash accounts of Terah's workshop—wherein a youthful Abram smashes the idols—symbolize generational confrontation between polytheism and covenant loyalty. While these stories are not canonical, they echo biblical motifs of faith tested within family structures. By examining Terah's occupational identity, we glimpse how material culture can both sustain and distort spiritual truths. This occupational legacy frames the household's religious climate, setting up the dramatic pivot wherein Abram abandons a lucrative trade for an invisible God.

1.2.2 The Move from Ur to Haran: Push-and-Pull Factors (Gen 11:31)

 Genesis 11:31 reports that Terah took Abram, Sarai, and Lot from Ur of the Chaldeans to go toward Canaan, but settled in Haran. Ancient historians debate whether this migration was prompted by economic opportunity, declining fertility of the land, or political instability. Ur's prosperity, tied to worship of the moon-god Sin, contrasts with Haran's strategic location on trade routes connecting Mesopotamia to Anatolia. Terah's decision may reflect pragmatic concerns—securing caravan income and avoiding regional conflicts. Yet divine providence uses these human motives to position Abram in a place of preparation. Haran's syncretistic religious environment, influenced by both northern and southern deities, would have presented Abram with fresh challenges to his ancestral faith. The geography of Haran, nestled near the Balikh and Khabur rivers, offered fertile grazing grounds but also cultural crosscurrents from Aramaean populations. Terah's settlement thus becomes a theological waypoint, where the promise originally spoken to Abraham will be reissued (Acts 7:4). Understanding these push-and-pull factors enriches our grasp of how God often guides through the very decisions shaped by human fear and hope.

1.2.3 Household Composition: Servants, Livestock, and Inherited Wealth

Terah's household extended far beyond a nuclear family; it included numerous servants and sizeable herds, marking him as a man of considerable means. In the ancient Near East, such wealth signified both social status and covenant responsibility—wealthy households were expected to provide hospitality and uphold communal obligations. Servants, often bound to the patriarch, formed a dependent class whose faith trajectories could mirror or diverge from their master's. Abram's command to "send away" Hagar (Gen 21:10) centuries later resonates with the fluidity of these servant-master relationships established under Terah. Livestock holdings—flocks of sheep, goats, and oxen—served as economic engines but also as cultic symbols, foreshadowing sacrificial motifs. Inheritance customs favored the firstborn, yet biblical narratives will later privilege faithfulness over birth order, as when Isaac supersedes Ishmael. Understanding the household's composition clarifies social dynamics that would later influence inheritance disputes and covenantal transitions. Terah's accumulated wealth thus sets the socioeconomic stage for Abram's call to forsake earthly riches for divine promise.

1.2.4 Terah's Lifespan and Death in Haran: Chronological Questions (Acts 7:4)

According to Genesis 11:32, Terah lived 205 years and died in Haran, after which God called Abram onward. Stephen, in Acts 7:4, suggests that Abram left Haran after Terah's death—an interpretation that invites chronological scrutiny. The LXX and MT differ slightly in lifespans and timelines, sparking scholarly debate on harmonizing these data points. Terah's death marks a dramatic family turning point: it severs paternal authority and frees Abram to heed God's call without filial obligations. Some propose that Abram's deference to his father's wishes delayed his departure, while others argue that cultural respect required his presence until Terah's passing. This familial obedience, while honorable, contrasts with the radical obedience Abram later demonstrates in leaving home at God's command. The end of Terah's life in Haran, then, can be seen as both a human constraint and a divine setup—closing one chapter of family history and opening another of covenant fulfillment. As Terah's chapter concludes, Abram stands poised at the threshold of transformative obedience, unencumbered by ancestral duties yet buoyed by the lineage he inherits.

With Terah's life and influence now fully explored, we turn to the dynamics among his children—Haran's premature death, Nahor's family, and Abram's emerging role—each shaping the household's future trajectory.

1.3 Sibling Dynamics: Nahor II, Haran, and Abram

1.3.1 Birth Order, Age Gaps, and Ancient Near-Eastern Inheritance Laws

In patriarchal Mesopotamia, birth order carried heavy legal and social implications: the firstborn son typically inherited a double portion of the estate (Deut 21:17). Haran, as the eldest, would have held preeminence in household governance, yet his early death disrupted normal inheritance flows. Nahor II, the next in line, assumed broader responsibilities for property and clan leadership, positioning him to arrange matrimonial alliances such as marrying Milcah. Abram, though politically junior, emerges in biblical narrative as spiritually preeminent—an inversion of expected primogeniture that underscores divine election. Age disparities among the brothers likely shaped their perspectives: Haran may have died in his early forties, while Abram, perhaps a decade younger, witnessed both the loss of his brother and consequent power shifts. These family changes influenced how Abram later negotiated with Lot over land (Gen 13:8), reflecting unresolved tensions about seniority and entitlement. The distortion of inheritance laws in practice foreshadows later covenant promises, where God elevates faith to override legal norms. Understanding these sibling dynamics illuminates the social backdrop against which Abraham's unique calling unfolds.

1.3.2 Haran's Early Death and Its Psychological Ripple (Gen 11:28)

Genesis 11:28 briefly notes that Haran died before his father Terah in the land of his birth. While terse, this notice carries emotional weight: the loss of an older brother would have disrupted familial cohesion and introduced trauma at an otherwise stable stage of life. Haran's death in Ur, rather than during migration, suggests a break in the family's trajectory, compelling survivors to reckon with grief amid change. Orphaned Lot, Haran's son, became Abram's ward, forging a bond that later shapes Lot's fate in Sodom. The psychological ripple of Haran's passing likely influenced Abram's protective instincts and his compassion-driven interventions—traits that recur in his diplomatic dealings with neighboring kings. Rabbinic tradition speculates that Haran's idolatry may have contributed to his demise, serving as a cautionary emblem for Abraham's own spiritual journey. Ultimately, this early death highlights the fragility of human plans and the preparedness God instills in Abram to lead a family through loss.

1.3.3 Nahor II and Milcah: Foundations of the Aramean Line (Gen 22:20–24)

Nahor II's marriage to Milcah, his niece, aligns with ancient Near-Eastern endogamous customs aimed at preserving clan property and influence. Their union produced eight children—including Bethuel, father of Rebekah—linking Abraham's line to later covenant developments in Isaac's story. The Aramean branch founded by Nahor and Milcah would become significant players in

Genesis narratives, as seen when Rebekah travels to marry Isaac (Gen 24). This interweaving of families cements kinship bonds across internal clan lines, reflecting diplomatic marriage strategies of the period. Nahor's household, firmly rooted in Haran, contrasts with Abram's pilgrimage--focused ethos, yet both strands trace back to a shared patriarchal heritage. Gen 22:20–24 underlines how these parallel lines contribute to God's broader blueprint: while one branch follows the promise through Isaac, the other disperses into Aramean tribes often interacting with Israel. The interplay of these lines underscores that divine purposes frequently involve multiple family networks, each with distinct roles in salvation history.

1.3.4 Orphaned Lot: Guardianship, Protection, and Future Entanglements

Lot, Haran's only recorded son, came under Abram's guardianship following his father's death and Terah's relocation. As a nephew and dependent, Lot occupies a liminal status: both family and servant, recipient of Abram's household religion yet participant in his uncle's flocks. This dual identity sets the stage for future tensions when resources dwindle and moral compromises arise (Gen 13:5–13). Abram's protective role toward Lot exemplifies covenant hospitality but also exposes him to responsibility for Lot's choices—most notably Lot's dwelling among the Sodomites. The episode illustrates how family loyalties can both enrich and imperil divine obedience. Lot's story, beginning here under Abram's roof, becomes a mirror for Israel's own exposure to surrounding cultures. Abram's early experiences as Lot's protector inform his diplomatic rescues later in life (Gen 14). Thus, Lot's presence in Terah's household is not a mere footnote but a formative relationship shaping Abram's leadership style and the clan's moral contours.

Having examined how sibling relationships, inheritance laws, and early loss molded Abram's immediate family, we now turn to the women of the clan—Sarai, Iscah, and Milcah—and their pivotal roles in the unfolding covenant narrative.

1.4 Matrilineal Threads: Sarai, Iscah, and the Women of the Clan

1.4.1 Sarai as Half-Sister and Wife: Legal Norms vs. Moral Tension (Gen 20:12)

Sarai's dual identity as Abram's half-sister (sharing the same father, Terah) and his wife reflects ancient Near-Eastern marriage customs designed to consolidate property and power within a clan. While legal in that context, the arrangement juxtaposes moral tension when viewed through later Mosaic prohibitions against close-kin marriage (Lev 18:9). Genesis 20:12 records Abram's candid defense to Abimelech: "She is indeed my sister; she is the daughter of my father though not of my mother." This confession underscores the complex interplay between social convention and divine ordinance. Sarai's role extended beyond marital alliance; as matriarch, she oversaw household management, hospitality protocols, and the upbringing of future covenant heirs. Her barrenness for decades—amplified by cultural stigma—created personal anguish and communal pressure, a tension that will later explode in the drama of Hagar's concubinage. Yet Sarai also functioned as Abram's confidante and partner, accompanying him through two relocations before God's promise of offspring transformed her status from barren to blessed (Gen 17:15–16). Her identity, rooted in patriarchal structures yet destined to transcend them by divine fiat, illustrates how God works through existing social norms to effect revolutionary covenant promises.

1.4.2 Iscah's Obscure Role: Rabbinic Proposals and Genealogical Gaps

Iscah appears only once in the biblical genealogy (Gen 11:29), yet Jewish tradition elevates her as a prophetess who recognized God's voice and foresaw Abraham's destiny. Some Rabbis equate Iscah with Sarah, suggesting her early spiritual insight earned Abraham's notice. Whether historical or interpretive embellishment, this rabbinic elevation points to the scriptural acknowledgment that women's spiritual perceptions often operate behind the scenes of patriarchal narratives. The absence of further biblical detail about Iscah highlights how genealogies can conceal as much as reveal, prompting communities of faith to fill gaps with oral traditions that honor unrecorded figures. As a sister-aunt figure, Iscah's presence in Terah's line reinforces that the covenant's spiritual heart was not confined to the male line. Her prophetic attribution serves as a reminder that God's call frequently intersects with individuals predisposed to spiritual sensitivity, regardless of their gender or social standing.

1.4.3 Milcah's Bridge to Rebekah and Laban (Gen 24:15; 29:5)

Milcah, Nahor II's wife and Sarah's niece, stands at a nexus between Abraham's branch and the family of Isaac's eventual bride. Gen 22:20–24 introduces her as mother of Bethuel, Rebekah's father, while Gen 24:15 and 29:5 depict Rebekah's and Laban's roles in continuing Abraham's covenant story. Milcah's offspring thus become key actors in the marriage arrangements that secure Isaac's lineage. Her Aramean heritage injects cultural diversity into the Abrahamic family, illustrating God's use of cross-clan alliances to advance redemptive history. The hospitality customs Milcah's household practiced would later be mirrored in Rebekah's willingness to water Abraham's servant's camels, a pivotal act of faith (Gen 24:45). Through Milcah, the narrative emphasizes that covenant continuity often depends on the faith and actions of women operating within relational networks. The link from Milcah to Rebekah also foreshadows the later influence of Laban—whose greeds and deceptions test Jacob but ultimately serve God's

25

purposes (Gen 29–31). Milcah's matrilineal thread thus weaves forward, reminding readers that divine intentions often unfold through extended family bonds.

1.4.4 The Importance of Matrilocal Alliances in Maintaining Covenant Purity

In ancient Near-Eastern societies, marriages often involved matrilocal arrangements—brides residing with their natal families until establishing their own households. Such customs could bolster clan solidarity and ensure bride-price transactions remained transparent. For Abram's clan, alliances through Sarai, Iscah, and Milcah reinforced intrafamily cohesion while exposing the household to external cultural influences. Yet God's covenantal design demanded both purity and expansion: Abraham's seed would emerge from within while blessing all nations beyond his immediate kin. Matrilocal alliances thus serve as microcosms of the wider tension between separation and mission. When Sarai sends Hagar back to her Egyptian mistress (Gen 16), it illustrates consequences when these alliances stretch beyond God's timing. Conversely, Rebekah's willingness to leave Haran for Canaan (Gen 24:58) demonstrates faith aligning with divine promises. By examining these matrilineal bonds, we see how women's movements between homes both preserve covenant identity and facilitate its geographic spread. The household boundaries these alliances establish are pivotal arenas where divine faithfulness meets human initiative.

Having explored the vital roles of Terah's daughters and daughters-in-law in shaping the covenant community, we will next consider the spiritual atmosphere of Ur and Haran, where competing deities and emergent monotheism set the stage for Abraham's radical call.

1.5 Household Deities and Hidden Faith: Spiritual Atmosphere in Ur and Haran

1.5.1 Moon-God Nanna/Sin Cult and Its Symbols in Ur and Haran

The city of Ur stood as the preeminent center for the worship of the moon-god Nanna (also called Sin), whose ziggurat towered over the Euphrates valley and dominated civic life. Daily offerings of incense and lambs consecrated to Nanna were carried out by priests and supported by artisans like Terah, whose reputation as an idol-maker linked him directly to temple economies. Astrological omens deciphered by temple scribes shaped political decisions, binding families—including Terah's—to a worldview in which cosmic forces governed human fates. In Haran, echoes of Ur's moon-cult persisted alongside regional storm-deity worship, creating a polytheistic tapestry that left little room for exclusive devotion to Yahweh. Idols carved from wood or stone bore the iconography of crescent moons and bull-horned crowns, symbols that communicated divine favor and protection. Children of the clan would have grown accustomed to daily ritual processions, where they learned both the practical skills of trade and the religious presuppositions of Mesopotamian theology. Abram himself later reacts against this heritage, suggesting its hold remained powerful even as he pursued the invisible God (Heb 11:1). Texts from Ebla and Mari corroborate the economic importance of temple estates in the third millennium BC, indicating that Terah's livelihood was inseparable from the cultic system. Yet within this environment, small clandestine gatherings may have preserved stories of Shem's God, hinting at underground currents of monotheism. These quiet remembrances would have provided Abram with a counter-narrative to the dominant pagan rites. The ubiquity of lunar symbols, then, serves as a stark backdrop against which Yahweh's later revelation shines in startling contrast.

1.5.2 Joshua 24:2 on Terah's Idolatry: Textual and Theological Analysis

When Joshua addresses Israel at Shechem, he recounts, "Your fathers... served other gods" and specifically mentions Terah, Abraham's father, as one who "served other gods" (Josh 24:2). This retrospective indictment situates Terah within a lineage of spiritual waywardness, highlighting the radical nature of Abraham's subsequent call. The terse biblical citation invites readers to probe deeper: why emphasize Terah's idolatry when recounting Israel's history? Theologically, it underscores that covenant faith must break decisively with ancestral sins. By invoking Terah's worship of wood and stone, Joshua demonstrates God's sovereign grace in rescuing a family from generational bondage to falsehood. Rabbinic commentaries suggest Joshua chose Shechem—a former Canaanite religious center—to contrast pagan high places with Abraham's altars, reinforcing the text's polemical thrust. In this light, Terah's household becomes emblematic of human religiosity detached from divine truth. The narrative placement in Joshua forms a literary bracket around Abraham's story, framing it as the decisive turning point from idolatry to covenant fidelity. Modern scholars debate whether this mention serves historiographical or homiletical purposes, but its impact remains clear: Abraham's obedience reverses an inherited pattern of spiritual drift. As subsequent generations remember Terah's error, they also celebrate God's initiative in calling Abram out of the darkness into covenant light.

1.5.3 Embers of Monotheism: Possible Oral Traditions from Shem

Amid the clamor of idol worship, the possibility remains that faint embers of pure monotheism burned within Terah's extended family, passed down from Shem through Eber. These precious fragments of oral tradition likely recounted the deluge narrative and Noah's covenant, preserving the silhouette of a single Creator. Patriarchs

28

such as Arphaxad and Selah may have served as guardians of these memories, recounting to their descendants the divine promise to never again destroy the earth (Gen 9:11). In Terah's household, these stories could have been whispered during tent gatherings or encoded in genealogical recitations. Archaeological findings of small, undecorated shrines in the countryside hint at informal worship spaces that predated grand temple cults. Such locales may have provided faithful families with refuge from mainstream polytheism. Abram later demonstrates familiarity with these traditions, as evidenced by his immediate willingness to set up altars in Canaan (Gen 12:7). The retention of covenantal lore, despite centuries of cultural assimilation, testifies to the resiliency of God's word within human hearts. By contrast with the public spectacle of idol worship, these private remembrances reveal how spiritual truth can persist in the margins, prepared to burst forth when God calls.

1.5.4 Preparing the Soil for Yahweh's Epiphany

The convergence of public idolatry and private monotheistic hope in Ur and Haran formed a fertile—but challenging—ground for God's impending revelation. Just as agrarian fields require plowing and preparation before planting, the spiritual terrain of Terah's household needed breaking before new life could take root. The tension between clashing worldviews—visible idols versus invisible promise—created a crisis of identity that Abram would soon resolve by embracing the latter. The presence of covenant whispers sustained him through Haran's diverse religious currents until God spoke directly, promising land and descendants (Gen 12:1–3). Terah's own spiritual vacillation, evidenced by his continued idol-making even as hints of true worship persisted, models the human struggle between inherited patterns and divine invitation. This intricate tapestry of devotion and drift set the stage for Yahweh's dramatic entrance into history, demonstrating that God often works through relational networks and cultural fault lines. As Malachi later laments Israel's return to idolatry, the memory of Abraham's departure from his father's gods stands as both warning and exemplar (Mal 2:10–11). With the soil now tilled by centuries of practice and hope, the time is ripe for the covenant seed to be planted in Abram's heart.

Having surveyed the spiritual milieu in which Abraham was raised, we now turn to the legal and social frameworks that governed Terah's clan—structures that shaped family dynamics and foreshadowed covenant administration.

1.6 Legal and Social Structures of the Terahite Clan

1.6.1 Patriarchal Authority and Clan Councils

In Terah's time, the patriarch wielded ultimate authority over household decisions, from land use to dispute resolution. Clan councils—comprising elder sons, married daughters-in-law, and senior servants—met under the patriarch's roof to adjudicate matters ranging from grazing rights to marital contracts. Decisions were guided by customary laws rather than codified statutes, yet principles of justice and hospitality were prized virtues (cf. Lev 19:33–34). The patriarch's word was both final judgment and covenantal promise, binding kin and dependents alike to collective responsibilities. Abram's later negotiations with Lot over pastureland (Gen 13:8) reflect his seasoned familiarity with such councils, demonstrating deference tempered by prophetic insight. Women's voices, especially those of matriarchs, carried weight in domestic councils, influencing choices on alliances and migrations. The absence of formal bureaucracy meant that loyalty networks were personal and fluid, yet they provided a semblance of order in a nomadic-agrarian economy. Elders interpreted omens or divine signs before major moves, blending the spiritual and social in governance. This patriarchal framework ensured continuity of property and faith traditions across generations. As we examine inheritance customs next, we see how these councils balanced competing claims with the overarching aim of clan survival.

1.6.2 In-House Adoption Practices: Servants as Heirs (cf. Gen 15:2)

When a patriarch lacked biological offspring, in-house adoption offered a solution to lineage continuity. Servants, often young men raised within the household from childhood, could be designated heirs, inheriting property and spiritual responsibilities. Abram's own anxiety over barrenness emerges in God's reassurance that an "offspring" from his own body would be his heir, contrasting with the common practice of adopting a servant as in Gen 15:2. This practice underscores how closely economic sustenance and covenant identity were intertwined. Adoption ceremonies involved symbolic acts—such as blessing and name-giving—mirroring divine adoption themes later echoed in New Testament theology (Eph 1:5). Servant-heirs were expected to uphold household deities and cultic obligations, reinforcing the patriarch's authority beyond his lifetime. However, these arrangements could spark conflict, as seen when Hagar's son Ishmael threatens Isaac's place until divine intervention resolves the dispute (Gen 21:9–12). The tension between servant inheritance and promise-born succession highlights God's radical reordering of human expectations. Adoption customs, while pragmatic, proved inadequate to contain Yahweh's expansive covenant plan, pointing forward to adoption by grace through faith (Rom 8:15).

1.6.3 Bride-Price Economics and Dowry Transfers

Marriages within Terah's clan adhered to bride-price and dowry customs that secured alliances and transmitted wealth. A prospective husband offered a bride-price to her family, compensating for loss of labor and affirming his capacity to provide. Conversely, the dowry—goods or livestock brought by the bride—bolstered the husband's household economy. When Nahor's children intermarried (Gen 22:20–24), these exchanges strengthened intra-clan bonds, ensuring property remained within extended family lines. Sarai's marriage to Abram likely involved similar negotiations, though the narrative frames it primarily as a half-sister union. The material dimensions of such contracts underscored marriage's dual nature as both spiritual covenant and economic partnership. Disputes over bride-price could lead to long-standing feuds, making elders' mediation crucial. In stipulating that a wife remained under her husband's guardianship until widowhood or divorce, these customs both protected women and reinforced patriarchal control. As Abram steps into God's promise, his readiness to send Hagar away (Gen 21:10) demonstrates how bride-price dynamics could be overridden by divine command, exposing the limits of human contractual frameworks.

1.6.4 Covenant-Making Customs Prefiguring Divine Covenants

Long before Sinai, Mesopotamian clans observed covenant-making rituals that foreshadow biblical analogues. These "cutting of the covenant" ceremonies involved solemn meals, animal sacrifices, and binding oaths—acts that communicated mutual obligations and divine witness. Abram's own covenant-meal with God in Genesis 15 (Gen 15:9–21) mirrors these practices: he brings animals, cuts them in two, and witnesses a blazing torch pass between the pieces. Whereas human covenants required two participants to walk between offerings, here only God appears, underscoring divine initiative. Terah's community, familiar with such rites, would have recognized the solemnity of Abram's encounter, even if its unilateral nature was unprecedented. Covenant meals in the household also accompanied adoption ceremonies and marriage contracts, embedding the idea that sacred promises create new kinship bonds. These customs provided the template upon which Yahweh would later expand, culminating in Israel's national covenant at Sinai. By highlighting pre-Israelite covenant forms, we see how God meets humanity in existing cultural frameworks before transcending them with transformative revelation.

With legal and social structures illuminating the fabric of Terah's clan life, we now shift our focus to the very landscapes—Ur, Haran, and the Fertile Crescent—through which this family migrated and upon which their story unfolded.

1.7 The Geographic Axis: Ur, Haran, and the Fertile Crescent Corridors

1.7.1 Ur of the Chaldeans: Urban Planning, Ziggurats, and Trade Routes

Ur's grandeur lay in its meticulously planned streets, mud-brick houses, and the towering Great Ziggurat dedicated to Nanna. Archaeological excavations reveal residential districts organized around courtyard homes, indicating strong emphasis on family compounds. Granaries, workshops, and temple precincts ringed the central plaza, reflecting a city whose economy blended agriculture with long-distance commerce. Caravans bearing textiles, metals, and exotic goods traversed the Euphrates corridor, connecting Ur to Dilmun, Magan, and distant Anatolia. Terah's household, likely owning livestock herds, would have contributed to this market system, exchanging wool and dairy for grain and pottery. Urban density also fostered social stratification: priestly elites, merchants, and artisans coexisted with agricultural laborers. The city's cosmopolitan character exposed its inhabitants to myriad religious influences, underscoring the cultural pressures that Abram would renounce. Yet Ur's prosperity and sophistication also provided skills in administration and building that later manifested in Abram's establishment of camps and altars. By mapping this urban center, we appreciate both the material wealth and the spiritual complexities confronting Abraham's family.

1.7.2 The Balikh and Khabur Rivers: Reasons Haran Became a Caravan Hub

Haran's strategic location beside the Balikh and Khabur rivers made it a natural nexus for trade routes linking Mesopotamia, Anatolia, and the Levant. Seasonal floods enriched valley soils, supporting flocks and orchards that sustained caravans passing through. Inns and caravanserai sprang up along these rivers, offering security to merchants braving bandits and extreme weather. Terah's decision to settle here (Gen 11:31) suggests an astute recognition of Haran's commercial advantages. The intermixed Aramaean tribes contributed linguistic and cultural diversity, creating multilingual markets where Akkadian, Aramaic, and early Semitic tongues coexisted. Religious syncretism thrived as merchants carried idols from foreign lands, while local deities gained new adherents. Amid this flux, Abram's call to separate himself foreshadows his later commitment to set apart Israel from competing spiritual influences. Haran's geography thus functioned as both economic boon and spiritual crucible, testing the household's fidelity to ancestral traditions.

1.7.3 Climate, Famine, and Nomadic Pressures Shaping Migration Decisions

The Fertile Crescent, though verdant, experienced cyclical droughts and famines that pushed settled families toward pastoralism. Periodic crop failures forced many clans to adopt nomadic or semi-nomadic lifestyles, following seasonal pastures. Terah's move from Ur to Haran may have been prompted by such environmental stressors, as scholars correlate archaeological evidence of a south Mesopotamian drought in the early second millennium BC. Nomadic pressures also facilitated interactions with desert peoples skilled in survival techniques—knowledge Abram would later apply in navigating the Negev. Famine narratives recur in Genesis (Gen 12:10; 26:1), highlighting how dependence on divine provision contrasted sharply with human contingency plans. Abram's willingness to descend into Egypt during famine (Gen 12:10) underscores his pragmatic response to environmental realities. Yet the pattern of hunger-driven migration sets the stage for God's promise of a land "flowing with milk and honey" (Ex 3:8), a pledge that transcends ecological uncertainty.

1.7.4 Strategic Positioning for God's Next Instruction

The intersection of trade routes, river valleys, and climatic factors rendered Terah's household ideally situated to receive God's call with maximum relational impact. Haran's connectivity meant that news of Abram's journey would ripple through multiple kingdoms, laying groundwork for the Abrahamic covenant's eventual global reach. From this vantage point, Abram could witness first-hand the limits of human planning, encountering both wealth and want, faith and falsehood. The plateau north of Mesopotamia offered open vistas for pilgrim camps, while still within reach of familiar comforts. Such positioning mirrors the later placement of Israel between Babylon and Egypt—nations whose histories would intertwine with Abraham's legacy. As God commands Abram to "go" (Gen 12:1), the physical geography underscores the radical departure required: leaving fertile corridors for unknown frontiers. This strategic backdrop thus transforms from mere setting into theological symbol, illustrating how God ordains the very landscapes through which His purposes advance.

With the geographic and social canvases fully rendered, our attention turns next to Abram himself—shaped by these forces yet called beyond them to a destiny that transcends earthly maps.

1.8 Literary Genealogies: From Genesis to Chronicles

1.8.1 Stylistic Features of Semitic Genealogical Lists

Semitic genealogies in Genesis present names and ages with rhythmic precision, emphasizing divine providence through generational succession (Gen 5; 11). Each entry follows a consistent formula—"When X had lived Y years, he fathered Z; and after he fathered Z, he lived A years and had other sons and daughters"—underscoring continuity and stability in God's unfolding plan. The repetition of life spans cultivates a sense of sacred time, where human history unfolds under divine sovereignty. Variations in the formula, such as the omission of "and had other sons and daughters" in later chapters, signal editorial shifts or thematic refocus. Hebrew parallelism appears as patriarchs live "X years" then "another Y years," reinforcing balance between their covenant duties and personal longevity. The genealogies often group ten names—a pattern that resonates with symbolic completeness in ancient Near-Eastern thought. Sparse narrative detail within these lists invites readers to ponder the hidden lives behind the names, encouraging faith in what lies beyond recorded history. The lists function less as mere ancestry charts and more as theological statements: God preserves a family line for covenant fulfillment. Scribal redactors employed chiasm and numerical structuring to link genealogies with broader themes, such as blessing through the tenth generation. This literary artistry aligns with ancient epics, yet Scripture repurposes such techniques to point readers toward Yahweh rather than pagan heroes. The genealogical sections serve as compositional anchors, dividing primeval history from patriarchal narratives while maintaining narrative momentum. Their placement at critical junctures signals transitions from creation and flood to promise and pilgrimage. These features reflect an intentional blending of form and function, where genealogical data convey theological truth. As we move to consider how the ten-generation formula shaped Israel's self-understanding, we see Scripture's literary craft in full view.

1.8.2 The Ten-Generation Formula and Its Theological Function

The recurring motif of ten generations from Adam to Noah (Gen 5) and again from Shem to Abraham (Gen 11) frames the primeval and pre-Abrahamic epochs with symmetrical precision. Ten functions as a number of completeness and divine order within both biblical and broader Mesopotamian symbolism. This decadal structure underscores that Abraham's arrival marks the culmination of God's preparatory work through preceding patriarchs. By positioning Abraham as the tenth link in the Shem-to-Terah line, the text highlights him as the divinely appointed fulcrum between dispersed humanity and covenant community. The theological function of ten emerges also in the ten commandments (Ex 20) and tithe practices (Lev 27:30), suggesting a rhythmic pattern to covenant life. Within Genesis, the ten-generation pattern conveys that God's timing is purposeful: promises mature precisely when prior stewardship has run its course. This literary device imparts a sense of destiny to Abraham's calling, as if cosmic history were calibrated to his obedience. Moreover, the ten-generation frame gives readers confidence that genealogical gaps and narrative ellipses do not represent oversight but rather divine conciseness. This compression invites meditation on the mystery between recorded names—what faith looked like in the lives of semi-anonymous forebears. The formula also reinforces covenant solidarity: just as ten gates in ancient cities provided protection, ten generations safeguard God's promise until it emerges in covenant form. As we compare these features to later editorial work in Chronicles, we gain insight into how Israel shaped its identity through carefully curated ancestry.

1.8.3 Comparison with 1 Chronicles 1:24–27: Editorial Purposes

In 1 Chronicles 1:24–27, the Chronicler revisits the Genesis genealogy with slight adjustments—names harmonized, variant spellings normalized, and some ages recalculated. This editorial retelling serves theological aims: to present Israel's history as continuous and divinely orchestrated from creation through monarchy. The Chronicler omits certain names found in Genesis, such as Joktan, focusing instead on the line most directly connected to Davidic kingship. Such selectivity underscores the Chronicler's emphasis on legitimacy and covenant fidelity through David's house. The prose style in Chronicles, more uniform and less repetitive, suggests a later scribal effort to streamline genealogical material for post-exilic audiences seeking restored identity. By truncating extended lifespans and adjusting genealogical sequences, the Chronicler signals that theological clarity may supersede strict historical detail. Yet the essential message—God's preservation of a sacred line—remains intact. This editorial work resonates with Ezra's and Nehemiah's concerns for reestablishing communal boundaries and worship practices in Jerusalem. The Chronicler thus transforms early genealogies into foundational texts for restored Israel, demonstrating how Scripture's compositional history itself participates in covenant renewal. As readers compare Genesis and Chronicles, they discern a dynamic interplay between memory, identity, and divine promise. With this understanding of biblical editorial artistry, we can appreciate how covenant memory is transmitted across diverse literary contexts.

1.8.4 Transmission of Covenant Memory through Genealogy

Genealogies functioned in ancient Israel as spoken liturgies, recited during festivals and taught to children to embed covenant identity deeply within communal consciousness. Lists of forebears served as mnemonic devices, enabling laypersons and priests alike to recall divine promises and past deliverances. Within Terah's household, such recitations likely occurred around evening fires, where patriarchs named ancestors to preserve oral history. This practice ensured that covenant faith remained alive even when written texts were scarce. The act of naming each generation invited reflection on God's faithfulness: each patrilineal link testified to divine preservation amid cultural upheaval. Moreover, genealogical recitations intersected with legal claims to land and leadership, reinforcing that covenant inheritance was both spiritual and material. As Israel matured, genealogical registers regulated priestly succession and tribal boundaries, rooting worship in ancestral legitimacy (Num 3; 1 Chron 24). The communal reading of genealogies on Sabbaths bound individuals to a corporate narrative, transcending personal identity. This transmission of memory also shaped Messianic expectations, as each generation awaited the promised seed. Thus, genealogies served as living tapestries— woven narratives that kept covenant hope ever before God's people. Having traced the literary and theological dimensions of genealogy, we now turn to how Abraham's lineage becomes the conduit for Messianic promise.

With the mechanics of covenant memory in view, we shift to explore how Terah's line foreshadows Christ, fulfilling Israel's deepest hopes.

1.9 Messianic Trajectory: How Terah's Line Points to Christ

1.9.1 Matthew 1:1–2 and Luke 3:34: Dual Testaments, Single Line

The Gospel of Matthew opens with a genealogy that deliberately begins, "The book of the genealogy of Jesus Christ, son of David, son of Abraham" (Matt 1:1), anchoring Jesus in Abraham's faith heritage. Matthew traces fourteen generations from Abraham to

39

David, fourteen from David to the Babylonian exile, and fourteen from the exile to Christ—an intentional structuring reminiscent of Genesis' decadal patterns. By contrast, Luke's genealogy (Luke 3:23–38) works in reverse, moving from Jesus back to Adam, yet it still intersects with Abraham at the ten-generation mark (Luke 3:34). These dual genealogies affirm that both Jewish and Gentile audiences recognize Jesus as the culmination of God's covenant with Abraham. Matthew's emphasis on Abraham first underscores legal entitlement to promise territory, while Luke's Adam-ward trace universalizes Jesus' messianic mission. The convergence at Abraham highlights that salvation history pivots on Terah's grandson, not merely as ethnic inheritance but as theological fulfillment. These New Testament authors, by echoing the structure of ancient genealogies, validate the scriptural tradition that God's redemptive work spans ages through a singular lineage. The messianic trajectory thus bridges Testaments, demonstrating that Christ stands firmly upon the foundation laid in Terah's household.

1.9.2 "Son of David, Son of Abraham": Linking Royal and Patriarchal Promises

The dual titling of Jesus as "Son of David, Son of Abraham" (Matt 1:1) weaves together two strands of Israel's hope: royal restoration and covenantal blessing. The Davidic promise (2 Sam 7:12–16) guaranteed an enduring throne, while the Abrahamic covenant (Gen 12:2–3) promised worldwide blessing through his seed. Jesus' identification with both fulfills prophetic anticipations—Isaiah's vision of a righteous shoot from Jesse (Isa 11:1) and Genesis' promise that in Abraham all families of the earth would be blessed (Gen 22:18). By invoking both lineages, the Gospels affirm Jesus as Israel's long-awaited Messiah, embodying the fullness of royal authority and covenant faithfulness. Early Christians preached this unity in Acts, arguing that Jesus' Davidic descent authenticated His messianic claim before Jewish audiences (Acts 13:23). Simultaneously, they proclaimed that Gentiles share in Abraham's blessing by faith (Gal 3:14). This composite title thus encapsulates the Gospel's core: Jesus reigns as king and redeemer, expanding Abraham's family to include every believer.

1.9.3 Typology of Exile and Return Foreshadowing Redemption

The exile motif, first hinted in Terah's departure from Ur, becomes a central typology in biblical theology: God's people leave homeland, experience alienation, and return under divine mercy. Abraham's journey from Haran to Canaan prefigures Israel's later exodus and return from Babylon, as well as the individual sinner's exile and restoration. New Testament writers adopt this typology to describe spiritual exile—believers estranged from God by sin—and return to fellowship through Christ's atoning work (Eph 2:12–13). The genealogical link from Abraham through David to Jesus thus charts a redemptive arc: out of foreign lands into promised relationship, culminating in the ultimate homecoming in God's kingdom. Hebrews draws on this pattern, portraying believers as "strangers and exiles on the earth" looking forward to a "better country" (Heb 11:13–16). Each generation in Terah's line both experiences and points toward this movement, making the messianic hope tangible across time.

1.9.4 Faith-Lineage vs. Blood-Lineage in Pauline Thought (Rom 4:11–17)

Paul revolutionizes the concept of lineage by asserting that true descendants of Abraham are not defined by physical descent but by sharing Abraham's faith (Rom 4:11–12). In Romans 4:11–17, he contrasts the "sign of circumcision" given to Abraham with the promise of righteousness credited to the uncircumcised, emphasizing that faith, not law or blood, secures covenant membership. This theological move democratizes Abraham's blessing, extending it to Gentiles who trust in Christ. Paul's argument hinges on Scripture's portrayal of Abraham as justified by faith (Gen 15:6), positioning him as prototype for all believers. The apostle thereby reframes the genealogical tapestry: its ultimate value lies in fostering faith lineage rather than mere genetic heritage. This shift undergirds New Covenant theology, where the church comprises spiritual offspring of Abraham (Gal 3:7–9). By reinterpreting Abraham's line through the lens of faith, Paul unites Jew and Gentile into one family, fulfilling the promise that Abraham would be "father of many nations" (Gen 17:5).

Conclusion Our exploration of Terah's household has shown that the roots of Abraham's faith run deep into a complex soil of family loyalties, cultural pressures, and half-remembered whispers of one true God. We have seen how stories of idolatry and exile, of sibling rivalry and dynastic marriages, served not to diminish the promise but to highlight its radical origin: a call to step out of the known into an unseen reality. In these ancestral currents, God's future covenant with Abraham already casts shadows—promises of land, of offspring, of blessing that transcend every human limitation.

As we leave behind the bazaars of Ur and the caravan routes of Haran, the stage is set for a dramatic encounter between heaven and earth. It is here, at the perimeter of Torch-lit altars and family tents, that God summons Abram to abandon the safety of inherited patterns and embrace a promise defined not by lineage alone but by divine initiative. The faith of his forebears, both bright and fractured, prepares him for a journey that will redefine nationhood and reshape redemptive history.

In the chapters ahead, we will follow Abraham as he heeds that summons—crossing deserts, negotiating with kings, and wrestling with doubts even as he clings to celestial assurances. But none of that is possible without first understanding the intricate tapestry from which he sprang. With his roots now unveiled, we turn to the man himself: Abram of Ur, a pilgrim called to walk by faith into the vast unknown of God's unfolding plan.

Chapter 2 – Before the Call: Abram in Mesopotamia

Before Abram ever heard the summons of the Almighty, his life revolved around bustling city markets, fertile fields, and the rituals that punctuated each Mesopotamian season. In Ur's grand courtyards and Haran's caravanserai, he learned the rhythms of trade, the hierarchies of temple worship, and the fragility of human plans when faced with drought or dynastic upheaval. Yet even amid the clamor of ziggurat festivals and the logic of family councils, Abram's heart stirred with questions no idol could answer, and his spirit longed for a promise that transcended the barter of goods and the rites of local deities. These formative years, spent balancing livestock accounts by day and listening to whispers of ancestral covenants by night, forged in him a resilience and restlessness that prepared him for the greatest journey of faith in history.

2.1 Ur of the Chaldeans: A World City on the Euphrates

2.1.1 Civic Layout and Ziggurat Districts

Ur's urban plan centered on a massive ziggurat complex dedicated to the moon-god Nanna, whose tiered structure dominated the skyline and served as both temple and administrative center. The ziggurat platform rose in successive receding terraces, each supporting shrines and offering spaces for priests to perform daily rituals. Surrounding the temple precinct lay courtyards paved with fired brick, where public festivals and royal proclamations took place. Beyond this sacred core, the city unfolded in concentric rings: the inner ring housed elite residences and government offices, while the outer ring contained artisan workshops, merchants' stalls, and commoners' dwellings. Streets ran in a rectilinear grid, intersecting at public squares that functioned as marketplaces for grain, textiles, and livestock. Wells and cisterns dotted the neighborhoods, ensuring access to water in an arid climate. City walls, reinforced by towers at regular intervals, provided defense against nomadic raiders but also symbolized communal identity. Sewage channels ran beneath major thoroughfares, a testament to sophisticated public works and concern for sanitation. Processional avenues connected the ziggurat to city gates, facilitating pilgrimages from surrounding villages during major lunar festivals. Archaeological excavations have unearthed inscribed boundary stones marking property divisions, illustrating the legal precision of Mesopotamian urban planning. Private homes often opened onto courtyards containing family altars, indicating that domestic and civic worship coexisted. Storage magazines for surplus grain and oil clustered near the city's periphery, reflecting a planned economic reserve against famine. Urban scribes kept detailed records on clay tablets, cataloging everything from temple offerings to tax quotas. This meticulous civic layout both facilitated and reflected the complex social order in which Abram matured.

2.1.2 Social Stratification: Priests, Merchants, and Artisans

At the apex of Ur's social hierarchy stood the priestly class, whose authority derived from temple control over land and labor dedicated to Nanna's service. Priests interpreted celestial omens recorded on clay tablets, influencing royal policies and legal judgments. Beneath them, temple administrators managed vast estates worked by dependent laborers, including captured war prisoners and indentured servants. Merchants formed a prosperous middle tier, organizing long-distance caravans that transported tin from Anatolia and lapis lazuli from Afghanistan. They negotiated treaties with city-state rulers along trade routes, securing safe passage in exchange for tribute. Artisans—potters, metalworkers, textile weavers—populated artisan quarters, supplying both temple needs and urban markets. Skilled craftsmen like Terah likely held esteemed positions, producing iconographic idols and household goods for wealthier families. Common laborers and agricultural workers occupied the lowest rung, living in simpler mud-brick dwellings outside the inner walls. Social mobility existed but was limited; a successful merchant could, over generations, purchase land or marry into higher strata. Women's roles varied by class: priestly women served in temple rituals, while merchant wives managed domestic finances and textile production. Children inherited their parents' status, but apprenticeship systems provided avenues for skill acquisition across classes. Legal codes such as the Code of Ur-Nammu formalized penalties and restitution, underscoring the social responsibilities of each group. Civic festivals temporarily blurred class distinctions, allowing commoners to participate in public worship alongside elites. This stratified environment shaped Abram's worldview, exposing him to both privilege and the plight of the marginalized.

2.1.3 Agricultural Hinterlands and Irrigation Systems

Ur's prosperity depended on extensive irrigation networks diverting Euphrates waters into canals feeding fields of barley, dates, and sesame. Canals required regular maintenance overseen by temple authorities, who mobilized labor gangs during the dry season. Dykes and sluice gates controlled floodwaters, ensuring silt-rich deposits replenished soil fertility each year. Date palms grew along canal banks, providing shade and exportable fruit used in offerings and trade. Peasant families lived in villages along feeder canals, paying tribute in grain and labor in lieu of taxes. Herds of sheep and goats grazed on reclaimed marshlands, producing wool traded in distant markets. Temple granaries stored tithes—one-tenth of each harvest—serving as famine reserves and redistribution centers during lean years. Seasonal festivals marked planting and harvest cycles, integrating agricultural rhythms with religious observance. Excavated seed deposits show crop diversity, indicating deliberate crop rotation to prevent soil exhaustion. Clay envelopes containing agricultural contracts and debt records reveal tensions between peasant borrowers and creditor temples. Irrigation-induced salinization posed long-term challenges, prompting experimental drainage ditches and fallow periods. These ecological dynamics influenced population movements, as failing plots drove families toward urban centers or nomadic pastures. Abram's later experience of famine-driven migration (Gen 12:10) echoes these historical patterns, illustrating how environmental pressures shaped Mesopotamian society. The sophistication of Ur's agricultural systems thus formed the material foundation for the household into which Abram was born.

Having surveyed the city that formed Abram's earliest horizons, we now turn to his immediate household—Terah's compound in Ur— where domestic rhythms and family structures further shaped his character.

2.2 Terah's Compound in Ur: Household Economy and Daily Rhythms

2.2.1 Livestock Management, Textile Production, and Trade Ledgers

Terah's household maintained sizable flocks of sheep and goats, managed by herdsmen who oversaw breeding cycles and grazing rotations. Wool from these animals fed into a dedicated textile workshop, where spinners and weavers produced cloth for trade and domestic use. Dyes derived from madder root and indigo traded with Anatolian merchants added value to the finished textiles. Surplus fabric was bargained in Ur's market squares for grain, pottery, and metal implements, illustrating a self-sustaining micro-economy. Trade ledgers inscribed on clay tablets recorded each transaction, noting the weight of goods, names of parties, and agreed exchange rates. Scribes trained in cuneiform maintained these accounts, ensuring transparency and reducing disputes over debts. Yields and profits were tallied annually during New Year festivals, when offerings were recalibrated according to the household's wealth. The same flocks provided milk, cheese, and lamb for domestic consumption and temple sacrifices. Herd migrations followed seasonal cycles, with sheep driven to higher pastures during the hot months. This integrated system of animal husbandry, textile manufacture, and record-keeping instilled in Abram both practical skills and an appreciation for meticulous stewardship. It also exposed him to the interdependence of household and temple economies, foreshadowing his later concerns for resource allocation and justice (Gen 18:25). The blend of pastoral and artisanal livelihood cultivated adaptability in Abram, equipping him to manage flocks and negotiations across diverse cultural settings.

2.2.2 Servants, Apprentices, and the Training of Young Abram

Within Terah's compound, a network of servants and apprentices formed the household workforce, each with defined roles and status. Young Abram, as a member of the patriarch's family, partnered with senior servants to learn livestock care—a task that required patience and knowledge of animal behavior. In the textile workshop, he observed apprentices mastering the loom and tablet weaving, absorbing techniques that combined artistry with precision. Domestic servants taught him meal preparation, hospitality protocols, and the management of grain stores, responsibilities he would later replicate when hosting divine visitors (Gen 18:1–8). Apprentices in the scribal school introduced him to cuneiform symbols, opening the door to literacy uncommon among his peers. These early lessons in reading and writing clay tablets laid cognitive foundations for understanding legal covenants and genealogical records. Relations between masters and servants followed customary obligations: servants owed obedience and labor, masters granted protection and provisions. Abram's childhood exposure to this system taught him both authority and empathy, as he witnessed the precarious position of bonded workers. The apprenticeship system also fostered cross-cultural exchange, as servants from conquered regions introduced foreign naming conventions and practical skills. Through this mosaic of personal instruction, Abram developed the competencies—communication, management, and care—that undergird his later role as covenant mediator and host.

2.2.3 Extended-Family Governance and Patriarchal Decision-Making

Terah presided over a broad household encompassing his three sons, their wives, grandchildren, servants, and apprentices. His governance model combined patriarchal decree with informal counsel from senior family members—often acting as a proto-council. During crises such as famine or external threat, Terah convened elders under the family tent to deliberate options, reflecting early Mesopotamian practices of communal consultation. Decisions on migration, trade routes, and marriage alliances carried weighty consequences, and the patriarch's role was to weigh risks while preserving clan coherence. Abram observed these gatherings, internalizing principles of leadership that balanced firmness with deference to collective wisdom. Disagreements were mediated by appealing to ancestral precedents or invoking divinatory omens interpreted by temple scribes. Marital arrangements, such as Nahor's union with Milcah, exemplified these decision-making processes, intertwining economic strategy with social alliance. The patriarch also adjudicated disputes over grazing rights and inheritance shares, grounding judgments in customary law rather than written codes. This lived experience sharpened Abram's sense of justice and process, later reflected in his intercession for Sodom (Gen 18:23–32). Through extended-family governance, Abram learned that wise leadership requires listening, adaptability, and moral courage—qualities that would define his obedience to the divine call.

With the operations of Terah's household understood, we now explore Abram's formal and informal education—how cuneiform schools and folk traditions equipped him to navigate both human and divine realms.

2.3 Formal Learning and Folk Wisdom: Abram's Early Education

2.3.1 Cuneiform Schools, Mathematics, and Astral Calendars

Abram's education began in the tablet-house (é-dubba), where young nobles attended classes on cuneiform writing, arithmetic, and astronomical observation. Sumerian and Akkadian scribal schools taught numerical tables used for surveying land and calculating grain rations. Abram learned to recognize wedge-shaped impressions on clay, mastering syllabic and logographic symbols for record-keeping. Teachers introduced him to base-60 mathematics, a system that underpinned timekeeping and calendrical calculations. Understanding lunar cycles allowed accurate prediction of festivals tied to agricultural seasons. Observations of planetary conjunctions held political and religious significance, interpreted by temple scholars to forecast omens. Abram's familiarity with such methods granted him status as an informed diplomat in later interactions with foreign rulers (Gen 20). The discipline of copying lexical lists instilled patience and attention to detail. School curricula included proverbs and moral exhortations, blending technical instruction with ethical formation. Seasonal recalibrations of the calendar—

50

intercalary months inserted to align lunar and solar years—demonstrated a respect for cosmic order. By mastering these academic disciplines, Abram gained intellectual tools crucial for covenant mediation and record-keeping, foreshadowing his later role in transmitting divine promises to future generations.

2.3.2 Oral Story Cycles: Flood Traditions and Fertility Myths

Beyond formal schooling, Abram absorbed oral narratives circulated in Terah's compound—stories of the great flood, heroic demigods, and fertility deities that shaped communal memory. Elders recounted how a righteous man survived divine judgment by building a large boat, tales that resonated with Genesis' Noah account and hinted at ethical imperatives. Fertility myths celebrated agricultural renewal, featuring gods who died and rose with seasonal cycles, symbolizing hope amid uncertainty. These folk narratives coexisted uneasily with nascent monotheistic threads, prompting Abram to question divine character and purpose. Drumming and song accompanied these recitations, embedding them in sensory experience and communal identity. Abram's exposure to variant versions across regions fostered discernment between cultural myth and deeper theological truth. Layers of embellishment—such as demonic figures and cosmic battles—revealed humanity's struggle to explain suffering and injustice. Abram later repurposed elements of these stories, contrasting polytheistic caprice with Yahweh's consistent character revealed in covenant (Gen 15:6). His familiarity with widespread myths enabled him to communicate the promise in culturally intelligible terms when addressing diverse audiences. Thus, folk traditions provided both context and contrast for Abram's emerging faith.

2.3.3 Skills in Diplomacy, Herding, and Caravan Logistics

Mesopotamian society prized skills in negotiation, and Abram's upbringing equipped him for delicate interactions with tribal chieftains and city-state officials. He accompanied Terah's elder servants on caravan missions, learning route-planning, supply-chain management, and risk mitigation against banditry. Identifying reliable guides and establishing tribute agreements with local sheikhs required cultural sensitivity and strategic foresight. Abram observed bargaining techniques in bazaar negotiations, where mastery of regional dialects and gift-exchange rituals could secure favorable terms. Herding skills acquired during pastoral migrations fostered resilience and ecological awareness, as flocks required rotation across grazing lands to prevent overuse. He learned to read animal behavior, detect water sources, and respond swiftly to health crises among the herd. These competencies translated into effective leadership during later crises—for example, rescuing Lot in the War of the Four Kings (Gen 14). Caravan logistics also involved medical knowledge of local herbs and first-aid, lessons Abram would recall when negotiating with Abimelech over well rights (Gen 21:25–34). The synthesis of diplomatic acumen and pastoral expertise thus prepared Abram for calling that fused moral authority with practical governance.

Having detailed Abram's cognitive and practical training, we now examine the religious environment of Ur and Haran—how temple rites and household piety framed his search for ultimate reality.

2.4 Religious Milieu: Temples, Talismans, and Personal Piety

2.4.1 Cult of Nanna/Sin and the Lunar Festival Cycle

The cult of Nanna/Sin in Ur revolved around a twelve-month lunar festival cycle, each month inaugurated by sighting the new moon. Priests performed elaborate rites—animal sacrifices, libations of beer and oil, and hymns praising the deity's perceived influence over fertility and fate. Abram's household participated indirectly through offerings delivered to temple courts by designated lodgers. Temple scribes maintained ritual calendars on clay prisms, dictating when specific ceremonies should occur. Festivals attracted pilgrims from distant regions, infusing Ur with cultural diversity and commerce. Observing these sacred rhythms taught Abram the power of communal worship and the human yearning for divine favor. Yet he also witnessed how ritual efficacy depended on priestly gatekeeping, leading him to question the accessibility of the divine through human intermediation. Over time, Abram's mind contrasted the ebb and flow of lunar-based festivals with the steadfast promises whispered by monotheistic traditions. The spectacle of temple processions thus stirred both awe and unease, sowing seeds for his later devotion to a God beyond calendar constraints.

2.4.2 Household Gods (Teraphim) and Ancestral Offerings

In many Mesopotamian homes, small clay or wooden figures—teraphim—served as household deities or ancestral proxies, believed to offer protection and guidance. These teraphim stood on domestic altars where families presented food offerings and incense at dawn and dusk. Affluence determined the quality and number of such figures, with wealthier homes displaying elaborate statuettes. Women often oversaw these household shrines, invoking teraphim for prosperity, fertility, and resolution of familial disputes. Biblical allusions to teraphim surface later in Rachel's theft from Laban (Gen 31:19), suggesting a continuity of practice into Abraham's extended family. Abram likely observed such customs in Terah's compound, weighing their spiritual merit against whispered memories of Yahweh's singular presence. While teraphim offered tangible symbols of divine care, Abram found them spiritually hollow compared to the covenant promises he inherited. His departure from his father's gods (Josh 24:2) thus represented both personal conviction and repudiation of domestic idolatry. Household gods, in Abram's formative milieu, exemplified the tension between tangible worship aids and authentic encounter with the living God.

2.4.3 Abram's Emerging Questions about Ultimate Reality

Amid this tapestry of temple festivals and household shrines, Abram's spiritual curiosity burgeoned as he pondered the efficacy of clay idols versus the unseen Creator. He noted that idols suffered decay and destruction, powerless to save their devotees from famine or conflict. Observing injustice—such as oppressive taxation and temple monopolies—Abram questioned the moral character of deities represented by human intermediaries. Late-night discussions with his brother Nahor and cousin Lot explored philosophical inquiries: Was there a supreme Being beyond local gods? Could such a Being be known without elaborate rituals? Abram's solitary vigils under desert stars stirred an awareness of cosmic vastness and divine sovereignty. These internal wrestlings laid groundwork for his later confession, "I believe that I shall surely become a great nation" (Gen 15:5), anchored not in human institution but in direct divine promise. His emergent faith contrasted sharply with communal piety, foreshadowing his radical obedience when God called him to leave his kinsmen. Abram's questions thus marked a turning point: personal seeking that transcended inherited religious forms and prepared him for covenant initiation.

Having mapped Abram's formative environment—city, household, education, and religion—we are now poised to witness the moment when the divine summons shatters his world and beckons him into covenant adventure.

2.5 Cross-Cultural Currents: Trade Routes and Foreign Merchants

2.5.1 Tin from Anatolia, Lapis from Afghanistan, and Gulf Incense

Long before Abram's departure, Mesopotamia thrived on a network of trade routes stretching from the Taurus Mountains to the Arabian

Gulf. Tin, essential for alloying bronze, arrived from Anatolia by caravan, passing through numerous city-states that levied tolls and exchanged local goods in return. Abram would have seen caravans bearing polished pieces of lapis lazuli from the rugged highlands of Afghanistan—stones so prized that they featured in temple jewelry and royal seals. Incense, frankincense and myrrh harvested in southern Arabia, traveled up the Gulf coast in small ships before transferring to camel trains bound for inland markets. Merchants from Dilmun and Magan conversed in Akkadian as a lingua franca, negotiating exchange rates inscribed on clay tokens sealed in bullae to guarantee authenticity. Coastal ports maintained warehouses where agents stored exotic commodities awaiting overland transport. Abram's household likely contributed wool textiles and dried fruit in barter, while his father's business contacts offered him early exposure to international commerce. These trade flows fostered economic interdependence across cultural lines, encouraging urban centers to develop cosmopolitan sensibilities. Archaeological finds of foreign pottery shards in Ur's sewage pits confirm the presence of distant goods within everyday life. Through these interactions, Abram learned that wealth and ideas moved along converging corridors, shaping identities and belief systems. Such exposure proved pivotal when he later navigated negotiations with kings and officials in Canaan and beyond. Recognizing that material exchange often carried spiritual influences, Abram's future faith would stand in contrast to syncretistic practices encountered along these routes.

2.5.2 Linguistic Diversity: Sumerian, Akkadian, and Early West-Semitic

Ur's status as a trade hub ensured continual mingling of languages: Sumerian persisted as the scholarly tongue of temple archives, while Akkadian functioned as the common language of administration and commerce. Abram, attending the é-dubba, would have memorized bilingual lexical lists to translate Sumerian loanwords into Akkadian equivalents. Semitic dialects—early West-Semitic speech forms ancestral to Hebrew—circulated among caravan crews and rural settlements. These dialects varied by region; in Haran, for example, Aramaic began to emerge as a distinct vernacular, setting the stage for its later use in imperial correspondence. Script styles—cuneiform and proto-alphabetic pictographs—coexisted, demonstrating an evolving literacy landscape. Abram's facility with multiple tongues prepared him to serve as an interpreter between peoples, a skill he employed when mediating between Lot's herdsmen and local shepherds (Gen 13:7). Multilingual proficiency also exposed him to diverse theological concepts embedded in language: divine names and epithets shifted subtly across cultural contexts. Recognizing the limits of language, Abram later relied on covenant signs—such as circumcision (Gen 17:11)—to communicate spiritual truths transcending mere words. The fluid linguistic environment of Mesopotamia thus sharpened his awareness of both human communication's power and its insufficiency in conveying ultimate reality.

2.5.3 Economic Treaties That Shaped Political Stability

City-states along the Fertile Crescent frequently entered into formal treaties to secure trade corridors and prevent conflict among merchant caravans. These treaties, often ratified by royal oaths sworn before temple deities, bound signatories to mutual non-aggression and tax-free passage for identified goods. Copies were stored in temple archives and ratified by public readings during festival gatherings. Abram's family, embedded in Terah's economic network, would have witnessed these ceremonies and understood the gravity of covenantal language echoing in later divine covenants (Gen 15:18). Enforcement depended on reciprocal benefit: city-states policed their borders to maintain merchant confidence and sustain revenue streams. Breaches could lead to punitive raids or trade embargoes, disrupting local economies and compelling families like Abram's to consider relocation. The political equilibrium maintained by these treaties fostered an environment where commerce thrived, yet also demonstrated the fragility of human agreements absent transcendental guarantee. Abram's later experiences—such as his treaty at Beersheba with Abimelech (Gen 21:27–32)—mirror these ancient practices, revealing how God repurposed familiar legal forms to establish enduring spiritual commitments.

While robust trade and diplomatic frameworks offered prosperity and relative peace, they could not insulate Terah's household from external shocks. In the next section, we examine the political upheavals and ecological stresses that pressured Abram's family to contemplate migration.

2.6 Harbingers of Change: Political Upheavals and Ecological Stresses

2.6.1 Royal Dynastic Shifts and Military Levies

Mesopotamia's political landscape in Abram's youth was marked by the ascendancy and decline of powerful city-states competing for hegemony. Rulers in Ur, Isin, and Larsa battled for control of water rights and trade tariffs, often drafting able-bodied men into military levies to secure caravan routes. Soldiers marched under banners bearing temple emblems, convinced that divine favor determined victory. Terah's household, though primarily civilian, could find itself drafting younger males for corvée labor or siege efforts, disrupting pastoral rhythms and causing anxiety over personal safety. The conscription of local youths into armies underscored the precariousness of urban prosperity: political alliances shifted abruptly, and families like Abram's had to weigh loyalty to city rulers against long-term survival. Historical records note periods when Ur's armies campaigned in Anatolia, reflecting the transregional ambitions of Mesopotamian kings. Abram's understanding of political volatility later informed his diplomatic strategies when interacting with foreign potentates. He learned that military might could secure land temporarily but that divine protection offered a more stable foundation. These lessons in realpolitik prepared him to trust in God's promise even when human power faltered.

2.6.2 Drought Cycles, Crop Failures, and Urban Food Rationing

Mesopotamia's irrigation-based agriculture thrived under predictable flooding, but extended droughts could devastate harvests and lead to widespread famine. Clay tablets from Ur and neighboring cities record years when canal silting and low river levels forced rationing of grain and oil. Bakeries and breweries, central to everyday diets, scaled back production, while temple granaries released stored reserves to prevent mass starvation. Urban authorities instituted limits on household consumption, fueling resentment among commoners who viewed aristocratic families as hoarding resources. Terah's compound, reliant on its own flocks and textile trade, nonetheless felt the pinch as market prices soared and trade caravans delayed. Environmental stress prompted local councils to debate digging new canals or abandoning fields in search of more fertile lands. Abram's exposure to these ecological cycles deepened his appreciation for divine provision, a theme he later articulates when God reassures him of descendants amid a land of famine (Gen 15:5–6). These patterns of scarcity and survival underscored human dependency on both natural rhythms and unseen sovereignty.

2.6.3 Family Council Deliberations over Migration Options

When drought and political strain intensified, patriarchs convened family councils to weigh migration versus resignation to local hardship. Clad in fine woolen cloaks—products of Terah's workshop—Abram and his kin gathered under a shaded tent to review caravan logistics and potential destinations. Debates considered Canaan's legendary fertility against the security of Mesopotamian alliances. Opinions clashed: some elders favored loyalty to ancestral lands despite uncertainty, while others argued for moving toward the hills of Haran or beyond the Euphrates. Women's voices, particularly Sarai's, influenced decisions by highlighting the toll of famine on childbearing and household harmony. Proposal and counterproposal followed customary protocols: oaths swore safe conduct, and diviners cast lots to discern favorable omens. Abram's analytical mind assessed risks but remained open to unseen possibilities—a tension culminating in his later obedience to an inexplicit divine command (Gen 12:1). These deliberations illustrate how human planning and divine invitation intersect, setting the stage for a covenant journey that would transcend conventional migration motives.

Having grappled with escalating crises, Terah's household moved from debate to action. In the next section, we trace the preparations and motivations that propelled Abram toward Haran.

2.7 Terah's Decision to Migrate: Motives and Preparations

2.7.1 Economic Opportunity versus Religious Conviction

Terah's choice to leave Ur balanced pragmatic concerns—securing caravan profits and escaping food shortages—with possible inklings of spiritual seeking. Caravan leaders promised lucrative trade agreements in Haran, inviting the family to capitalize on fresh markets and pastoral lands. Yet rumors of Yahweh's promise to Abram may have circulated in private gatherings, planting seeds of conviction that transcended material incentives. As patriarch, Terah weighed tangible benefits against intangible longings for a promised land, reflecting the dual drives of survival and hope. His willingness to uproot a prosperous household testifies to the persuasive power of both human enterprise and emerging faith traditions. Preparations included liquidating urban properties at fair market value, documented in sale receipts now lost to history. Family assets—trade caravans, livestock herds, and business contacts—were organized into discrete units for easier relocation. Terah's deliberations thus blended the calculable metrics of commerce with the immeasurable stirrings of covenant expectation.

2.7.2 Caravan Organization: Routes, Supplies, and Security

Organizing a caravan of several dozen people, animals, and goods required meticulous planning. Terah appointed trusted stewards to assemble supplies: dried meat, grain sacks, water skins, and fodder for livestock. Merchants from Ur contracted camel brigades familiar with desert terrain, ensuring reliable transport across shifting sands. Guides were hired to navigate volatile tribal territories, and agreements forged with local chieftains provided protected way-stations. Security measures included arming select servants with bronze-tipped spears and shields, while itinerant blacksmiths prepared spare tools for caravan repairs. Detailed itineraries charted daily distances and rest points, accounting for water source availability and seasonal weather patterns. Abram observed these logistics closely, mastering the art of resource allocation—a skill later evident when he managed flocks across Canaan (Gen 13:5–12). Caravan cooks and quartermasters prepared communal feasts at campfires, fostering unity and morale on the long trek. Through this process, Abram internalized principles of leadership, foresight, and mutual reliance critical for his future role as covenant head.

2.7.3 Farewell Rituals and Legal Transfer of Urban Holdings

On the eve of departure, Terah's household conducted farewell rituals blending Mesopotamian custom and nascent covenant practice. Servants burned incense before household teraphim, seeking their ancestral protection for the journey. Scribes finalized property sale contracts, witnessed by elders and sealed with clay bullae bearing Terah's emblem. Family members performed acts of remembrance—sharing stories of Ur's streets and temple festivals— to anchor communal identity amid change. Sarai prepared garments and personal ornaments for the journey, mindful of negotiating her status in Aramean regions. Abram, standing beside his father, offered a silent blessing to the family altar, foreshadowing his later role as spiritual intercessor. These rituals provided psychological closure and legal clarity, allowing the household to depart without dispute over residual claims. As dawn broke, the caravan moved under a lead camel carrying Terah's standard—a symbol of unity and divine accompaniment. This blend of practical and ceremonial acts illuminated how human transitions often combine legal formality with spiritual resonance.

With urban ties severed and preparations complete, Abram's family embarked on the storied route to Haran—a journey that would redefine their destiny and his faith.

2.8 Transit to Haran: The Journey Along the Fertile Crescent

2.8.1 Way-Stations, River Crossings, and Nomadic Encounters

The caravan's route followed established way-stations—clustered at natural springs and rocky outcrops—where travelers exchanged news and replenished supplies. River crossings at the Diyala and Balikh rivers required construction of temporary rafts or use of primitive fords, a logistical challenge that slowed progress and demanded collective labor. At each ford, local nomadic tribes gathered to trade milk and meat for pottery and metal tools, offering hospitality in exchange for safe passage through tribal lands. Abram observed the semi-nomadic Bedouin-style hospitality—

tent-dwelling traditions and communal feasts—as differing from Ur's urban culture. Dust storms and flash floods tested the caravan's resilience, forcing unexpected detours that extended the journey by days. These encounters honed Abram's crisis management skills, as he coordinated water rationing and adjusted timelines to account for environmental hazards. Camels, prized for their endurance, carried majority of goods, while sheep and goats grazed on sparse scrub along the route. This convergence of pastoral, nomadic, and settled cultures provided Abram with a panoramic view of the region's human ecology. Each day's progress underscored the delicate balance between independence and interdependence inherent in long-distance travel.

2.8.2 Altered Family Dynamics on the Road

Life on the move reshaped Terah's household relationships: authority structures became more fluid, with younger men shouldering responsibilities as scouts and water-finders. Women organized communal childcare and meal preparation at campfires, drawing on experiences from Sarai's leadership in Ur's compound. Kinship bonds strengthened through shared hardship, yet tensions surfaced over resource allocation and pace of travel. Abram, though younger than Nahor, emerged as a mediator when disputes arose between shepherds and camel drivers. The physical proximity of tents fostered nightly discussions around firelight, where elders recounted ancestral stories and younger members voiced hopes for the new land. Children born on the road—nominally citizens of neither Ur nor Haran—embodied the transitional nature of the journey. These dynamics foreshadowed Abram's later role in managing household cohesion amid external pressures. The journey taught the family adaptability, mutual care, and the necessity of trust when confronting uncertainty.

2.8.3 First Glimpses of Haran's Trading Colonies

Approaching Haran, the caravan passed through satellite trading colonies—small settlements with rustic bazaars and simple lodgings for merchants. Mud-brick storage vaults held olive oil and grain destined for market towns, while rudimentary caravanserai offered shelter for travelers. Abram noted the interchange of Aramaic and Akkadian in market calls, and the sight of clay seals marking goods for distinct city-states signaled Haran's administrative reach. Local shrines, devoted to storm-god Hadad and moon-goddess Sin, sat alongside open-air stalls, illustrating Haran's syncretistic religious environment. The terrain rose into rocky ridges, providing vantage points to survey caravan approach—a defensive measure against bandit raids. Seasonal festivals in Haran attracted merchants from the Levant, broadening the cultural mix Abram encountered. These early impressions of Haran's strategic importance and religious pluralism set the stage for Terah's decision to settle, while planting in Abram's mind questions about divine sovereignty amid competing deities.

Having reached Haran's outskirts, Terah's family prepared to establish a new home in a land of both promise and uncertainty. In the next chapter, we will explore Abram's life in Haran as a liminal season of waiting.

2.9 Life in Haran: A Liminal Season of Waiting

2.9.1 Re-establishing Commerce and Herd Expansion

Terah's household, upon settling in Haran, swiftly re-established its trading operations by negotiating new market stalls and caravan partnerships. Merchants in Haran valued Ur's reputation for quality wool, prompting Terah to dispatch flocks northward along established trade corridors. Abram supervised the selection of grazing lands near the Balikh River, ensuring fresh pasturage for sheep and goats during spring and autumn seasons. He coordinated with local Aramean herders to exchange breeding stock, enhancing the household's genetic diversity and wool yield. Textile production resumed under the supervision of his sister-in-law, producing dyed fabrics that fetched premium prices in Haran's bazaars. Clay tablets recording these transactions were archived in a modest household temple, reflecting a hybrid of urban record-keeping and tribal hospitality. As caravan traffic picked up, Abram arranged for shared guard duties with neighboring clans, fostering mutual security agreements. The prosperity of these ventures tempered the psychological strain of displacement, offering tangible proof that God's blessing could accompany them even outside Canaan. Yet Abram sensed that material success alone could not satisfy deeper longings, anticipating a promise that extended beyond commercial gain. His nights often ended with solitary counting of stars, echoing the covenant promise yet unspoken in Haran's alleys. This period of economic rebuilding thus served both as practical training and spiritual test, teaching Abram resilience and resource stewardship.

2.9.2 Abram's Observations of Aramean Culture and Religion

In Haran's cosmopolitan environment, Abram encountered a tapestry of Aramean customs, from nomadic tent-life to settled brick-house architecture. He observed local festivals honoring Hadad, the storm-god, during which priests conducted ritual dances and bull sacrifices to secure rain for crops. Market stalls displayed wooden idols and terracotta figurines representing a pantheon of deities, each with distinct iconography and cultic paraphernalia. Abram noted how religious devotion permeated daily life: before any business negotiation, merchants offered incense to household gods, while travelers invoked protective spirits at caravanserai thresholds. The Aramaic tongue, with its guttural consonants and fluid vowel sounds, contrasted with the Akkadian he learned in Ur, drawing him into comparative linguistics of divine names. He recorded scribal notes on talismanic incantations used to ward off illness, a practice he found both fascinating and troubling in its transactional approach to the sacred. Women in Haran practiced communal childbirth rituals invoking fertility goddesses, illustrating social solidarity but highlighting Sarai's own unfulfilled desire for children. Abram's growing discomfort with polytheism sharpened his inner conviction that true power resided not in carved images but in the Creator behind all creation. His reflections during walks along the Khabur River, where he admired natural order unmediated by priests, deepened his burgeoning monotheistic awareness. These cultural engagements in Haran enriched Abram's understanding of human religiosity and prepared him for the divine call that would upend familiar patterns.

2.9.3 Spiritual Restlessness and the Seeds of Monotheistic Faith

Despite the comforts of Haran's commerce and the richness of its culture, Abram experienced a profound spiritual disquiet that no idol or ritual could assuage. He wrestled with questions born of witnessing injustice: wealthy landowners evicting destitute families during famines, and temple authorities prioritizing tribute over compassion. These observations prompted midnight dialogues with Sarai and Lot about the nature of justice and mercy, foreshadowing Abram's later intercessory role (Gen 18:23–25). In private moments, he revisited ancestral stories of Shem and Eber, recalling fragments of covenant promise passed down by word of mouth. Abram began marking simple cairns in the fields, offering silent prayers to an unseen God, a nascent form of the altars he would erect in Canaan (Gen 12:7). His restlessness intensified during seasonal worship festivals in Haran, where he felt like an outsider even as a privileged resident. Dreams and visions occasionally disturbed his sleep, hinting at divine communication through symbols and celestial imagery. These experiences sowed seeds of faith that would germinate when God's voice finally called him to leave Haran behind. Abram's spiritual tension in Haran thus functioned as both crucible and preparation, refining his heart for covenantal obedience.

As Abram's inner life matured amidst Haran's contrasts, personal crises and hidden encounters further shaped his readiness for the divine call.

2.10 Formative Crises: Personal Losses and Silent Epiphanies

2.10.1 Grieving Haran's Death and Guardianship of Lot

The sudden death of Abram's brother Haran cast a long shadow over the family's migration, reopening wounds even after the bustle of relocation. Abram, still young but growing in stature, assumed protective oversight of his orphaned nephew Lot, comforting the boy and mediating his grief. Haran's passing, noted in Genesis 11:28, reminded Abram how fragile human enterprises can be, despite careful planning. The family council convened to discuss Lot's future, balancing inheritance rights with educational needs, and Abram vowed to secure both material provision and moral guidance. He accompanied Lot to nearby well sites, teaching him to find water and avoid dangerous wildlife—lessons in survival that bonded them as mentor and ward. Abram's empathy deepened as he witnessed Lot's sorrow, fostering a parental concern that later influenced his rescue mission in Genesis 14. This period of mourning catalyzed Abram's understanding of loss as formative rather than merely tragic, laying emotional groundwork for his later reliance on divine comfort. His silent prayers for strength and wisdom, offered at unattended roadside shrines, signaled a turning inward toward unseen help. Through grief, Abram internalized that true security rests not in household wealth but in divine companionship.

2.10.2 Sarai's Barrenness in Cultural Perspective

In Haran's patriarchal setting, Sarai's continued barrenness became a source of communal pity and personal anguish, as childbearing solidified women's status and lineage security. Abram faced social pressure to produce offspring to perpetuate Terah's name and safeguard inheritance protocols. During market visits, he observed other families' young children playing at his feet, reminders of Sarai's silent womb. Sarai's shame, culturally rooted in perceived divine disfavor, manifested in her longing gaze toward other mothers and daughters. Abram comforted her with promises drawn from ancestral faith—recalling that descendants would come "like the stars of heaven" (Gen 15:5)—even before any formal divine revelation. His support contrasted with local customs where childless women faced marginalization or were encouraged to adopt servants as heirs. Sarai's distress led Abram to explore alternative solutions, such as adopting a nephew or servant, reflecting Mesopotamian norms (Gen 15:2). Yet his faith resisted such measures, foreshadowing the later promise of Isaac's birth by divine intervention. This intimate struggle deepened Abram's relational empathy and fueled his hope in God's power to fulfill impossible promises.

2.10.3 Private Altars and Unrecorded Prayers

In moments too personal for public ritual, Abram constructed modest altars at the fringes of the family camp, using stones gathered from field boundaries. He anointed each altar with oil drawn from Terah's household stores, a silent offering signaling devotion to a God not yet named among Haran's deities. At these secluded shrines, Abram whispered prayers for guidance, protection, and the fruitfulness of Sarai's womb. No temple scribe recorded these petitions, yet they shaped his spiritual trajectory more profoundly than formal festival rites. The stones themselves, piled in deliberate stacks, served as mnemonic devices, recalling each answered prayer and divine encouragement. Abram's private worship contrasted starkly with public sacrifices at temple courts, underscoring his emerging preference for personal encounter over ceremonial formality. These altars foreshadowed the Bethel and Ai monuments he later erected in Canaan (Gen 12:8; 13:3), demonstrating continuity between hidden devotion and covenant landmarks. Though unheralded, these early worship acts forged Abram's identity as a worshiper of Yahweh, laying the groundwork for the theophanies to come.

In grappling with loss and longing, Abram cultivated virtues and skills that prepared him for leadership; we now turn to those competencies he honed before God's call.

2.11 Skills and Virtues Forged in Mesopotamia

2.11.1 Strategic Foresight, Hospitality, and Conflict Mediation

Abram's management of trade caravans and herds required strategic foresight, anticipating seasonal shifts and tribal rivalries. He planned grazing rotations months in advance, ensuring that livestock had year-round resources without depleting any single pasture. His hospitality toward visiting merchants—from preparing communal feasts to offering medical care using local herbs—built alliances that later facilitated safe passage for his family. When conflicts arose between shepherds over water rights, Abram stepped in as mediator, convening elders under his tent and invoking ancestral customs to negotiate fair agreements (cf. Gen 13:7–9). His balanced judgments won him respect among diverse groups, a testament to his integrity and cultural fluency. These skills would prove invaluable when interceding for Sodom or negotiating treaties at Beersheba (Gen 14; 21). Abram's reputation for fairness enhanced his household's standing, demonstrating that economic success and social harmony often depend on just leadership.

2.11.2 Resource Stewardship and Seasonal Mobility

Navigating an environment of fluctuating resources, Abram mastered the art of seasonal mobility—relocating flocks between uplands in summer and lowland pastures in winter. He tracked rainfall patterns and grass regeneration cycles, adjusting migration routes to avoid overgrazing and erosion. Water management included constructing simple troughs and repairing ancient cisterns, ensuring flock health during dry spells. Abram instituted household conservation measures—rotating grain stores and salvaging unthreshed barley during reaping—to buffer against famine. He trained servants in efficient butchering and food preservation techniques, extending supplies through lean months. This holistic stewardship reflected a theology of care rather than exploitation, aligning with later biblical mandates for land rest and resource equity (Lev 25). Abram's approach to resource management embodied faith in God's provision, balanced by human responsibility—a principle he would later articulate when trusting in promised land abundance (Gen 15:13–16).

2.11.3 Ethical Sensitivities Shaped by Urban–Nomad Tension

Torn between the structured norms of city life and the egalitarian rhythms of nomadic pasturing, Abram developed ethical sensibilities that embraced both stability and mobility. He recognized the vulnerability of urban poor to taxation, advocating for fair levies among his merchant peers. Equally, he respected the autonomy of nomadic bands, negotiating peaceful grazing accords rather than imposing territorial dominion. His awareness of these contrasting lifestyles informed his later guidance to Lot—urging separation to prevent strife over shared resources (Gen 13:8). Abram's ethical compass prioritized human dignity over rigid adherence to custom, allowing him to challenge both temple tax collectors and tribal chieftains when they imposed harsh terms. This moral flexibility, grounded in covenant values, distinguished him from other leaders and predisposed him to champion justice within a broader divine framework.

Having surveyed the competencies and convictions Abram acquired, we now see how these combine to create readiness for the climactic moment of divine revelation.

2.12 Prelude to Revelation: Setting the Stage for Divine Encounter

2.12.1 Convergence of Cultural Exposure and Spiritual Longing

Abram's years in Mesopotamia immersed him in the pinnacle of human culture—urban sophistication, international commerce, and ritual grandeur—yet simultaneously awakened a yearning for a reality beyond finite institutions. His mastery of multiple languages, familiarity with diverse religious rites, and skill in negotiation equipped him for cross-cultural mission. At the same time, his grief over Haran's death and Sarai's barrenness fueled an existential longing unfulfilled by idols or ancestral gods. These parallel trajectories—cultural competence and spiritual restlessness—converged in his character, preparing him to perceive and respond to a transcendent call. Abram's life in Ur and Haran thus represented both the height of human possibility and the limits of creaturely achievement, setting the stage for God's voice to penetrate where human promises could not suffice.

2.12.2 Theological Vacuum Awaiting Covenant Voice

Despite Mesopotamia's elaborate pantheons, Abram perceived a theological vacuum at the heart of communal religion. Ritual precision and temple wealth masked moral failings: greedy elites, corrupt priests, and social disparities unaddressed by religious rites. Abram's private altars and unrecorded prayers testified to a silent hunger for authentic communion with the true God. His exposure to conflicting divine claims—Sin, Hadad, and myriad local deities—revealed the inadequacy of constructed gods in answering questions of origin, purpose, and destiny. This void within established

70

frameworks made him receptive when Yahweh's promise finally broke through the silence. Abram's readiness for covenantal revelation thus depended on both cultural saturation and spiritual longing—conditions His spoken word would transform.

2.12.3 Transition to Chapter 3: The Voice of Destiny—Yahweh Calls Abram

As Abram reached the zenith of his formative journey, every skill acquired and every question wrestled had conspired to prepare him for the divine summons. The stage was set for a radical departure from Mesopotamian religion, family bonds, and economic certainty, ushering in a covenant relationship that would redefine human history. In the next chapter, we witness the moment when the Voice of Destiny shatters the familiar horizon and beckons Abram into uncharted obedience.

Conclusion By the time Abram settled into Haran's crossroads, he had already been shaped by loss, responsibility, and glimpses of a reality beyond Mesopotamian pantheons. The skills he honed—strategic planning, compassionate leadership, and an unsettling openness to the unseen—became the very tools God would use to call him away from every familiar anchor. As we leave Abram on the threshold of his divine appointment, we see a man whose identity has been tempered by the world's challenges yet remains malleable to heaven's design. In stepping out of Ur's prosperity and Haran's security, Abram prepares to trade every earthly certainty for a venture defined solely by obedience to a voice still to be heard.

Chapter 3 – Voice of Destiny: The Divine Call and Covenant

In the quiet dawn at Haran's edge, Abram's world pivoted on a single, unspoken question: what does it mean to follow a voice that demands everything yet offers more than any city or kinship could provide? When Yahweh called him to "go" beyond familiar streets, to step into territory uncharted by human maps, Abram embarked on a journey that would redefine not only his own destiny but the very contours of redemptive history. This chapter traces the unfolding of that divine summons—from the first echo of "Lek-lekha" (leave yourself) to the solemn covenant rituals that bound heaven and earth together. As Abram uproots his life in obedience, God's multifaceted promise—land to inhabit, offspring to inherit, and blessing to extend to all nations—takes shape through encounters with kings, altars hewn of stone, and visions beneath the night sky. Here we witness how faith is forged not in ease but in the crucible of trust, as Abram learns that a voice calling into the unknown is the purest invitation to discover the heart of the Almighty.

3.1 The Theophany at Haran—"Leave Your Country" (Gen 12:1–3)

3.1.1 The Imperative Command: Linguistic Nuances of "Lek-lekha"

The Hebrew phrase "לֶךְ-לְךָ" (lek-lekha) carries a double imperative, compelling Abram both to "go" and to "for yourself" undertake the journey. This dual meaning emphasizes personal responsibility: Abram must leave not only his geographic homeland but also his self-reliant identity. The verb "לֵךְ" (lek) commands movement, implying decisiveness and urgency, while "לְךָ" (lekha) adds an inward focus—this call is Abram's alone to embrace. Ancient Near-Eastern treaty texts often hinge on similar verbs that demand unilateral departure from former allegiances, yet here the suzerain is Yahweh inviting Abram into a unique covenant. The absence of a specified destination heightens the act of faith; Abram must trust God's promise without visible evidence of fulfillment. Rabbinic commentary highlights how "lek-lekha" initiated a spiritual uprooting, severing ties with familial gods and ancestral customs. The command's directness bypasses negotiation—Abram cannot request clarifying terms. By addressing Abram personally rather than through Terah or Sarai, God elevates him as covenantal head, responsible for future generations. The imperative resonates through Scripture whenever God invites individuals into mission: Moses at the burning bush, Jonah to Nineveh, and the disciples to follow Jesus. Each call mirrors the double imperative, demanding external movement and internal transformation. Thus, "lek-lekha" frames the divine-human relationship as one of sovereign invitation and radical trust, setting the tone for Abram's lifelong obedience.

3.1.2 Severing Kinship Ties: Psychological and Legal Implications

To obey "lek-lekha," Abram needed to relinquish not only land but also legal rights tied to inheritance under Mesopotamian custom. In his culture, elder sons inherited land and leadership roles; by leaving, Abram formally renounced these privileges. Psychologically, departure from one's family fostered profound insecurity: social identity, economic security, and religious belonging all rested on clan membership. Abram's willingness to face isolation underscores the depth of his emerging faith. His wife Sarai and nephew Lot joined him, yet he stood as principal signatory to the covenant promise. Legal documents from Ur illustrate how migration often involved notarized renunciations of property rights; Abram's move likely entailed similar ritual acts. Anthropologists note that departing clans often underwent symbolic rituals—handing over tokens, reciting farewell oaths—in order to legitimize separation. Israelite tradition echoes this, with Joshua recalling how Abraham left "his people and his father's house" (Josh 24:2) to follow Yahweh. Abram's psychological distancing from his birthplace set a precedent for spiritual pilgrimage: his true "family" would be determined by divine affiliation rather than blood alone. This radical redefinition of kinship emerges later when Jesus speaks of those who do God's will as his true family (Mark 3:35). Abram's legal and emotional detachment thus foreshadows a covenant community defined by faith rather than descent.

3.1.3 Promise Framework: Land, Seed, Universal Blessing

God's promise to Abram unfolds in three interlinked strands: land to inherit, offspring to multiply, and blessing extended to all nations. The grant of land anticipates Israel's eventual possession of Canaan, a "country that I will show you" (Gen 12:1)—though its borders remain unspecified at first, marking a divine land grant rather than a human-mediated purchase. The promise of a "great nation" invokes images of demographic flourishing, contrasting Sarai's barrenness with future fertility (Gen 12:2). The third clause—"and in you all the families of the earth shall be blessed"—introduces universal scope, anticipating the messianic mission embodied in Christ (Gal 3:8). Ancient treaties often list obligations and benefits; here, God's obligations far exceed Abram's minimal response of migration. The triad of promise parallels royal grant formulas in Mesopotamian texts, yet Yahweh alone possesses authority to fulfill such cosmological pledges. Covenant theology later emphasizes that land belongs to God (Ps 24:1), and offspring result from divine blessing (Ps 127:3). Paul explicates that Gentile inclusion springs from Abram's faith (Rom 4:13), cementing the global dimension of the promise. Abram's story thus redefines covenant: it is neither anthropocentric nor local but cosmic, designed to reshape human history through one man's obedience.

Having examined the profound weight of God's inaugural command and promise, we turn to Abram's tangible steps of faith as he organizes his departure and navigates the unknown.

3.2 First Steps of Obedience—Logistics of a Faith Journey

3.2.1 Assembling the Caravan: People, Provisions, Protection

Abram's initial act of obedience required mobilizing a diverse caravan of family members, servants, livestock, and provisions. He designated key lieutenants—trusted servants well-versed in caravan management—to inventory livestock, including sheep, goats, and camels, ensuring the herd's size matched Sarai's needs and Lot's flock. Food stores—dried figs, barley loaves, and goat cheese—were measured against projected journey duration. Water skins were sealed, and spare amphorae prepared for potential fording of rivers. Abram also negotiated with local mercenaries for protected passage, offering a share of caravan profits as compensation for their watchful guard. His diplomatic skill secured peace accords with neighboring clans, preventing ambushes and toll extortion. The caravan's organization mirrored temple processions in structure and discipline, but its purpose was pilgrimage rather than ritual homage. Women and children received instruction on camp routines, including gathering firewood and assembling makeshift tents. Abram's faith manifested in allocating resources for an uncertain destination, trusting God's guidance to replenish what nature and providence could not sustain. The meticulous planning and reliance on human instruments balanced by reliance on the divine exemplify the synergy of obedience and trust.

3.2.2 Navigating Unknown Terrain: Mapping by Constellations and Wells

Without detailed maps, Abram's caravan relied on star positions to maintain direction as they crossed deserts and valleys. Skilled astronomers among Abram's retinue charted the Pleiades and Orion to approximate latitudes, while local guides identified natural landmarks like the Ridge of Emath and wells known only by tribal knowledge. Caravan crews recorded the locations of freshwater springs on clay tablets for future reference, pioneering early travelogues of the Fertile Crescent. Pilgrims observed prayer rituals at sunset and dawn, invoking Yahweh's protection using the very stars as divine witnesses. Abram commemorated each successful waypoint with brief altars, signifying gratitude and claiming the territory for the promise yet unfulfilled. His ability to combine celestial navigation with terrestrial intelligence demonstrated practical wisdom born of Mesopotamian training, now directed by a higher mandate. When storms blinded travelers or sand dunes obliterated tracks, Abram rallied his people with reminders of God's guiding presence, sustaining morale. The journey's navigational challenges thus became opportunities to affirm faith through successful passage, laying spiritual and physical markers that pointed ahead to Canaan's beckoning horizons.

3.2.3 Early Tests: Detours, Delays, and Silent Divine Guidance

No sooner had Abram embarked than hazards emerged: flooded wadis forced lengthy detours, and seasonal nomadic raids threatened supplies. On one occasion, a broken axle left pack animals stranded until villagers from a nearby oasis offered aid in exchange for Abram's hospitality. He responded by sharing grain and shelter, modeling covenant generosity even before formal promise fulfillment. Abram's caravan paused at a shrine dedicated to Baal-Lebanon, where he resisted the temptation to appease local spirits, choosing instead private prayer by the well. His faith faced silent tests when months passed without explicit divine communication; yet he continued forward, guided by conviction rather than visible confirmation. At times, gut instincts led him to alternate routes that proved safer, decisions he later attributed to unseen divine prompting. These early challenges honed Abram's discernment between human counsel and divine direction, teaching him to wait for God's timing before making critical moves. His perseverance through adversity solidified leadership credibility and strengthened the caravan's cohesion for trials ahead.

With Abram's obedience now tested on the road, the narrative shifts to the pivotal moments when he first erects altars in the land—public testimonials of faith in the face of surrounding idolatry.

3.3 Altars of Arrival—Shechem, Moreh, and Bethel (Gen 12:6–8)

3.3.1 Sacred Trees and Canaanite Shrines: Conquest Foreshadowed

At Shechem near the Oak of Moreh, Abram encountered ancient Canaanite shrines venerating groves and sacred trees. These local high places served as focal points for fertility rites and ancestor worship, featuring stone pillars and cistern-fed altars inscribed with tribal symbols. Abram's choice to build his own altar adjacent to these sites constituted a deliberate challenge to prevailing cultic practices, signaling Yahweh's supremacy over regional deities. He purged the stone altar of local talismans, replacing them with uncut stones gathered from the field—echoing later Israelite injunctions against graven images (Deut 27:5–6). The confrontation of shrines demonstrated Abram's recognition that worship must occur in native soil, not merely within temple precincts. His act foreshadowed the conquest's spiritual dimension: before military advancement, worship must assert divine claim on land. Local observers, intrigued by Abram's silent ritual, spread word of a foreign patriarch honoring a mysterious God. This subversive worship laid groundwork for Israel's future altar practices under Joshua, who instructed building stones to remain unhewn (Josh 8:31). Abram's altars thus inaugurated a new spiritual geography within a land steeped in idolatry.

3.3.2 Stone and Soil: Theology of the First Altars

Abram's altars comprised simple piles of field stones, signifying impermanence yet divine permanence. Each stone represented a thanksgiving monument, a physical marker of covenant presence in foreign territory. Soil taken from around the site formed an earthen base inviting future pilgrims to step onto altar ground with reverence. Abram anointed the stones with oil—an act reserved for consecration—and poured wine libations, aligning with broader sacrificial customs yet distinct in its absence of animal sacrifice at this stage. The tactile elements—stone, soil, oil, and wine—combined earth and heaven, symbolizing the union of human response and divine initiative. These altars anticipated the more elaborate sacrifices later described, but their simplicity highlighted relational immediacy over ritual complexity. Through them, God communicated that true worship requires only a heart willing to honor Him wherever He leads. Abram's theology of altars set a precedent for later patriarchs and Israelite kings who built altars to commemorate divine encounters (1 Sam 7:17). Each monument stood as a tangible footprint of faith arranged on consecrated ground.

3.3.3 Public Witness: Worship in the Presence of Pagan Onlookers

Unlike clandestine groves, Abram's altars were visible to passing Canaanites and traders, serving as public testimonials of allegiance to Yahweh. Word spread through local networks as curious pilgrims paused to inquire about the foreign patriarch's devotions. Abram welcomed their questions, explaining that his God had shown him this land for promise, sowing seeds of monotheistic curiosity among indigenous populations. His open-air worship contrasted with secretive rituals of local cults, offering transparency and hospitality rather than gatekept access through priestly intermediaries. Some locals mocked, viewing Abram's God as one among many, yet others intrigued began to question their own practices. Abram's witness at Bethel foreshadowed later Israelite prophetic outreach, where altars and prophetic proclamations broke Canaanite spiritual hegemony. Though his audience was limited, Abram's public worship initiated a spiritual campaign preceding Israel's military conquests. His altars thus functioned as evangelistic outposts, embodying the universal blessing promised in his call.

Having established worship practices on Canaanite soil, we now explore the deeper covenant motifs—land, seed, and universal blessing—that underpin Abram's journey.

3.4 Covenant Motifs—Land Grant, Descendants, and Global Mission

3.4.1 Land as Divine Inheritance Versus Royal Donation Charters

In ancient Near-Eastern cultures, kings granted land to loyal subjects through formal charters, often sealed with witnesses and symbolized by boundary markers. Abram's divine grant resembles these royal gifts yet differs fundamentally: God, as sovereign

Creator, required no intermediary to confer territory. The promise of "all the land that you see" (Gen 12:7)—extending "from the river of Egypt to the great river, the river Euphrates" (Gen 15:18)—far surpassed any human grant's scope. God's self-designation as "I will give" undercuts notions of land as commodity, reframing it as a gift rooted in divine fidelity. Theological reflection in Leviticus underscores this: "The land shall not be sold in perpetuity, for the land is mine" (Lev 25:23). Abram's inheritance thus introduces a paradigm where divine ownership precedes human stewardship. This motif emerges again in Israel's conquest narratives, where boundary stones serve as reminders of God's original promise (Josh 24:13). Abram's land grant, framed by covenant language, establishes a sacramental geography, sanctifying space through divine word rather than regal decree.

3.4.2 Seed Promise: Biological Line and Messianic Trajectory

The promise of offspring—"I will make your offspring as the dust of the earth" (Gen 13:16)—addresses Sarai's barrenness head-on, asserting supernatural fertility ahead of natural possibility. In the ancient world, childlessness equated to divine curse; Abram's seed promise thus subverts expectations, inaugurating a new theology of divine miracle. Subsequent narratives emphasize the tension between human meddling (Hagar and Ishmael) and divine timing (Isaac's birth at ninety-nine years old), reinforcing that the primary seed flows through God's initiative. This biological promise also carries messianic dimensions: Galatians affirms that "the promise... was spoken to Abraham and to his seed. He does not say, 'And to seeds,' as of many, but as of one, 'And to your seed,' who is Christ" (Gal 3:16). Thus, the covenant seed extends beyond ethnic Israel to encompass all who share Christ's faith. Abram's seed promise bridges immediate generational hope with eschatological fulfillment in the Messiah, integrating familial lineage into cosmic redemption.

3.4.3 Blessing for the Nations: Missional Vocation of Abraham's Call

God's declaration that "in you all the families of the earth shall be blessed" (Gen 12:3) infuses Abram's personal journey with a global mandate. Unlike localized patron-client pacts, this covenant projects beyond ancestral holdings to the benefit of every nation. Abram's household, though small, becomes the conduit for universal blessing, foreshadowing Israel's prophetic vocation to be "a light to the nations" (Isa 42:6). Early Jewish interpretation saw this promise fulfilled in the Torah's blessing obligations, while Christian theology locates its consummation in Christ's atonement. Abram's call thus plants missional DNA in the faith community: worship and covenant are not ends in themselves but means to impart divine life across cultural boundaries. His journey inaugurates a new anthropology—people defined by divine blessing rather than ethnic origin. As Abram moves forward in obedience, he carries not only hopes for personal descendants but also the weight of God's global redemptive purpose.

Having unpacked the foundational covenant motifs, we proceed to Abram's sojourn into Egypt—an episode that tests promise under foreign oppression and reveals God's protective advocacy.

3.5 Under Egyptian Shadow—Famine, Flight, and Divine Protection (Gen 12:10–20)

3.5.1 Ethical Ambiguity: Abram's Half-Truth Strategy

As the famine in Canaan deepened, Abram faced a dire choice: remain obedient to God's promise of inheritance or secure survival through human strategy. He opted for the latter, instructing Sarai to present herself as his sister rather than wife (Gen 12:11–13). This half-truth exploited cultural norms—where brothers could claim sisters without repercussion—but placed Sarai at moral and physical

81

risk. Abram's decision reflects the tension between faith in God's provision and reliance on human ingenuity when promises seem suspended by crisis. His fear of potential violence from Pharaoh (Gen 12:12) reveals both prudent self-preservation and wavering trust. The narrative underscores Abram's flawed humanity; even the friend of God stumbles when circumstances grow bleak. Yet Sarai's dignity and Abram's responsibility for her safety emerge as central concerns, shaping his later role as protector. This episode foreshadows recurring themes of ethical compromise under pressure, later mirrored in Abraham's treatment of Abimelech and Isaac's deception (Gen 26:7–11). The half-truth strategy introduces a sobering reminder: faith journeys often include missteps that require divine correction. Though Abram's choice endangered Sarai, God's covenantal initiative prevailed, preserving the promise despite human frailty.

3.5.2 Plagues on Pharaoh: God's Covenant Advocacy

When Pharaoh took Sarai into his palace, intending her as a wife, God intervened with plagues falling upon the Egyptian household (Gen 12:17). These divine afflictions—whether disease, infertility, or economic calamity—demonstrate Yahweh's protective advocacy over His covenant family. Pharaoh, perceiving the causal link between Sarai's presence and his people's suffering, confronted Abram with moral urgency, rebuking him for deception (Gen 12:18–19). God's plagues mirror later exodus judgments, presenting a miniature deliverance narrative where Israel's patriarch benefits from the same divine power that would later free the nation from Egypt. The episode highlights God's sovereignty to override human authority and cultural privilege in defense of covenant integrity. Abram's rapid restoration to favor following the plagues underscores God's mercy and the primacy of the promise over human schemes. This divine advocacy affirms that no worldly ruler can nullify God's vow, and that Abram's missteps, though serious, do not thwart the unfolding plan. The Egyptian interlude thus serves as a dramatic testament to Yahweh's commitment to protect Abraham and Sarah for the future birth of Isaac.

3.5.3 Exodus Prototype: Foreshadowing Israel's Future Deliverance

Abram's retreat from Egypt, laden with gifts from Pharaoh (Gen 12:16), foreshadows Israel's exodus in several key aspects: departure under threat, divine plagues to compel release, and refusal to remain under foreign dominion. The familial exodus anticipates the larger national deliverance that would shape Israel's identity in memory and worship (Ex 13:3–9). Abram's emergence "very rich in livestock, in silver, and in gold" parallels Israel's exodus with spoils from Egypt (Ex 12:35–36), underscoring the theme that God repays His people's obedience. His journey northward, avoiding the Nile's delta and seeking refuge in Canaan, models the directed migration under divine guidance later seen in the wilderness wanderings. The narrative link between Abram's Egyptian episode and Israel's subsequent liberation invites readers to see the patriarch as a microcosm of corporate salvation. This prototype functions liturgically: Israel's Passover reflections echo Abram's deliverance, embedding his story within communal observance. Thus, Abram's Egyptian sojourn serves both as a covenantal apprenticeship and as a theological precursor to the grand deliverance that defines Israel's covenantal self-understanding.

Having witnessed God's protective hand in foreign lands, Abram's faith now matures through covenantal vision, where promises deepen beyond spoken words.

3.6 The Starry Covenant—Righteousness Credited by Faith (Gen 15:1–6)

3.6.1 "Fear Not, Abram": Vision, Shield, and Reward

In the aftermath of Abram's Egyptian encounter, God spoke again: "Fear not, Abram, I am your shield; your reward shall be very great" (Gen 15:1). Addressing Abram's lingering anxiety, this initial reassurance combines divine protection ("shield") with promise recompense ("reward"). The term "shield" evokes imagery of a warrior deity defending His servant against cosmic and earthly threats. In Mesopotamian treaties, vassals often invoked their sovereign's shield for security; here, Yahweh adopts that role unilaterally. Abram's reward, though unspecified at first, ties directly to his offspring and land inheritance. This opening verse frames the subsequent unfolding of covenant content, preparing Abram's heart for deeper revelation. God's words counterbalance Abram's fear-induced deception, indicating restoration of covenantal relationship. The vision that follows invites Abram to gaze at stars, linking divine defense to cosmic assurance. This intimate dialogue transcends the remote pronouncement in Haran, establishing a personal bond characterized by divine empathy. Abram's response of faith inaugurates a new paradigm: righteousness becomes linked to trusting God's character more than to performing cultic rites.

3.6.2 Celestial Arithmetic: Counting Stars as Prophetic Assurance

God's command—"Look now toward heaven, and number the stars, if you are able to number them" (Gen 15:5)—transforms a simple survey into prophetic arithmetic. The immeasurable multitude of stars symbolizes offspring beyond calculable bounds, promising Abram descendants like cosmic dust. In ancient Near Eastern thought, stars often represented deities or spirits; here, the inversion

84

lies in God using star imagery to illustrate faith in His promise rather than heavenly pantheon. Abram's act of stargazing connects human frailty to divine infinitude, teaching that faith expands vision beyond earthly confines. The promise combines quantitative and qualitative dimensions: quantity (numerous descendants) and quality (righteous offspring). Later Jewish reflection would see this event commemorated in festivals tied to lunar months, reinforcing the covenantal memory. Abram's celestial encounter thus blends astronomy, prophecy, and trust into a singular moment of covenant initiation. His willingness to believe the unseen fosters a righteousness credited by God—a theme Paul later amplifies in Romans 4.

3.6.3 Justification Theme: Pauline Echoes in Romans 4

Scripture records that Abram "believed the LORD, and he counted it to him as righteousness" (Gen 15:6), introducing the doctrine of justification by faith. This concept reverberates through the New Testament, with Paul citing Abram as prototype: "Abraham believed God, and it was counted to him as righteousness" (Rom 4:3). The linkage affirms that obedience and faith precede law, positioning Abram outside and before Mosaic legislation. Justification by faith becomes the cornerstone of apostolic preaching, uniting Jews and Gentiles as heirs of Abram's promise (Rom 4:16–17). Early Christian apologetics leveraged this precedent to demonstrate that righteousness arises through trust in God's promises rather than through ritual observance. Abram's covenantal stargazing thus transcends its original context, informing universal theology on grace. The theological trajectory from Genesis to Romans underscores the continuity of redemptive revelation, with Abram's faith as a linchpin for New Covenant identity.

With Abram's faith established as righteousness, God deepens the covenant through solemn oath rituals, binding promise with sacrificial symbolism.

3.7 Cutting of the Pieces—Blood-Bound Oath (Gen 15:7–21)

3.7.1 Ancient Near-Eastern Treaty Parallels: Vassal and Suzerain

In the Ancient Near East, treaties between lesser vassals and sovereign suzerains were ratified through bilateral animal sacrifices, binding both parties under divine witness. Gen 15:9–11 describes Abram preparing heifers, goats, a ram, a turtledove, and a pigeon—symbolic pairings signifying the gravity of covenant vows. Unlike human treaties, only the suzerain passed between the carcasses, as indicated by prophetic darkness (Gen 15:17), illustrating God's unilateral commitment while Abram observed. The ceremonial cutting and arrangement of animals mirrored Hittite vassal treaties, yet Yahweh's sole procession through the pieces emphasized divine initiative. Abram's silent participation underscores his role as beneficiary rather than contractor. The theological import: God assumes full responsibility for covenant fulfillment, relieving Abram of performance-based liability. This act elevates the Abrahamic covenant above political alliances, marking it as cosmic covenant ratified by the Creator Himself.

3.7.2 Smoking Firepot and Flaming Torch: Theophanic Symbols

Genesis 15:17 recounts a "smoking firepot and a flaming torch" passing between the sacrificial pieces, classical theophanic symbols representing Yahweh's presence. Fire and smoke in biblical theophanies often signify God's holiness, judgment, and purifying presence (Ex 13:21–22; Isa 4:5). The imagery communicates both warmth and warning—divine blessing for obedience and judgment for breach. Abram, standing as covenant participant, witnessed these symbols, internalizing the seriousness of the vow. The mobile fire also foreshadows Israel's pillar-of-fire guidance during the exodus (Ex 13:21). By linking Abram's covenant to later national experiences of God's guiding flame, the narrative weaves thematic continuity through redemptive history. These theophanic elements underscore that covenant promises rest not on human words but on divine presence enacted in tangible phenomena.

3.7.3 Prophetic Timeline: Four-Hundred-Year Sojourn and Exodus

God's pronouncement following the covenant ceremony includes a prophetic timetable: "Know for certain that your offspring will be sojourners in a land not their own, and will be enslaved and oppressed four hundred years" (Gen 15:13). This timeline anticipates Israel's Egyptian bondage and ultimate exodus (Ex 12:40–41), linking Abram's covenant to national destiny. The prophecy of affliction underscores that covenant blessing often entwines with trial, shaping character and legacy through suffering. Yet the promise concludes with deliverance—"they shall come out with great possessions" (Gen 15:14)—assuring that God's purposes transcend immediate hardships. Abram's passive hearing of this grim forecast demonstrates deep trust, as he accepts both yoke and promise without recorded protest. The prophetic timeline thus provides historical orienting points, connecting Abraham's personal narrative to collective Israelite identity. As exilic communities later reflected on their history, this prophecy became a touchstone affirming God's faithfulness across centuries of upheaval.

Transition to Section 3.8: Emerging from the solemn oath, Abram and Sarai next grapple with human impatience in fulfilling the seed promise—a drama that unfolds through Hagar and Ishmael.

3.8 Hagar and Ishmael—Human Expediency Meets Divine Patience (Gen 16)

3.8.1 Cultural Norms of Surrogacy and Concubinage

In Mesopotamian and patriarchal cultures, surrogacy through maidservants like Hagar offered a socially accepted remedy for elite barrenness. Sarai's proposal that Abram conceive through Hagar aligns with customs preserving family lineage when wives remained childless. The practice of concubinage granted secondary wives limited rights yet affirmed offspring's integration into the primary household. Abram's acquiescence demonstrates deference to Sarai's status and prevailing social protocols. However, the narrative highlights tensions between legal custom and divine intention; reliance on human expedience disrupts covenantal timetable. Later Jewish tradition would view Hagar's status ambiguously—both as captive and as mother of a prophetic line (Gen 21:18). The episode reveals how cultural norms, though legitimate, can conflict with God's unique promises, necessitating divine correction and deeper reliance on grace over human contrivance.

3.8.2 Angel of the LORD at Beer-lahai-roi: Mercy in the Wilderness

After Hagar flees Sarai's harsh treatment, an "angel of the LORD" appears at Beer-lahai-roi, offering comfort, promise, and direction (Gen 16:7–11). The location—"well of the Living One who sees me"—symbolizes divine watchfulness in desolation. The angel's messages include a prophecy of Ishmael's future: a "wild donkey of a man," his hand against all and all against him (Gen 16:12). This nuance reveals Ishmael's significant legacy yet distinct from Abraham's covenant seed. The encounter underscores God's compassion for the marginalized, affirming Hagar's dignity and ensuring her survival. The theophanic presence prefigures later divine interventions in Israel's wilderness journeys, reinforcing the theme that God meets individuals in liminal, distressing places. Hagar's return to Sarai's household, under divine instruction, initiates a fragile family dynamic that will later again require God's intervention to preserve covenant purity.

3.8.3 Ishmael's Destiny: Twelve Princes and Nations in Tension

The angelic prophecy that Ishmael would father twelve princes prefigures the rise of tribes in Arabian and Aramean regions (Gen 25:12–16). This multiplicity of leaders echoes Abraham's promise of many descendants, yet Ishmael's line remains parallel to, not synonymous with, the covenant-seed trajectory through Isaac. The tension between Ishmael and Isaac foreshadows later geopolitical and theological conflicts between Israel and neighboring peoples. Ishmael's wilderness upbringing, coupled with divine blessing, illustrates that God's providence extends beyond the primary covenant line, shaping a broader human tapestry. His tribal descendants would interact with Israel throughout biblical history— from Isaac's descendants to the exilic period—highlighting the interconnectedness of Abraham's extended family. The narrative nuance balances divine impartiality with covenantal priority, respecting Ishmael's humanity while preserving Isaac's unique role. In subsequent centuries, Jewish and Christian interpreters wrestled with Ishmael's status, shaping interfaith dialogues to this day.

With human expediting yielding mixed results, God returns to deepen and clarify the covenant through personal name changes and the institution of circumcision in the next section.

3.9 Covenant Name Changes—From Abram to Abraham, Sarai to Sarah (Gen 17:1–16)

3.9.1 El Shaddai's Self-Revelation: "Walk Before Me and Be Blameless"

In Genesis 17:1, God identifies Himself to Abram as "El Shaddai," a title rich with connotations of sufficiency and nourishment, underscoring that the covenant rests on divine power rather than human merit. The command "walk before me" summons Abram into ongoing relational intimacy—every step of his life now oriented toward God's presence. "Be blameless," or "tamim" in Hebrew, does not demand sinless perfection but wholehearted devotion, reflecting covenantal integrity rather than legalistic flawlessness. This invitation echoes the call later given to Israel: to follow God in purity (Deut 18:13). El Shaddai's self-revelation marks a shift from nomadic promise to personal encounter, transforming Abram's identity at the core. Where "Yahweh" emphasizes God's covenant faithfulness, "El Shaddai" highlights sufficiency, assuring Abram that whatever trials lie ahead, God's provision is all-surpassing. The doubling of the divine name in subsequent chapters (e.g., "God Almighty blessed Noah," Gen 9:1) reinforces that God's sustaining power extends to future generations. Abram's response of bowing his face (Gen 17:3) exemplifies reverent acceptance of both promise and obligation. This posture models humility for covenant participants: worship emerges not from entitlement but from awe at divine initiative. El Shaddai's revelation thus reframes Abram's pilgrimage: it is not merely geographic but spiritual, a lifelong walk under God's nurturing care. Subsequent biblical writers draw on this term to assure the faithful of divine sustenance in hardship (Num 24:4; Ps 91:1). In Christian tradition, "God Almighty" resonates with Christ's promise of living water and bread (John 6:35), linking Abram's sufficiency motif to Messianic fulfillment. The call to "walk" implies motion—Abram's faith is active, not static. And "blameless" challenges every reader to integrity rooted in trusting God's sufficiency above structural ritualism. Through El Shaddai, Abram's name change becomes a theological pivot: from scarcity to abundance, from isolation to covenantal camaraderie under divine care.

3.9.2 Semitic Semantics: Breath Sounds Added to Covenant Names

The alteration of Abram to Abraham and Sarai to Sarah involves the insertion of the Hebrew letter "ה" (he), often vocalized as a breath sound "ah," signifying divine involvement in their identities. In Abram, "אַבְרָם" ("exalted father"), the added "ה" transforms it to "אַבְרָהָם" ("father of many"), marking God's promise concretely inscribed within his name. Sarai's "שָׂרַי" ("my princess") becomes "שָׂרָה" ("princess"), generalizing her role from personal to dynastic, reflecting that she too will be mother of nations. This semitic semantic shift parallels other biblical name changes—Jacob to Israel (Gen 32:28)—as markers of new mission and character. The letter "he" may evoke the breath of God (ruach), intimating that divine life force animates Abraham's renewed vocation. Grammar specialists note that Hebrew name changes frequently coincide with covenantal turning points, encoding God's word into personal identity. Theophoric elements—like the "el" in Israel—fuse human names with divine titles; here the silent "he" serves as a subtle yet profound divine signature. In ancient epigraphy, adding a single letter could distinguish between common and sacred status, showing how script functioned as theology. Abram's transformation thus becomes public proclamation: his name now proclaims the universal promise to descendants. Similarly, Sarah's new name signals her shift from private wife to matriarch of nations—a role she would fulfill in laughter and joy (Gen 21:6). These changes underscore that God's covenants affect both external circumstances and internal self-understanding. By breathing divine essence into their names, God ensures that Abraham's identity carries theological resonance across generations. Later prophets echo this naming motif: Isaiah calls Zion "Jehovah our righteousness" (Isa 33:16), integrating divine presence into communal identity. Abram and Sarai's new names thus stand as linguistic landmarks in redemptive history, testifying that every believer's identity is reshaped by covenant encounter.

3.9.3 Royal Motherhood: Sarah's Laughter Turned to Promise

Sarah's laughter in Genesis 18:12, born of incredulity at conceiving in old age, contrasts with her later proclamation at Isaac's weaning: "God has made laughter for me" (Gen 21:6). This linguistic play on "laughter" (צְחֹק, tzchok) transforms initial doubt into testament of joy, modeling how divine promise converts human skepticism. In ancient royal courts, the queen mother (gebirah) held significant political influence; Sarah's elevation to "mother of nations" parallels this office, granting her spiritual matriarchy over Abraham's lineage. Her role anticipates the "queen of Sheba" who comes to honor Solomon (1 Kings 10), illustrating how women in Scripture often embody covenantal grace. Sarah's late-life fruitfulness—Isaac's birth at ninety—defies natural calculation, affirming God's sovereignty over biology itself (Gen 17:17–19). Jewish midrash praises Sarah's hospitality and righteousness, linking her deeds to her reward of motherhood, revealing that covenant blessing often aligns with virtuous character. Christian commentators see Sarah as type of the Church, barren until filled by the Spirit, birthing spiritual heirs through faith. Her laughter shifts from incredulity to praise, framing her life as testament to God's reversal of human expectations. Sarah's weaning of Isaac at age three (Gen 21:8) formalizes his covenant status, acknowledging her active participation in covenant faith. Through Sarah's story, covenant motherhood emerges as both spiritual and literal, influencing how communities value women's roles in God's plan. Her laughter-turned-joy motif resonates in Pauline theology: "And where sin increased, grace abounded all the more" (Rom 5:20), tracing covenant reversal from curse to blessing. Sarah's legacy thus intertwines personal transformation with cosmic promise, illustrating that covenant name and vocation reshaping extend equally to men and women.

Having deepened understanding of identity transformation through covenant names, we next examine the formal sign that sealed belonging—circumcision—as symbol and seal of divine promise.

3.10 Sign of Circumcision—Seal of Belonging (Gen 17:9–27)

3.10.1 Ritual Practice: Surgical, Social, and Spiritual Dimensions

Circumcision, performed on every male in Abram's household on the eighth day (Gen 17:12), combined medical precision with profound communal meaning. Surgically, the removal of the foreskin required clean instruments and healing protocols, reflecting advanced ancient understanding of ritual hygiene. Socially, the ceremony marked entry into covenant community: servants, sons, and Isaac himself passed under the knife, signaling equality in divine promise regardless of ethnic origin. Spiritual dimensions ran deep: the visible mark on flesh reminded each generation that their bodies belonged to God, prefiguring later New Testament metaphors of "circumcision of the heart" (Rom 2:29). Jewish tradition highlights eighth-day significance, connecting circumcision to creation cycles and completion motifs. In Deuteronomic law, circumcision delineates Israel from surrounding nations (Deut 30:6), ensuring covenant fidelity through embodied sign. Abram's perfect compliance—obeying God's command without delay—contrasts Hagar's earlier hesitancy, underscoring obedience as the pathway to covenant seal. The ritual's communal feast that followed (Gen 17:27) combined celebration with covenant education, as elders recounted God's promises to assembled clansmen. Circumcision thus functioned as both private rite and public testimony, a boundary marker visible in communal gatherings. The surgical act introduced covenantal symbolism into the very substance of life and lineage, embedding promise in progeny. This bodily sign sets Abram's covenant apart from fleeting human contracts, invoking a sacred permanence. Over centuries, the practice shaped Israel's identity, surviving exile and diaspora as a sign of chosen status. In Christian theology, Paul reinterprets the sign as metaphorical "circumcision made without hands" (Col 2:11), emphasizing inward fidelity over physical ritual. Abram's institution of circumcision thus initiates a ritual tradition whose meanings evolve yet retain original covenant resonance.

3.10.2 Generational Scope: Eight-Day Infant and Household Inclusion

The stipulation that every male be circumcised on the eighth day ensures covenant continuity from birth, weaving the sign into earliest memory and family identity. Eight days after birth permitted sufficient healing, recognizing infant resilience and suggesting divine provision in biological processes. The inclusion of household servants in the rite (Gen 17:12) expands the covenant community beyond bloodline, foreshadowing later New Covenant openness to Gentile believers. Abram's command that even slaves from foreign origins receive the sign underscores God's sovereignty over all creation, not merely a single ethnic group. The attendant feast shared by free and bond exemplifies covenant hospitality, dissolving social barriers under divine order. Jewish law later prescribed synagogue readings of patriarchal narratives during circumcision ceremonies, teaching covenant history to successive generations. The ritual's familial nature—performed by patriarchs or elders—imbued the sign with paternal blessing, echoing God's fatherly role. Infant circumcision also shaped socialization: children born into covenant carried the mark as lifelong reminders of divine claim. This

94

embodied tradition distinguished Israel in diaspora, as circumcised and uncircumcised identities forged communal boundaries. The generational scope of circumcision highlights covenant as intergenerational promise, not isolated event. By instituting the sign at life's threshold, God binds future hopes to present obedience, weaving the promise into the fabric of family life. Abram's household thus becomes prototype for covenant communities throughout redemptive history, modeling inclusive yet structured belonging.

3.10.3 New-Covenant Anticipation: Heart Circumcision in Prophets and Paul

While physical circumcision signified external covenant membership, prophetic voices soon envisioned an inner transformation—circumcision of the heart—as hallmark of genuine devotion (Jer 4:4; Deut 30:6). Ezekiel prophesied a time when God would remove the "stony heart" and give a "heart of flesh" (Ezek 36:26), pointing to deeper spiritual renewal. In the New Testament, Paul emphasizes that true followers of Christ, whether Jew or Gentile, participate in a "circumcision made without hands" (Col 2:11), indicating an inward reality of faith over external rite. This reinterpretation does not negate Abraham's institution but fulfills its spiritual purpose: covenant membership mirrored first in flesh, then in spirit. The synoptic Gospels record Jesus' teachings on purity of heart over ritual compliance (Matt 23:25–28), resonating with prophetic calls for authentic worship. Early Christian communities wrestled with the necessity of physical circumcision, ultimately affirming inclusion by faith in Christ (Acts 15). The trajectory from Abram's sign to Pauline theology illustrates the dynamic interplay of body and spirit in covenant life. Heart circumcision becomes marker of covenant grace for all nations, embodying the universal blessing promised to Abraham (Gen 12:3). Abram's institution thus serves as foundation for evolving covenant understanding, from visible marker to internalized transformation. The dual aspects—

physical and spiritual—underscore that true belonging requires both outward allegiance and inward devotion.

With bodily and spiritual signs securing Abram's belonging, we now explore how covenant affirmed among kings—Melchizedek and Abimelech—reinforced the divine promise in political contexts.

3.11 Covenant Affirmed Among Kings—Melchizedek and Abimelech

3.11.1 Bread, Wine, and Blessing: Melchizedek's Priestly Typology (Gen 14:18–20)

Following Abram's victory over the four kings, Melchizedek—king of Salem and priest of God Most High—brought out bread and wine to meet Abram (Gen 14:18), introducing sacramental elements later echoed in Christian liturgy. The simple offering of bread and wine symbolizes sustenance and covenant fellowship, aligning Melchizedek's priesthood with Abram's divine patron. Melchizedek blesses Abram: "Blessed be Abram by God Most High, Possessor of heaven and earth" (Gen 14:19), acknowledging Yahweh's sovereignty over cosmic realms. Abram's tithe to Melchizedek (Gen 14:20) marks the first biblical instance of giving a tenth, foreshadowing Israel's tithe system (Lev 27:30). The interaction transcends ethnic boundaries: a Canaanite king-priest recognizing and honoring Abram's God, illustrating covenant's capacity to bridge political divides. Hebrews 7 later interprets Melchizedek as type of Christ—"without father or mother, without genealogy" (Heb 7:3)—highlighting eternal priesthood beyond Levitical lines. Abram's reception of blessing and tithe exchange cements his legitimacy before human rulers and divine authority. The bread and wine motif prefigures the Eucharist, connecting Abram's experience to New Covenant worship. Melchizedek's dual role as king and priest invites reflection on integration of spiritual and temporal

96

power under God Most High. This event demonstrates that covenant promise extends beyond family into global leadership structures. Abram's recognition by Melchizedek underscores that true kingship honors God's covenant channels. The typology invites readers to see Christ as ultimate Melchizedek, offering true bread of life and living wine to His people.

3.11.2 Tithes and Treaties: Economic Ethics in a Faith Context

By giving Melchizedek a tithe of all spoils, Abram institutes an economic ethic where victory yields responsibility to support God-appointed priests and ministers. Tithing became codified in Mosaic law as mechanism for sustaining Levites and the poor (Num 18:21–24; Deut 14:28–29), rooted in Abram's precedent. The practice underscores that material abundance flows from divine blessing and thus belongs in part to divine service. Abram's voluntary tithe, not coerced by law, exemplifies generosity as authentic response to grace. Economic treaties in the ancient world often included sacrificial offerings to deities, but Abram's tithe to a human priest typifies a new model: supporting earthly mediators of divine worship. This ethic safeguards against materialism by embedding redistribution within covenant framework. Later prophets condemn neglect of tithe as breach of covenant justice (Mal 3:8–10), tracing their critique back to Abram's example. The economic dimension of covenant thus emerges as integral to spiritual fidelity. Abram's tithe signals that faithfulness manifests not only in ritual but in stewardship. His act prefigures Christian giving principles, where believers support ministry through systematic offerings. By integrating treaty symbolism with tithing, Abram's covenant life models holistic devotion—spiritual, military, and economic. This holistic ethic contrasts with pagan tribute systems, where wealth served rulers rather than God's purposes. Abram's tithing thus becomes a template for sacrificial generosity under divine covenant.

3.11.3 Oath at Beersheba: Wells, Witness, and Boundary Stones (Gen 21:22–34)

In Genesis 21, Abram and Abimelech conclude a treaty at Beersheba, swearing oaths and erecting a boundary-separating monument called "Beersheba" (well of the oath). Beersheba's name combines "beer" (well) and "sheba" (oath or seven), linking water source with covenant vow. Abram dug a new well, contested by Abimelech's servants, prompting diplomatic negotiation reflective of earlier family councils. The agreement included sworn promises not to harm each other, witnessed by Abraham and the Philistine king, binding future relations in trust. Boundary stones served as physical reminders of treaty terms, akin to ancient practice of erecting pillars at political agreements. The well provided life-sustaining water for flocks, symbolizing mutual provision and peace. Abram's insistence on well rights illustrates covenant's practical dimensions—protecting economic livelihood under divine protocols. This treaty demonstrates how covenant principles translate into social justice and resource sharing. Biblical law later codifies well protection and neighborly rights (Ex 22:5; Deut 24:19), echoing Abram's example. The oath at Beersheba underscores that divine covenant fosters human peace accords grounded in fairness. Abram's covenant life thus extends from personal faith to regional diplomacy. The Beersheba encounter prefigures prophetic visions of justice flowing like waters (Amos 5:24). By marking the site with a named monument, Abram memorializes God's blessing and human responsibility, weaving spiritual dedication into landscape.

With covenant affirmed across cosmic, communal, and political spheres, we now trace its unfolding from Abraham through prophets to the Messiah, demonstrating continuity of divine promise.

3.12 Theological Trajectory—From Abraham to the Messiah

3.12.1 Covenant Continuity: Isaac, Jacob, and Israel's National Charter

The Abrahamic covenant finds successive affirmations in Isaac (Gen 26:2–5) and Jacob (Gen 28:13–15), ensuring that the promise moves beyond one man into corporate destiny. Isaac's sojourn and blessing at Gerar mirror his father's Egyptian episode, yet his focused trust in God secures covenant continuation. Jacob's ladder vision at Bethel extends Abram's altar motif, linking heaven and earth through divine assurance. These patriarchal reaffirmations consolidate covenant into national charter, culminating in Israel's formation under Moses (Ex 19–24). Moses' restatement of Abram's promise (Ex 32:13) reminds the people of their ancestral heritage amid disobedience at Sinai. The Deuteronomic formulation "to you and to your offspring" (Deut 29:14) reinforces inclusivity of tribal heads beyond immediate family. Israel's establishment in Canaan under Joshua echoes Abram's initial steps of obedience, marking land inheritance fulfillment. The pattern of calling, promise, and reaffirmation shapes Israel's liturgical calendar, with feasts recalling patriarchal milestones. David's enthronement invokes Abram's blessing, linking monarchy to covenant lineage (2 Sam 7). The prophetic corpus repeatedly points back to Abram's promise as metric of divine fidelity (Isa 41:8; Mic 7:20). The covenant's trajectory thus moves from individual promise to communal reality, tested and confirmed across generations. This continuity sets the stage for Messianic hopes, as covenant line descends through Judah to David and ultimately to Christ. Abram's initial call thereby anchors historical faith communities in unbroken divine purpose.

3.12.2 Prophetic Resonance: Isaiah's Servant and Micah's Ruler from Bethlehem

Prophetic literature amplifies Abrahamic promise by announcing a servant-king from Judah (Isa 11:1; 42:1) and a ruler born in Bethlehem (Mic 5:2), weaving covenant hopes into messianic expectation. Isaiah's servant songs depict one who embodies divine justice and brings light to the nations, fulfilling Abraham's universal blessing. Micah's oracle locates the birthplace of future ruler in David's hometown, underscoring covenant line continuity. These prophecies interpret Abram's promise through lenses of royal redemption and global mission. The servant's role as suffering redeemer echoes Abram's own trials—departure from home, exile in Egypt, and covenant testing. The prophetic imagination expands covenant scope from physical land to spiritual restoration. New Testament authors cite these oracles in affirming Jesus' messianic identity (Matt 2:6; Acts 13:47). Thus, prophetic resonance situates Abram's call within trajectory leading to Christ, the ultimate heir of covenant promises. The alignment of Abrahamic and Davidic lines in prophetic texts showcases theological weaving across centuries. Covenant theology thus integrates patriarchal, monarchical, and prophetic strands into cohesive redemptive narrative. Abram's initial trust in God anchors prophetic anticipation of universal salvation.

3.12.3 Pauline Synthesis: Justification by Faith and Inclusion of the Nations (Gal 3:6–9)

Paul articulates Abraham's significance for Gentile inclusion: "So then those who are of faith are blessed along with Abraham" (Gal 3:9), collapsing ethnic barriers in covenant community. He emphasizes that justification by faith, not law-keeping, marks true descendants of Abraham (Gal 3:7–8). This Pauline synthesis unlocks Abram's promise for all believers, linking Abrahamic blessing to gospel proclamation. The apostle cites Abram's belief counted as righteousness (Gen 15:6; Rom 4:3), establishing faith as covenant

100

entry point. The result is that "there is neither Jew nor Greek... for you are all one in Christ Jesus" (Gal 3:28). Paul's theology reframes covenant as cosmic reconciliation, fulfilling Abraham's universal blessing promise. Gentile believers thus inherit status as "offspring" (σπέρμα) of Abram, sharing in promise of the Spirit (Gal 3:14). The synthesis underscores that covenant faith transcends ethnic lineage, uniting diverse peoples. In Romans, Paul further roots this inclusion in Abraham's example, showing that covenant grace preceded Mosaic law, making covenant inherently open (Rom 2:28–29). The New Covenant church thus embodies the climax of Abrahamic trajectory, inaugurated by Christ's work. Abram's ancient call echoes in every gathering of faith where believers from all nations worship God together. This Pauline perspective completes the theological arc from Abram's obedience to global church mission.

Conclusion By the close of these covenantal encounters, Abram stands transformed: no longer merely a migrant of Haran, he is now Abraham, "father of many nations," marked by both divine words and earthly ordinances. The initial command to leave home blossoms into a tapestry of promises sealed by smoke and fire, star-counting assurances, and the cutting of sacrificial pledges. Even when human fear leads him to Egypt or expedient schemes with Hagar, God's patience and sovereign purpose prevail, shaping Abram's faith through both peaks of obedience and valleys of doubt. These chapters of call and covenant reveal that true relationship with God demands radical departure from all that binds us, coupled with the willingness to bear a sign—even in flesh—that proclaims belonging to a higher King. As Abraham moves forward, his footsteps echo through every altar he builds and every treaty he honors, pointing beyond himself to the ultimate fulfillment in the One who would come from his line—the Messiah, the living embodiment of every promise God ever spoke.

Chapter 4 – Places of Pilgrimage: Residences and Altars

Abram's journey of faith was not confined to inner conviction alone but was vividly inscribed upon the landscapes through which he passed. Every campsite became a sanctuary, every well a witness, and every altar a testament to God's unfolding promise. From fertile valleys to arid plains, Abram paused at key sites—some chosen by divine leading, others seized in moments of human need—to acknowledge God's presence, renew his trust, and mark pivotal encounters. These waypoints formed a spiritual map, guiding him through foreign territories and domestic challenges alike, each one shaping his identity as a pilgrim in search of a heavenly homeland. In this chapter, we explore the rich tapestry of Abram's residences and altars, revealing how geography and worship intertwined to deepen his covenant relationship and chart the course of redemptive history.

4.1 Shechem and the Oak of Moreh—First Footfall in Promise

4.1.1 Geo-Political Setting between Ebal and Gerizim

Situated in the heart of Canaan, Shechem occupied a vital crossroads between the northern and southern highlands, nestled between Mount Ebal and Mount Gerizim. Control of this junction meant dominion over principal caravan routes that funneled goods from Mesopotamia to Egypt and vessels from the Mediterranean to inland markets. As Abram arrived, local city-state allegiances lay fragmented, with Amorite chieftains vying for tribute and religious authority. The fertility of Shechem's terraced fields contrasted sharply with adjacent arid slopes, fostering both agricultural prosperity and pastoral competition. Archaeological remains reveal tumuli and fortification walls dating to the early second millennium BC, indicating a fortified settlement prepared for conflict yet open to trade. Religious shrines dotted the hillsides, each claiming patronage over rain and harvest, reflecting Canaanite polytheism. Political treaties, often sealed by blood oaths at sacred landmarks, bound neighboring tribes into transient alliances. Amid this volatile landscape, Abram's entry represented a new locus of divine claim, unsettling established power structures. His presence prompted local leaders to observe his foreign practices, curious about his uncircumcised yet authoritative posture. The strategic importance of Shechem ensured that word of Abram's altar and vows spread quickly through merchant and military networks alike. As Abram paused under the Oak of Moreh, he surveyed not only fields but potential footholds for a nascent faith community. His choice to worship in this contested zone signaled Yahweh's intent to supplant Canaanite deities with covenant worship. Thus, Shechem's geo-political tapestry formed both backdrop and stake for Abram's inaugural act of praise, foreshadowing Israel's later conquest under Joshua (Josh 8:30–35).

4.1.2 The Maiden Altar: Stones, Soil, and Spoken Promise

Abram's first altar at Shechem consisted of uncut field stones—each hewn only by God's providence rather than human hands—piled upon exposed earth. He scattered fresh soil at the base, creating a symbolic foundation for divine visitation in a land not yet fully under his possession. Offering no animal blood at this stage, Abram's altar emphasized relational proximity over sacrificial liturgy, focusing on spoken commitment to Yahweh's promise. He anointed the stones with oil brought from Haran, recalling his household's earlier worship while redefining oil's use as consecration in Canaan. Abram's prayer, though unrecorded, likely echoed Gen 12:7, acknowledging God's word and inviting the Almighty to dwell in this new territory. The simple materials—stone and soil—demonstrated that sacred space depends on divine presence rather than architectural splendor. Abram's solitary worship contrasted with communal Canaanite rites, highlighting Yahweh's accessibility to individual faith. Local onlookers, accustomed to temple priests and formal rites, found Abram's solitary act both perplexing and provocative. Through this altar, Abram instituted a pattern: first personal worship, then communal invitation. Future generations of Israel would replicate this model at Bethel and Gilgal, affirming that altars mark transgression points into covenant relationship. Abram's Maiden Altar thus became theological primer: places of promise begin with simple faith gestures before evolving into complex sacrificial systems. The intimacy of this first altar set tone for Abram's Canaanite journey, establishing stone markers of memory along his pilgrimage.

4.1.3 Canaanite Sacred Trees and Covenant Counter-Witness

The Oak of Moreh, revered by local pagans as dwelling place of tree spirits, formed natural cathedral for Canaanite deities. Abram's choice to erect an altar under this sacred tree constituted a direct challenge to indigenous worship norms, reclaiming the tree's shadow for covenant testimony. Whereas Canaanites poured libations to appease arboreal spirits, Abram poured oil to consecrate a grove to Yahweh's name. The dense canopy that once obscured sun-gods and storm-spirits now sheltered Abram's declaration of land promise. In situ, the tree's annual rings bore witness to centuries of pagan invocation, yet Abram's presence invigorated the site with new spiritual significance. His altar signaled an alternative worship narrative, supplanting dread of tree deities with confidence in Yahweh's providence. Local traditions held that childless couples visited Moreh's trees seeking fertility, but Abram's solitary act focused instead on divine promise of innumerable descendants. This counter-witness underlined covenant's capacity to reframe cultural symbols, redirecting sacred geography toward Yahweh. Subsequent Israelite practice at this site, as seen in Joshua's renewal of covenant (Josh 24:1–28), honored Abram's initial act. The Oak of Moreh transformed from Canaanite shrine to Israelite altar, illustrating faith's power to repurpose pagan landmarks. Abram's counter-witness under the tree thus stands as emblem of covenant creativity: God claims the very places once devoted to false worship.

Having inaugurated covenant altars at Shechem, Abram's pilgrimage climbed to Bethel and Ai, where worship ascended twin ridge heights and deepened relational intimacy with Yahweh.

4.2 Bethel–Ai Ridge—Prayer between Twin High Places

4.2.1 Topography of the Central Hill Country

Bethel and Ai rest along a strategic ridge in the central hill country, forming a natural amphitheater overlooking fertile valleys and terraced slopes. Ancient cartographers note these sites as visible sentry points controlling highland–lowland transitions, where east-wind storms clash with Mediterranean breezes. The steep ascent from the valley floor required pilgrims to traverse narrow goat paths, heightening anticipation of sacred encounter upon reaching each summit. Bedrock outcrops and natural cisterns near Bethel provided water storage for camp rituals, signaling divine provision in rocky terrain. Ruins at Ai reveal an Early Bronze Age fortress, indicating the site's longstanding military significance prior to Abram's pilgrimage. Panoramic views from the ridge span from Jericho's oasis to Hebron's hills, reminding Abram of the land's expanse and God's sovereign domain. The twin peaks echoed the symbolism of Mount Sinai and Horeb, linking Abram's altars to later Israelite theophanies. Windswept pines and terebinths clung to crevices, providing canopies for makeshift tents and altars. Abram's deliberate choice to worship at these heights underscored covenant's elevation above mundane valleys. The hill country's topography thus framed Abram's prayer as both humble ascent and transcendent dialogue.

4.2.2 Calling on the Name of Yahweh: Liturgy at the Look-Out

At Bethel, Abram "called upon the name of the LORD" (Gen 12:8), inaugurating formal liturgical patterns that Israel would later codify. Calling on God's name involved vocal invocation—pronouncing covenant titles like Yahweh or El Shaddai—binding memory and entreaty in spoken word. Abram likely recited ancestral prayers, weaving personal testimony with cosmic promises. Surrounded by windswept ridges, his voice carried across valleys, proclaiming Yahweh's sovereignty to unseen onlookers. As dawn broke, Abram's liturgy at the look-out included prayers for offspring, land security, and divine accompaniment. The act of prayer in elevated locale symbolized bringing heaven-ward petitions from earth below. Subsequent Israelite festivals would adopt "calling on the name" as communal act (Ps 116:4), tracing roots to Abram's high-place worship. Abram's liturgical innovation combined private devotion with prophetic proclamation, making each prayer an altar in the air. His calling on the name thus transformed Bethel into locus of divine-human dialogue.

4.2.3 Bethel's Echo through Jacob, Judges, and Prophets

Bethel's theological resonance reverberated through Israel's history: Jacob dreamt of ladder vision at this site (Gen 28:12–17), linking Abram's altars to visionary revelations. Judges record Israel's moral lapses and subsequent calls to repentance at Bethel (Judg 1:22–26), illustrating covenant's cyclical renewal. Prophets denounced idolatrous high-place worship at Bethel (Amos 5:5; Hos 10:8), yet the site remained locus for genuine repentance and rededication. Hezekiah's reforms sought altar removal at Bethel (2 Kings 18:4), acknowledging its dual potential for true and false worship. Jeremiah mourned Bethel's fall, lamenting its betrayal of Abram's initial devotion (Jer 7:12–14). In return from exile, Bethel regained prominence as place of communal prayer and sacrifice (Ezra 3:2). Mounting liturgical calendar cycles referenced Bethel's primacy, affirming covenant memory. Bethel's narrative tapestry thus weaves Abram's first high-place acts into Israel's collective conscience.

Descending from high-place reflections, Abram's pilgrimage pressed into the Negev's pastoral fringes, where tents and wells testified to covenant reliance amid scarcity.

4.3 Negev Encampments—Tents near the Famine Frontier

4.3.1 Pastoral Routes and Wells in the Southern Steppe

The Negev's rolling plateaus demanded agile movement of flocks along seasonal routes, following sparse rain-fed grasses. Wells, often known only to Bedouin sheikhs, punctuated these migratory paths, each controlled by competing tribal factions. Abram, familiar with well diplomacy, negotiated access through grain tribute or medical aid, securing life-saving water for his household. The harsh environment sharpened Abram's leadership: he assigned caretakers to maintain well covers and repair windlass ropes. Tent encampments clustered around oases like Beersheba and Engedi offered temporary reprieve, yet Abram avoided permanent settlement pending divine direction. Each well became a marker of covenant faith: Abram trusted God to confirm the next water source before setting camp. The interplay of tent and well embodied pilgrimage: temporary dwelling sustained by living water. This dynamic shaped Abram's identity as sojourner rather than landowner. Later Israelite nomads traced these same pastoral routes, enshrining Abram's Negev travels in national memory.

4.3.2 Transitional Altars: Dependence in Dry Seasons

In drought years, Abram built small cairn altars near wells, acknowledging dependence on divine provision of water. He offered small sacrifices—loaves and oil—rather than costly animal offerings, reflecting resource scarcity. Each altar stood beside troughs where sheep drank, reinforcing that sustenance flows from Yahweh. Abram's prayers at these altars included petitions for rain, echoing Deuteronomic laws on tithes and gleaning for landless travelers (Deut 24:19–21). Local nomads recognized these altars as tokens of Abram's unique God, fostering informal dialogue and exchange of folk wisdom about desert survival. Abram's transitional altars thus became both practical and spiritual lifelines, linking physical thirst to spiritual thirst in covenant relationship. These desert altars prefigured Elijah's confrontation with Baal prophets on Mount Carmel (1 Kings 18:30–39), where divine provision through drought-ending rain would affirm Yahweh's supremacy. Abram's dependence-driven altars thus anticipate national narratives of divine sustenance amid Israel's wilderness wanderings.

4.3.3 Lessons from Scarcity: Faith Refined on the Edge

Abram's Negev encampments tested faith at every turn: depleted herds, water disputes, and proximity to Philistine territories demanded trust beyond human resources. These trials refined Abram's character, nurturing humility and perseverance. He learned to discern God's guidance through unexpected events—wells found by dream or random conversation—understanding that divine provision often arrives through ordinary means. Scarcity fostered generosity: Abram shared scarce water with passing nomads, practicing covenant hospitality. His willingness to feed strangers amid lean times paralleled Abraham's later welcoming of the three visitors at Mamre (Gen 18:1–8). Desert hardship also revealed Abram's tendency toward anxiety, as seen in his flight to Egypt, teaching him the limits of human planning. Yet, each test drew him closer to covenant reliance, teaching that promise fulfillment often requires walking through dry valleys. These lessons carried forward into Israel's broader exile experience, where prophets called the people to trust God in barren lands (Isa 40:3–5). Abram's Negev journey thus stands as archetype for faith's refining fire on the margins of promise.

From desert thresholds, Abram's pilgrimage ascended to Hebron's fertile groves, where a permanent residence and profound hospitality awaited beneath the Oaks of Mamre.

4.4 Hebron and the Oaks of Mamre—Heartland Residence

4.4.1 Acquiring the Grove: Diplomatic Settlement with Amorites

Hebron's strategic importance lay in its natural springs and defensible ridges, making it valuable territory coveted by Amorite clans. Abram negotiated purchase of the cave of Machpelah resting beneath the Oaks of Mamre with Ephron the Hittite (Gen 23:8–16), employing local customs of public negotiation before city elders. He insisted on full monetary payment—400 shekels of silver—to secure unambiguous title, demonstrating respect for Amorite legal procedures. The transaction, recorded in writing and witnessed, preempted future disputes over burial rights. Abram's diplomatic acumen balanced firmness in covenant principle with cultural sensitivity to local norms. The grove's ownership symbolized not just a burying place but a foothold in Canaan, an anchor for Abram's household. This settlement contrasted earlier nomadic existence, signaling transition toward permanent patrimony. The successful acquisition underlined covenant's movement from promise to possession, establishing Hebron as patriarchal headquarters.

4.4.2 Hospitality under the Terebinths: Three Visitors and a Promise

Under the aged terebinths of Mamre, Abram welcomed three visitors—a theophanic visitation of Yahweh and two angels—proffering washed feet, bread, and tender veal (Gen 18:1–8). The hospitality ritual required quick preparation: choosing the finest flour for baking, selecting a choice calf, and serving curds and milk—meals emblematic of covenant abundance. Abram's reverential posture, bowing low as he stood by the tent entrance, acknowledged the visitors' divine status. The dialogue that followed included reaffirmation of the seed promise, with Sarah overhearing laughter at the prospect of bearing a son in old age. This scene interweaves hospitality ethics with prophetic proclamation: as Abram ministers, he also receives cosmic promise. The three-visitor motif later echoes Trinitarian reflections in Christian theology, seeing in Abraham's tent a foretaste of divine fellowship. Local lore held the terebinths as spirits' abodes, yet Abram's worship reframed these trees as witness to divine fellowship. The Mamre hospitality thus models covenant interplay of service and reception, foreshadowing spiritual feasts in heavenly banquet imagery (Rev 19:9).

4.4.3 From Tent to Tomb: Hebron as Patriarchal Capital

Abram's pitched tent at Hebron functioned as more than dwelling; it was mobile chapel, administrative center, and meeting hall for surrounding clans. The tent's vestibule hosted covenant councils and legal deliberations, while inner chambers served as private prayer space. As Abram aged, he designated this site for final rest, instructing that Sarah and later himself be buried in Machpelah, linking life and death within covenant geography. Hebron thus matured into patriarchal capital, a central node connecting spiritual and political spheres. Jacob, returning from Paddan-Aram, would later reside here (Gen 35:27), while David's kingship would begin and end in Hebron (2 Sam 2:4; 1 Kin 2:10). The persistent significance of Hebron across generations attests to Abram's foundational choice. The Oaks of Mamre witnessed covenant feasts and transitions of power, embedding Abram's legacy in national memory. Through tent and tomb, Hebron bridged Abram's temporal pilgrimage and eternal heritage.

Having established both desert and heartland altars, Abram's pilgrimage turns to the Valley of Siddim, where covenant worship intertwines with martial deliverance and royal blessings.

4.5 Valley of Siddim—Rescue, Royal Blessing, and Battlefield Worship

4.5.1 War of the Four Kings: Strategic Movements and Alliances

The Valley of Siddim, located near the Dead Sea's southwestern shore, formed a natural battleground where four Mesopotamian-backed kings clashed with five Canaanite city-state rulers. These alliances mirrored broader geo-political tensions, as east-bank princes like Kedorlaomer of Elam asserted tribute over rebellious western cities. Abram's nephew Lot, living in Sodom, became collateral in this power struggle, prompting Abram's martial response. Mobilizing his trained household servants—numbering several hundred—Abram crossed the Jordan under cover of night, demonstrating tactical surprise. He divided his forces into strategic units, encircling the coalition's rear and cutting off escape routes toward the Salt Sea. The nocturnal assault culminated in a rout, with Abram recovering Lot, his possessions, and captives from allied towns. This military campaign showcased Abram's leadership and covenant-driven courage, as he pursued justice over plundering zeal. His pursuit extended to Hobah, north of Damascus, indicating logistical endurance and knowledge of regional geography. The battle underscored that covenant faith entailed not only worship but righteous defense of kin and justice. Abram's rescue operation disrupted the prevailing tribute system and reshaped local power balances. Egyptian and Hittite chariot corpora observed from ridges, noting Abram's audacity in challenging imperial vassals. Sometime later, word of his triumph spread along trade routes, enhancing Abram's reputation among Canaanite and Mesopotamian elites. His ability to unite disparate servants under a just cause presaged Israel's later national armies. The strategic mastery displayed at Siddim thus inaugurated covenant imperatives beyond altars: active intervention for righteousness.

4.5.2 Melchizedek's Salem Table: Bread, Wine, and Benediction

After victory, Abram met Melchizedek—king of Salem and priest of God Most High—who brought out bread and wine to refresh the combatants (Gen 14:18). This spontaneous provision resembled later sacramental motifs, symbolizing spiritual sustenance awarded to those who uphold divine justice. Melchizedek blessed Abram: "Blessed be Abram by God Most High, Maker of heaven and earth" (Gen 14:19), affirming that true victory belongs to the covenant God. Abram responded by giving Melchizedek a tithe of all recovered spoils, establishing a model of grateful reciprocity. The pairing of bread and wine signaled both physical restoration and covenant fellowship, foreshadowing communal meals in later Israelite and Christian worship. Melchizedek's dual role as king and priest demonstrated that political authority and spiritual mediation could coexist under Yahweh's sovereignty. Abram's deference to Melchizedek, despite holding martial ascendancy, emphasizes humility in leadership. The episode transcends ethnic boundaries: a patriarch from Ur receives blessing from a Canaanite ruler-priest, illustrating covenant's cross-cultural reach. Subsequent Jewish tradition celebrated Melchizedek's priesthood as eternal, lacking genealogical record, prefiguring Messiah's priestly order in Hebrews 7. Abram's tithe to Melchizedek also initiates Israel's tithe tradition under Mosaic law (Lev 27:30–34). The Salem table thus embodies covenant integration of worship and ethical warfare. Abram's encounter affirms that God honors justice and sustains His people through unexpected mediators. Local lore later identified Salem with Jerusalem, connecting Abram's experience to the city's enduring sacred status. Through this blessing, Abram's pilgrimage entwines martial deliverance with liturgical innovation.

4.5.3 Righteousness Revealed: Worship in the Wake of Victory

Following the conflict at Siddim, Abram offered worshipful thanksgiving at the scene, laying his own altar on the battlefield site. This act signified that the victory was not for personal glory but for divine vindication. Abram's worship involved burnt offerings from his recovered flocks, integrating sacrificial rites with militant triumph. The site's transformation from battleground to altar underscores covenant theology: righteous warfare culminates in restored worship. Local Canaanite survivors observed Abram's altar, some forsaking former deities in intrigue over his God's power. Abram's liturgy likely included recounting God's faithfulness, establishing oral tradition among his household. Archaeological surveys of the Siddim plain reveal flint cairns that may mark ancient altars, echoing Abram's practice. The battlefield-altar motif becomes later a model for Israel's vow altars after victory (Judg 1:20; 1 Sam 7:12). Abram's pattern shows that war against injustice must conclude in worship, aligning human action with divine purpose. The dual reality of witness—military and liturgical—strengthened Abram's covenant identity. His worship at Siddim affirms that God's deliverance invites both communal gratitude and theological reflection. Abram's altar thus serves as point of convergence for faith and action, a template for future covenant encounters. This seamless transition from combat to covenant worship distinguishes Abram's pilgrimage as a journey of integrated discipleship.

From the eastern battle plains, Abram's pilgrimage turns southward to Beersheba, where covenant oaths crystallize around life-giving wells.

4.6 Beersheba Wells—Covenant of Water and Witness

4.6.1 Swearing the Sevenfold Oath with Abimelech

At Beersheba, Abram and Abimelech negotiated a non-aggression pact, each swearing an oath witnessed by seven elder men of the city (Gen 21:22–23). The sevenfold element—"sheba" in Hebrew—associated with completeness and covenant affirmation (cf. Num 29:35). Abram dug a new well here, contesting ownership with Abimelech's servants, who reopened an old site Abram's herders had sealed (Gen 21:30). The ensuing dialogue invoked sacred promises: Abimelech's oath ensured Abram's descendants would inherit peaceful pasture rights, while Abram pledged non-aggression. Sealing the treaty with an oath before assembled elders and rising dawn light anchored the covenant in communal memory. The pact transcended temporary alliances; it embedded mutual respect into local governance. Abimelech's delegation recognized Abram's God as arbiter of oaths, lending monotheistic weight to their promise. Both parties formalized terms with verbal formula and witness, paralleling royal treaty customs yet under divine sovereignty. The event underscores that water rights in arid regions demand legal clarity and spiritual accountability. Abram's insistence on formalizing well usage reflects covenant obligations toward neighborliness and fair resource distribution. This oath at Beersheba influenced future Israelite boundary stipulations (Deut 11:24), linking Abram's practice to national land laws. The sevenfold oath thus becomes nexus of faith, law, and survival in covenant pilgrimage.

4.6.2 Planting the Tamarisk: Living Altar of Perpetual Praise

Upon concluding the treaty, Abram "planted a tamarisk" (shittah tree) under which he "invoked the name of the LORD, the Everlasting God" (Gen 21:33). The tamarisk, known for durability in desert climates, symbolized perpetual remembrance of covenant and divine provision. Its wide canopy offered shade for travelers and hospitality for wayfarers, extending Abram's legacy of openness. The living altar contrasted with stone cairns, infusing covenant memory into growth cycles and seasons. Abram's planting anticipated Israelite commandments to "plant trees along the way" as reminders of the Lord's deeds (Deut 20:19). The evergreen herbage of the tamarisk suggested resilience of faith amid arid trials. This living monument intertwined ecological stewardship with liturgical practice. Abram's words beneath its branches likely included thanksgiving for water, life, and neighborly peace. Generations later, prophets would reference planting as metaphor for stability and growth under God's blessing (Jer 17:7–8). The tamarisk thus served dual purpose: ecological marker of treaty site and liturgical symbol of enduring covenant. Its continued existence invited future pilgrims to ponder God's everlasting faithfulness. Abram's living altar thus advanced covenant signs beyond static monuments into dynamic creation.

4.6.3 Southern Gate of the Patriarchs: Beersheba in Later Israelite Memory

Beersheba emerged as "the southernmost" point of Israel's territorial promise, later known as the "gate of the wilderness" (Judg 20:1).

Pilgrimage routes from Hebron and Jerusalem converged here, linking heartland centers to desert frontiers. Israelite caravans carried tributes and tithes past the wells, recalling Abram's treaty and resting under the tamarisk. The site's name—"house of the oath"—ritually reminded travelers of covenant commitments. During the monarchy, kings dispatched envoys through Beersheba to secure southern alliances. Prophetic texts reference "holy Olives at Beersheba" as symbols of covenant faith (Amos 5:5). Ezra and Nehemiah mention reestablishment of boundaries reaching Beersheba, confirming its enduring legal significance (Neh 11:25). Jewish pilgrims ascending to Jerusalem included Beersheba prayers in liturgical cycles, honoring Abram's foundational acts. The southern gate thus became theological conduit between desert margins and sacred centers. Its wells continued to serve Bedouin communities, embedding Abram's practice in everyday survival. The enduring memory of Abram's covenant at Beersheba fortified Israel's sense of national identity. Thus, Beersheba stands as liturgical and legal portal in the landscape of faith, linking patriarchal initiative to communal heritage.

Having solidified covenants through wells and living altars, Abram's journey culminates at Mount Moriah—site of ultimate trust demonstrated through the sacrificial test of Isaac.

4.7 Mount Moriah—Altar of Ultimate Trust

4.7.1 Three-Day Journey: Geography of Anticipation and Dread

Mount Moriah lay some three days' journey north of Beersheba, requiring Abram and young Isaac to traverse arid plains and rocky wadis—terrain marked by sparse vegetation and unpredictable water sources. The multi-day trek demanded rigorous planning: provisions had to be rationed, herds secured, and sufficient wood gathered for the impending sacrifice. Abram's decision to travel this distance reflects profound obedience to divine instruction, preparing both patriarch and son for the ultimate test. Each day's progress brought new topographical features—dry riverbeds, precipices, and vantage points—that compounded emotional tension. Abram explained to servants that he and Isaac would return, instructing them to stay behind with beasts—a directive underscoring faith in God's promise. As they ascended, Isaac carried wood and firepan, oblivious to the true purpose of the journey, while Abram bore the knife and covenant weight. The psychological landscape mirrored the physical ascent: each rocky step intensified anticipation and dread. Their arrival at Moriah's designated height signified reaching the brink of divine-human drama. The geography of Moriah thus shaped the narrative's emotional arc: a pilgrimage of trust through wilderness desolation to sacred summit. Abram's traversal of Mount Moriah anticipates later pilgrimages of Israel to temple mount, where descendants would similarly climb for worship and covenant renewal. The three-day journey also parallels Israel's sojourns, testing faith through time and terrain. Abram's ascent remains paradigmatic of faith's pilgrimage: moving toward divine encounter through hardship and hidden purpose.

4.7.2 Binding and Substitution: Ram Caught in Covenant Thicket

At Mount Moriah's summit, Abram bound Isaac, situating him on the altar's woodpile in resolute obedience (Gen 22:9). The act of binding ('asah) conveyed complete submission—both father and son laid aside personal will for divine command. Just as Isaac's hands were bound, Abram's heart wrestled with promise and command intertwined. When an angel intervened, Abram's eyes beheld a ram caught by its horns in a thicket—a providential substitute for his son. The ram's provision exemplifies divine substitutionary mercy, establishing theological foundation for later sacrificial systems and typology of Christ as Lamb (John 1:29). Abram renamed the site "Yahweh Yireh" (Jehovah Jireh), meaning "The Lord will provide," embedding provision theology into place name (Gen 22:14). The

117

substitution narrative emphasizes that God's covenant requires both obedience and grace. The thicket's tangled branches convey entrapment transformed into deliverance. Abram's act of offering the ram in Isaac's stead demonstrated that obedience does not preclude divine intervention. This episode shapes Israel's sacrificial rituals where innocent animals stand in for the guilty, pointing forward to ultimate atonement. Mount Moriah thus became locus for both judgment and mercy, sanctified by Abraham's obedience and God's provision. Later temple worship on Moriah would incorporate these dual themes in daily sacrifices and Yom Kippur rites. Abram's sacrifice typology thus resonates through centuries of redemptive ritual, anchored in Moriah's sacred soil.

4.7.3 Prophetic Vista: From Abraham's Altar to Solomon's Temple

Jewish tradition identifies Mount Moriah with the temple mount in Jerusalem, where Solomon would build the First Temple (2 Chron 3:1), linking Abram's altar site to national worship center. Solomon's selection of this hill acknowledges divine preference revealed first to Abraham, centering Israel's spiritual geography on covenant provision. Prophets Isaiah and Jeremiah reference "the mountain of the LORD's house" as place of instruction and restoration (Isa 2:2; Jer 31:38–40), echoing Moriah's covenant origins. The temple's lasting dedication ceremonies paralleled Abram's altar—burnt offerings, incense, and communal prayer—fulfilling promise of divine dwelling among His people. The sacrificial system that developed within temple courts drew theological legitimacy from Abraham's original test. Ezekiel's temple vision (Ezek 40–48) situates the altar as heart of restored worship, echoing Moriah's primacy. In the intertestamental period, Jewish pilgrims ascending to Herod's Temple Mount chanted hymns recalling Abraham's faith. Christian tradition further associates Mount Moriah with Calvary, teaching that God's provision lamb from Moriah prefigures Christ's atonement (Heb 13:12). The prophetic vista thus extends Abram's altar from private covenant drama to cosmic worship locus. Mount Moriah stands as focal point where divine promises, human obedience, temple worship, and messianic hope converge across redemptive history.

From the heights of Moriah, Abram's pilgrimage descends to Hebron's Machpelah, securing a burial plot that testifies to covenant hope beyond death.

4.8 Machpelah near Hebron—Purchase of a Promised Plot

4.8.1 Negotiation with Hittite Elders: Legal Title Deed Secured

After Sarah's death, Abram approached the Hittite leaders of Hebron to secure a burial site, insisting on a formally negotiated purchase rather than accepting a gift (Gen 23:3–9). He stood before the "sons of Heth," publicly declaring his intention to acquire the cave of Machpelah for full silver payment, thereby preventing future disputes over ancestral burial rights. The Hittites, moved by Abram's sincerity and status, offered the land and cave as gracious gift, but Abram—honoring covenant integrity—asserted the necessity of legal formality. He weighed out four hundred shekels of silver, ratifying the sale "in the hearing of the sons of Heth" (Gen 23:16). This transparent transaction, witnessed by city elders, created an irrefutable title deed. The process mirrored Mesopotamian land sale conventions, which required public witnesses and sealed payment to establish permanent ownership. Abram's insistence on paying full price underscored his respect for local laws and for the sanctity of covenant promises. The negotiation ceremony likely included ceremonial presentation of silver ingots on clay bullae, signifying divine witness to the covenant purchase. By securing Machpelah, Abram anchored his family's hope of resurrection and fulfillment in tangible geography. This legal transaction stands as only property deed recorded in Genesis, emphasizing significance of burial places in covenant theology. Abram's methodical approach to Machpelah's purchase models stewardship of divine gifts with legal propriety.

4.8.2 Cave of the Patriarchs: Theology of Hope in Burial

The cave of Machpelah—natural limestone formation beneath a grove of terebinths—became family mausoleum for Sarah, Abram, Isaac, Rebekah, Jacob, and Leah (Gen 50:13), embodying anticipation of resurrection and continuity beyond death. Burial within family land signified hope in God's promise that descendants would inherit the earth. The cave's interior chambers, carved by erosion, provided intimate spaces for interment and mourning. Abram's burial of Sarah here established theological precedent: even in death, covenant membership secures place in God's unfolding plan. Later Jewish pilgrims visiting Machpelah regarded it as access point to patriarchal presence, offering stones and prayers at the sacred site. Cave burials contrasted with cremation or communal tombs, underscoring belief in bodily preservation for future restoration. Machpelah's layered burials became physical genealogy, linking covenant generations. Christian reflection sees Machpelah as sign of hope in resurrection, paralleling New Testament tomb imagery. The cave's endurance through centuries of political upheaval testifies to power of covenant memory embedded in place. Abram's theology of hope in burial thus transforms Machpelah from simple grave to monument of divine promise.

4.8.3 Pilgrimage Center across Generations and Faith Traditions

Throughout Jewish history, Machpelah remained site of annual pilgrimages, drawing cohorts from distant regions to commemorate patriarchal faith. During Second Temple period, pilgrims recited Genesis passages at the entrance, reaffirming covenant bonds.

Christian pilgrims also venerated Machpelah, associating it with the roots of salvation history. Islamic tradition identifies the site as "Ibrahim's" burial, reflecting Abraham's centrality across monotheistic faiths. The shared reverence underscores Machpelah's capacity to bridge doctrinal divides through common patriarchal memory. Crusader-era churches built chapels above the cave, symbolizing layered spiritual claims to the place. Ottoman authorities recognized its sanctity by constructing protective enclosures, preserving access for worshippers. Modern archaeological surveys have mapped subterranean tombs, confirming multi-period usage. Machpelah's status within Hebron's Old City reinforces its ongoing role as pilgrimage nexus. Its layered architecture—cave, mosque, synagogue—testifies to living faith traditions converging on Abraham's deed. Through Machpelah, Abram's legacy continues to inspire communal journeys of remembrance and hope. The site's endurance affirms that covenant places, once consecrated, remain sacred across millennia.

Having traced Abram's altars from battlefield to burial cave, we now turn to eastern highland pastures—seasonal worship circuits where covenant observance extended into tribal partnerships.

4.9 Eastern Highland Pastures—Seasonal Circuits of Worship

4.9.1 Transhumance Paths and Boundary Pillars

The eastern hill country beyond the Jordan hosted seasonal transhumance routes where Abram's herds and those of allied clans followed summer pastures to higher elevations and winter flocks down to lower valleys. These pathways were ancient by Abram's day, marked by weathered stone pillars—"matzevot" or boundary stones—inscribed or deliberately arranged to demarcate grazing rights. Abram respected these markers, negotiating passage and sharing water sources in accordance with local custom, thus

121

maintaining peaceful relations with nomadic tribes. The pillars often stood near springs or grazing clearings, serving both legal and ritual functions: shepherds paused to offer brief prayers of thanksgiving before moving on. Abram's familiarity with transhumance law (cf. Deut 11:24) reflected his Mesopotamian upbringing, yet his worship among these routes introduced Yahweh's covenant into regions previously known only for clan totems. The boundary stones, under Abram's gaze, gained new significance as silent witnesses to divine promises rather than tribal claims. In later Israelite practice, boundary pillars became central in Deuteronomic curses and blessings (Deut 27:2–8), linking land ethics to covenant obedience. Abram's observance of transhumance protocols thus foreshadowed Israel's legal codifications on land and neighbor. The seasonal circuits established a rhythm of pilgrimage, where spiritual reflection accompanied flocks' movement. By intertwining worship with agricultural economy, Abram modeled a holistic covenant life that transcended fixed sanctuary spaces. Transhumance paths became liturgical circuits, with Abram's altars and boundary stones charting a sacred geography across eastern heights. These seasonal journeys underscored that covenant faith must adapt to life's cycles, embedding worship in daily labor. Abram's respect for existing boundary traditions, combined with his introduction of Yahweh's presence, transformed eastern pastures into nodes of covenant memory and blessing. The intersection of pastoral livelihood and pilgrimage thus enriched Abram's faith journey and laid groundwork for Israel's own pasture-shaped identity.

4.9.2 Stone Cairns and Communal Offerings with Allied Shepherds

In collaboration with allied shepherd groups, Abram participated in building small stone cairns—"galgalim"—to commemorate shared acts of deliverance or divine provision along pasture margins. These cairns, stacked at crossroads of grazing plots, served as focal points for brief communal sacrifices: handfuls of flour, pressed olive oil, or small portions of fresh meat. Abram's leadership ensured that these offerings honored Yahweh rather than local deities, persuading allied clans to adopt new covenant language in their memorial rites. The ritual involved communal circumambulation of the cairn, reciting covenantal psalms, and anointing stones with oil, reinforcing solidarity under Yahweh's lordship. Local traditions held that cairns once symbolized warrior victories; Abram repurposed them to memorialize spiritual victories—mercies received on the move. These communal observances fostered cross-cultural spiritual networks, sowing seeds of monotheism beyond Abram's immediate household. The cairns also functioned as navigational beacons in otherwise featureless landscape, guiding shepherds to fresh water or grazing ground. Abram's integration of commemorative cairns into pastoral life reflects a theology of memory: covenant grace is both topic of daily work and cause for shared celebration. Later Mosaic law would echo these memorial stones in instructions to "write the words of this law on the stones" (Deut 27:2), embedding Scripture in public memory. The collaborative offerings at cairns thus prefigure Israel's corporate worship, where individual families and tribal units converge under shared covenant markers. Abram's practice illustrates how everyday work—shepherding—can be sacralized through simple, yet profound, collective acts of remembrance. The stone cairns and their rituals underscore that faith communities flourish when work and worship intersect in tangible landmarks. Abram's cairn-building among eastern shepherds thus transforms pastoral cooperation into spiritual fellowship.

4.9.3 Stewardship of Land: Ethics of Grazing and Gratitude

Abram's seasonal grazing required careful stewardship to prevent overgrazing, erosion, and depletion of fragile highland flora. He instructed shepherds to practice rotational grazing—moving flocks among pasture subdivisions every few days—to allow regrowth of grasses and prevent soil compaction. Abram also designated fallow periods for certain slopes, aligning with later Israelite practices of sabbatical land rest (Lev 25:4). His emphasis on sustainable pasture management demonstrated that covenant faith includes care for creation, anticipating biblical mandates on environmental ethics. At each new grazing location, Abram held brief ceremonies of gratitude—pouring oil near springs and offering animal tithes at cairns—acknowledging that life-sustaining resources originate from divine generosity. These thanksgivings fostered an ethic of sufficiency, discouraging hoarding of forage or water in lean seasons. Abram's stewardship extended to wildlife: he issued unspoken decrees to shepherds to avoid hunting rare mountain gazelles, preserving biodiversity. Collaborating with Bedouin allies, Abram learned additional land-care techniques, sharing his own wisdom in turn, creating a culture of mutual respect for ecological balance. His integrated approach contrasts with exploitative practices of some Canaanite chieftains who deforested lands for short-term gain. Abram's pastoral ethics exemplify biblical vision of humans as caretakers rather than conquerors of creation (Gen 2:15). By linking grazing practices with covenant remembrance, Abram taught that right living flows from grateful recognition of God's provision. The eastern highland stewardship thus emerges as a vital chapter in Abram's faith, translating covenant into concrete ecological responsibility. His example resonates for modern readers grappling with sustainable land use, showing ancient roots for environmental care within covenant theology.

From pastoral circuits and stone memorials, we now turn to the overarching theology of place and pilgrimage—how Abram's repeated returns to altars mapped a covenant landscape shaping his faith and legacy.

4.10 Mapping the Covenant Footprint—Theology of Place and Pilgrimage

4.10.1 Rhythms of Return: Revisiting Altars over Decades

Abram's habit of revisiting altars—at Shechem, Bethel, Hebron, and beyond—established a rhythm of covenant reaffirmation punctuating decades of pilgrimage. Each return involved not simply repeating past rituals but layering fresh testimony onto existing monuments: additional anointing, new sacrifices, and verbal recounting of intervening mercies. These cyclical visits created concentric circles of memory, where covenant promises were rearticulated in the context of lived experience—victory, loss, famine, growth. Abram's returns served as personal debriefings, comparing original expectations with current reality and adjusting faith trajectories accordingly. For instance, revisiting Bethel after the Egyptian sojourn would have prompted thanksgiving that God had indeed preserved land promise despite earlier fears. Such rhythmic revisiting mirrors Israelite festivals of pilgrimage—Passover, Pentecost, Tabernacles—where communal memory renews covenant bonds (Ex 23:17). Abram's personal festival calendar thus prefigured national liturgical cycles, anchoring spiritual identity in sequential place-based worship. His repeated altars became time-stamped waypoints, charting a covenant journey that spanned generations and incarnated promise in geography. This pattern demonstrates that faith develops through reflective practice—return, remember, recommit. Abram's pilgrimage rhythm underscores that covenant is both event and ongoing relationship, sustained over time through intentional revisitings of sacred sites. His example invites believers to mark anniversaries of divine encounter, ensuring memory remains dynamic rather than fossilized. The theology of rhythms reveals that place-based worship fosters spiritual resilience across life's fluctuating seasons. Abram's repeated altar pilgrimages thus model how faith communities can sustain generational fidelity to divine promise.

4.10.2 Spatial Memory: How Geography Shapes Faith Narrative

The physical terrain of Abram's journey—hills and wells, valleys and caves—served as mnemonic devices imprinted on his mind and heart, shaping theology through spatial associations. Each topographical feature embedded narrative elements: the Oak of Moreh for promise, Beersheba wells for covenant oath, Machpelah cave for hope in death. Abram's spatial memory operated like a divinely curated pilgrimage map, where recalling one site brought to mind associated promises and lessons. This geographical theology finds echoes in Psalms, where writers speak of meditation "on Your Word" as one walks the "wilderness" (Ps 119:55), linking terrain to spiritual reflection. Israel's later sacred map—Jerusalem, Gilgal, Gibeon—traced from Abram's footsteps, affirmed that land itself communicates divine story. Ancient believers inscribed altars and boundary stones to teach children covenant history through walkable paths. Abram's integration of place and narrative prefigured Israel's establishment of Levitical cities as living catechism (Josh 21). Modern pilgrims following Abram's route benefit from similar spatial memory, reenacting geography to connect with origins of faith. Geography shapes faith narrative by providing tangible anchors for abstract promises, enabling believers to inhabit Scripture physically. Abram's pilgrimage thus models the pedagogical power of sacred landscape, a practice embraced by later traditions of holy land pilgrimage. His spatial theology demonstrates that God reveals truth not only through words but through carved contours of earth. Place-based memory anchors identity, ensuring covenant narrative remains embodied across terrains and generations.

4.10.3 Transition to Chapter 5: Defining Incidents after the Call

Having mapped the contours of Abram's covenant footprint—residences, altars, wells, and memorial stones—we stand at the threshold of Chapter 5, poised to examine how the profound places of pilgrimage intersect with defining incidents that tested, refined, and confirmed Abram's faith. The altars and sites charted here provide the sacred backdrop for encounters with famine, warfare, divine vision, and covenant negotiation. As Abram moves from place-based worship to relational crises and covenant deepening, we will see how each location's spiritual significance informs his responses to subsequent trials. In Chapter 5, these sites will transition from static monuments to dynamic theaters of faith in action, illuminating how covenant promises hold through the crucible of defining life events.

Conclusion By tracing Abram's footsteps across these sacred locales—from dispute-settling wells to life-affirming groves and peaks of worship under ancient oaks—we witness how physical places became catalysts for spiritual milestones. Each residence and altar recorded a divine encounter, knitting together memory and promise in the very soil that would later bear witness to Israel's national identity. As Abram moved between seasons of plenty and seasons of testing, these established sites anchored his faith, reminding him—and future generations—that God's fidelity transcends both the map's borders and the heart's uncertainties. With these foundational waypoints now in view, we turn to the next defining incidents after the call, where covenant convictions are tested and refined in trials far beyond the threshold of familiar altars.

Chapter 5 – High-Stakes Tests: Defining Incidents after the Call

Having pledged his life and legacy to a voice that beckoned him beyond homeland and kin, Abram's faith journey quickly moved from spiritual milestones to crucibles of real-world trial. In the crucible of pastoral disputes, tribal warfare, and moral dilemmas, his commitment to God's promise faced its most demanding tests. These defining incidents—whether navigating the delicate split with Lot, charging into battle to rescue family, or wrestling with divine justice on behalf of a corrupt city—revealed the depth of Abram's trust, the frailty of human expedience, and the steadfast provision of the covenant-keeping God. Each test served not merely as a challenge to his obedience, but as a refining fire, sculpting Abram's character and faith for the galaxy-wide promise of blessing to all nations.

5.1 Parting Paths with Lot—Vision versus Immediate Gain

5.1.1 Pastoral Quarrels: Herd-Size, Water Rights, and Range Anxiety

Abram's wealth in livestock and servants, a sign of divine blessing, soon led to resource pressures when both his and Lot's shepherds vied for grazing land and water (Gen 13:5–7). In semi-arid Canaan, access to springs and seasonal streams was critical; pasturing too many flocks in one valley risked overgrazing and communal conflict. Shepherds began quarreling, stirring fear that the household unity—so vital to covenant stability—might fracture. Abram, recognizing the gravity of these disputes, summoned Lot and his herdsmen for mediation rather than allowing tensions to escalate into violence. He proposed a peaceful solution: separation of flocks and herds to avoid contention, embodying his commitment to maintain relational harmony. Abram's willingness to relinquish prime grazing land demonstrated his prioritization of covenant obedience over material advantage. This leadership act mitigated fear among servants, preventing flight or rebellion within his contingent. By modeling conflict resolution based on generosity and trust in God's provision, Abram set a precedent for righteous leadership. His shepherd-mediators learned that generosity, not greed, fosters sustainable pastoral practices. Abram's approach reflects later Mosaic instructions for gleaning and land sabbath (Lev 19:9–10), ensuring the poor and guest benefit from fields. This pastoral quarrel, though seemingly mundane, became a theological lesson: God's promise transcends immediate gain, requiring faith to release control. Abram's strategic de-escalation prevented civil strife, preserving household integrity. His example informs biblical ethics on resource sharing and conflict management in community. The pastoral quarrel thus becomes first high-stakes test, preparing Abram for subsequent moral and spiritual challenges.

5.1.2 Lot's Jordan-Valley Choice: Edenic Lure and Moral Fault-Lines (Gen 13:10–13)

Presented with the choice, Lot surveyed the Jordan Valley's lush plains, "like the garden of the LORD" in its fertility, contrasting with Abram's highland tent (Gen 13:10). The valley's proximity to Sodom and Gomorrah, though visually appealing, masked moral degradation and idolatrous worship practices. Lot's decision revealed his inclination toward immediate abundance over covenantal trust, as he advanced first, staking claim to the best lands. Abram's silent blessing followed Lot's departure, demonstrating faith that God's promise did not depend on visible prosperity. Lot's move sowed seeds of future conflict, exposing the perils of prioritizing material comfort over spiritual discernment. His tents near Sodom entangled him in the city's sin, ultimately requiring Abram's rescue. Lot's choice illustrates how aesthetic allure can obscure moral and spiritual pitfalls, a recurring biblical theme (cf. Ps 106:37–38). Abram's hands-off approach respected Lot's agency yet underscored divergent worldviews: one rooted in divine assurance, the other in worldly incentives. Lot's enmeshment with Sodom's culture would later estrange him from Abram's household, fracturing family ties. The moral fault-lines revealed here presage Israel's own settlements in Canaan where kings compromised covenant ethics for land. Abram's response provides a corrective: blessing those who choose their own path without resentment or manipulation. This episode underscores that faith sometimes requires letting go, trusting God to fulfill promise beyond immediate circumstances. Abram's contrast with Lot reaffirms that true inheritance arises from obedience, not opportunistic land grabs. The Jordan-Valley choice thus becomes a defining incident, framing subsequent tests of faith and family loyalty.

Having demonstrated trust by releasing Lot, Abram's next trial thrust him into the geopolitical arena, where he would don arms to rescue kin and uphold justice.

130

5.2 Night Raid and Rescue—Abram the Warrior-Patriarch

5.2.1 Kedorlaomer's Coalition: Imperial Tribute Networks and Rebel Cities

In the fourth year of their sojourn, a coalition of Mesopotamian vassal kings—led by Chedorlaomer of Elam—launched punitive expeditions to reassert tribute from rebellious Canaanite cities including Sodom and Gomorrah (Gen 14:1–4). These imperial networks functioned much like modern spheres of influence, demanding annual levies of gold, silver, and goods from client states. When Sodom withheld tribute, it faced siege alongside other allied towns, demonstrating the high-stakes realities of covenant land. Lot's association with Sodom rendered him vulnerable to these power dynamics; he and his possessions were taken captive in the aftermath (Gen 14:12). The rescue mission thus transcended family concern—it became defense of tribal autonomy against imperial overreach. Abram's awareness of Kedorlaomer's army size and tactics came from merchants and scouts traveling trade routes, highlighting his long-standing connections across cultures. The initial coalition's swift victory underscored the precariousness of Canaanite polities lacking stronger alliances. Abram's subsequent mobilization foreshadows Israel's later fights for territorial security under Joshua and Judges. Understanding imperial tribute systems equips readers to grasp the strategic depth of Abram's military response. Chedorlaomer's geopolitical move set stage for Abram's decisive intervention, marking first clash between covenant faith and imperial force.

5.2.2 Tactical Pursuit to Dan and Hobah: Divided Forces and Surprise Maneuvers (Gen 14:14–16)

Responding to Lot's plight, Abram assembled 318 trained men born in his household—veteran fighters skilled in desert warfare and

131

archery. He pursued the coalition northward, crossing the Euphrates under cover of darkness to Dan, the coalition's supply base, catching the oppressors off-guard. Dividing his forces into three units, Abram executed a flanking maneuver that cut off enemy retreats toward Hobah, north of Damascus. The split-unit tactic, advanced for its time, prevented the larger army from regrouping, inducing panic and flight. Abram's knowledge of local terrain, gleaned from transhumance circuits, enabled him to choose routes inaccessible to heavy chariots. His pursuit covered over 150 miles in a single night and following day campaign, a testament to logistical prowess. The rescue operation freed Lot and other captives, along with recovered possessions spanning several occupied cities. Abram's decisive leadership contrasted with cautious approaches of contemporary tribal chiefs. The victory underscored that covenant heroes sometimes engage in righteous violence to uphold justice and protect the innocent. Abram's battlefield conduct earned him renown among Canaanite and Mesopotamian elites alike. His swift rescue prefigures Israel's breakthrough campaigns under Joshua's night attack on Ai (Josh 8). The tactical triumph at Dan and Hobah closes this chapter of military enterprise, leading directly to covenant reaffirmation under Melchizedek.

5.2.3 Spoils, Oaths, and Public Integrity before the King of Sodom

After routing the coalition, Abram returned with all spoils and captives to the Valley of Siddim, where the King of Sodom approached him with offers of wealth (Gen 14:17–21). Abram's refusal to accept any share beyond provisions for his men—"I have lifted my hand to the LORD, God Most High" (Gen 14:22)—demonstrated unwavering integrity. By declining Sodom's wealth, Abram affirmed that victory belonged to God alone and that he would not risk moral compromise through political patronage. His stance set a powerful precedent for stewarding divine blessing without succumbing to worldly enticements. Abram's oath before

Sodom's king effectively insulated him from future debt or obligation to a corrupt city. His refusal also shielded Lot from being a pawn in larger political games, preserving family honor. The public nature of the refusal, witnessed by local chieftains, conferred broader reputational capital upon Abram's household. Abram's discernment—accepting only what he needed—modeled covenant restraint in the face of political pressure. This moment foreshadows Israel's later refusal of Achan's illicit spoils (Josh 7). Abram's handling of spoils secured both spiritual purity and political autonomy for his descendants. His integrity before Sodom's king cemented trust in his vow before Yahweh, highlighting covenant faith in action. The intersection of military success, political negotiation, and moral witness in this incident underlines its status as a defining test after Abram's call.

Having demonstrated justice through decisive rescue and integrity in victory, Abram's faith now engages with prophetic vision and sacrificial covenant in the Covenant of the Pieces.

5.3 Covenant of the Pieces—Flame, Darkness, and Prophetic Timeline

5.3.1 "Fear Not, Abram": Shield-Promise after Battlefield Fatigue (Gen 15:1) Exhausted from the night-long pursuit and the aftermath of battle, Abram received a divine word of reassurance: "Fear not, Abram, I am your shield; your reward shall be very great" (Gen 15:1). The term "shield" evokes imagery of divine protection, signaling that God continues to guard Abram even after human successes. Battlefield fatigue often fuels doubt in warriors, but Yahweh's direct address restored Abram's courage and affirmed that promise fulfillment is God's work, not human valor alone. This moment mirrors earlier theophanies yet deepens relational intimacy: God acknowledges Abram's weariness and personally comforts him. The promise of "very great reward" returns Abraham's thoughts from past rescue to future inheritance, redirecting focus from temporal spoils back to covenant scope. Ancient Near-Eastern warriors often dedicated spoils to patron gods; here, Abram dedicates both spoils and self to Yahweh's shield. The timely reassurance at Abram's low moment underscores that divine covenant often appears amid exhaustion. Abram's experience demonstrates that faithful leaders receive divine care when earthly means wane. The shield-promise thus becomes part of Abram's spiritual armor, referenced by later psalmists: "My shield is God Most High" (Ps 91:1). This divine affirmation forms prelude to the deeper covenantal ratification in the pieces ritual. Abram's soul, buoyed by Yahweh's promise, readies for the solemn sacrificial ceremony ahead.

5.3.2 Sacrificial Geometry: Heifer, Goat, Ram, Dove, and Pigeon Arranged God instructed Abram to bring a heifer, a goat, a ram—all three three-year-old—and a turtledove with a pigeon (Gen 15:9), arranging them in paired symmetry before he "cut them in two." The tri-pair selection reflects covenant completeness—a numerical symbolism akin to "threefold" emphasis in royal decrees. Abram laid the carcasses side by side, creating a sacrificial pattern resembling treaty-binding between suzerain and vassal. The inclusion of both cattle and birds signifies universal scope, uniting earth's creatures under God's promise. The meticulous arrangement—east-west orientation facing Abram—allowed him to stand between divided halves, witnessing divine oath. Though Abram fell into deep sleep during the ritual (Gen 15:12), the sacrificial geometry spoke covenant language beyond words. In later Israelite cult, sacrificial layouts continued to follow divinely prescribed orders (Lev 1–7), situating Abram's ritual as archetype. The symmetry and species choice conveyed that covenant embraces land, herds, and people—every facet of creation. Abram's silent witness to sacrificial geometry underscores that covenant participation requires both human action and divine movement. This

structured sacrifice planted visual grammar for interpreting later temple offerings. Abram's arrangement thus communicates theology through ordered space, preparing hearts for the divine procession through the pieces.

5.3.3 Smoking Fire-Pot, Blazing Torch, and Four-Century Forecast (Gen 15:12–21)
As dusk fell, Abram saw a smoking fire-pot and a flaming torch pass between the sacrificial halves, God's theophanic signature ratifying the covenant unilaterally (Gen 15:17). The fire-pot's smoke denotes divine presence in a portable form, while the blazing torch symbolizes holiness and judgment, underscoring that covenant entails blessing for obedience and warning for breach. The ominous darkness that followed (Gen 15:12) marked a transitional moment, reminiscent of Sinai's darkness (Ex 20:21). God then revealed a prophetic timeline: descendants would sojourn in foreign land, be afflicted four hundred years, but exit with great possessions (Gen 15:13–14). This forecast connected Abram's personal story with Israel's corporate destiny, providing historical anchors for future generations. The prophetic timeline also foreshadows the exodus, embedding national memory in Abram's narrative. Abram's continuity of covenant from battlefield fatigue to sacrificial oath illustrates the seamless integration of action and vision in faith. The divine overture through smoking and flame established covenantal theology that blends mercy with righteous accountability. Abram's participation affirmed human trust in unseen realities, a motif echoed in Hebrews' account of faith (Heb 11:1–2). The covenant of the pieces thus becomes multi-layered: legal treaty, prophetic revelation, and sensory theophany. Abram's response to this profound moment set the template for all subsequent covenant renewal ceremonies in Israel's history. With the pieces covenant sealed, Abram's faith matured to embrace both promise and prophetic suffering.

Emerging from solemn covenant establishment, Abram soon faced a moral test as he interceded for Sodom, negotiating divine justice on behalf of the righteous few.

5.4 Interceding for Sodom—Negotiating Divine Justice

5.4.1 Three Visitors at Noon: Hospitality that Unveils Judgment (Gen 18:1–8)

Abram's tent-door vigil under the Oaks of Mamre brought three visitors at midday, whom he hosted with oil for feet, water for washing, and a lavish meal of bread, butter, and a tender calf (Gen 18:1–8). His hospitality ritual—offering water and shade before food—reflected covenantal hospitality virtues taught later in Lev 19:34. As he stood by them, the visitors revealed one as Yahweh in human form, outlining plans to judge Sodom. Abram's immediate response was to serve rather than question, demonstrating faith-in-action even as divine judgment unfolded. The midday timing underscores boldness: giving hospitality when heat was greatest and privacy most valued. The unfolding revelation transformed Abram's celebration into somber contemplation, linking generosity to moral responsibility. His entreaty would transform from host to intercessor, illustrating that faithful hospitality often leads into prophetic engagement. Abram's openness thus positioned him to negotiate divine justice on behalf of a condemned city. His example informs biblical patterns of hospitality preceding prophetic discourse.

5.4.2 Counting Righteous Souls: The Descent from Fifty to Ten

Upon hearing God's plan to destroy Sodom, Abram interceded: "Will You indeed sweep away the righteous with the wicked?" (Gen 18:23). He negotiated God's justice down from fifty righteous to ten, each decrement respecting divine mercy and human advocacy:

"What if there are forty? thirty? twenty? ten?" (Gen 18:24–32). Abram's respectful questioning modeled courage to speak truth to divine power, embodying prophetic boldness. His negotiations maintained reverence—"Far be it from You"—while pressing for mercy, illustrating the tension between divine holiness and mercy. Each step revealed Abram's strategic mind, understanding that spared few could salvage a remnant. The descent to ten righteous hinted at Israel's later ten-member rabbinical courts (Sanhedrin) tasked with communal justice. Abram's intercession underscored that covenant relationship invites human participation in divine justice processes. Though Sodom ultimately lacked ten righteous, Abram's advocacy stands as archetype for intercessory prayer on societal behalf. His boldness transformed private faith into public plea, bridging personal and communal redemption. Abram's counting prayer thus becomes liturgical pattern for mercy petitions by later prophets and psalmists.

5.4.3 Sulfur, Salt, and Sunrise: Rescue of Lot and Cost of Compromise

The morning found Sodom engulfed in sulfur and fire, yet God remembered Abraham's intercession, sending angels to rescue Lot (Gen 19:24–29). Lot's flight, urged by angelic command, underscored that intercession yields practical deliverance for the faithful remnant. Lot's wife's glance back to salt pillar fate warned of the cost of divided loyalties, reflecting Abram's earlier choice to let Lot go (Gen 13). The sunrise-to-judgment arc dramatized swift divine action once mercy's threshold closed. Abram, watching from Mamre, saw smoke rising like a furnace, affirming that God's justice executes swiftly but hears intercession first. The narrative contrasts Lot's compromise—living in Sodom's shadow—with Abram's resolute independence, highlighting covenant integrity. Lot's salvation through Abraham's advocacy exemplifies generational impact of faithful intercession. The salt pillar motif became shorthand for divine judgment against disobedience (Luke 17:32).

Abram's prayer thus safeguarded family legacy despite Lot's flawed choices. The rescue episode underscores that covenant blessings include protection for those associated by faith. Through sulfur and salt, Abram's intercession echoes in Israel's exodus deliverance narratives. His engagement in divine justice shapes later biblical themes of intercession, judgment, and mercy.

With Abram's intercession complete, his household faces the consequences of human convenience in Hagar's episode—another test blending culture and covenant.

5.5 Hagar and Ishmael—When Expedience Meets Providence

5.5.1 Surrogacy Customs and Household Power Dynamics (Gen 16:1–4)

Sarai's barrenness, a source of social stigma, led her to propose surrogacy through Hagar, her Egyptian maidservant, reflecting accepted Near-Eastern practice for perpetuating elite lineages. As custom dictated, a maid-surrogate's son would carry the primary wife's status, maintaining property and covenant rights within the household. Abram's assent to Sarai's plan honors her authority yet illustrates how patriarchal deference can unwittingly complicate God's timing. The power differential—mistress over maid—quickly became fraught: Hagar's pregnancy emboldened her, leading her to despise Sarai. Household tensions escalated, revealing a fault line between cultural expedience and divine promise. Abram's passive stance highlights patriarchal conflict management: attempt to preserve domestic peace at the cost of spiritual clarity. Servants and slaves witnessed the growing animosities, undermining Abram's leadership credibility. This surrogate arrangement sowed long-term discord, later echoed in sibling rivalries between Isaac and Ishmael. Their respective statuses—covenant-child versus surrogate-child— would frame family dynamics for generations. The incident underscores that cultural solutions to covenant challenges risk unintended consequences. Abram's willingness to follow Sarai's counsel here contrasts with his later decisive obedience to God's direct commands. The surrogacy crisis thus becomes a high-stakes test of covenant faith versus human rationale. Abram's eventual recognition of God's corrective intervention marks a pivotal lesson in discerning divine will over cultural norms. This event teaches that even well-intentioned customs cannot override divine promises' timetable. It sets up God's next act of providence in Hagar's wilderness encounter.

5.5.2 Flight to the Spring: "Beer-lahai-roi" and the Seeing God (Gen 16:7–14)

Driven by Sarai's harsh treatment, Hagar fled into the wilderness, reaching a spring "Beer-lahai-roi" (Well of the Living One who Sees Me), a site for divine revelation amid desperation. There, an "angel of the LORD" found her, asking, "Hagar, servant of Sarai, where have you come from and where are you going?" reflecting divine concern for the marginalized. The angel's address honored Hagar's personhood beyond her servant status, revealing God's inclusive care. He instructed her to return and submit, promising that Ishmael's numerous descendants would arise—a nod to Ishmael's eventual tribal leadership. Hagar's naming of the well acknowledges God's omniscience and mercy, even in unplanned covenant complications. This wilderness theophany parallels Moses at the burning bush—God meets His covenant people where they are, despite failures. Hagar's encounter also foreshadows Israel's desert experiences, where God's presence sustains the lost. The promise to Ishmael balances divine patience and covenant priority: Ishmael receives blessing without displacing Isaac's lineage. Hagar's empowerment through prophecy instated her as a progenitor of nations, illustrating God's sovereign plan includes more than the primary covenant line. The well's name endures, marking a sacred geography of God's attentive love. Abram's household, learning of

Hagar's deliverance, gains fresh insight into God's care for all involved in covenant drama. This incident redresses surrogacy's tensions by redirecting Hagar's despair into hope. The spring's waters symbolize living mercy emerging from covenant conflict. Abram's appreciation of "the God who sees" would deepen his own trust in divine oversight. The Beer-lahai-roi narrative thus reaffirms that God's providence transcends human schemes.

5.5.3 Twelve Princes Promised: Ishmael's Line beside, not within, the Covenant

The angel's prophecy declared that Ishmael would father "twelve princes" and become "a great nation" (Gen 16:12), echoing Abraham's own promised numerous descendants. This parallel blessing highlights God's generosity but also clarifies that Ishmael's line runs alongside Isaac's future covenant family. Each of the twelve princes is later named in Genesis 25:12–16, establishing Ishmael's tribal configuration distinct from Israel's twelve tribes. Ishmael's descendants dwell in wilderness and desert regions, engaging in pastoral and trade networks that intersect with Israel's history. Biblical narratives record interactions—both cooperative and conflictual—between Israel and Ishmaelite groups, underscoring the intertwined destinies seeded in this promise. God's inclusive blessing demonstrates divine concern for all Abraham's progeny, yet covenant continuation focuses on Isaac. The distinction between promise line and subsidiary blessing models divine precision in fulfilling specific redemptive plans. Ishmael's narrative also informs later interfaith considerations, as Islamic tradition regards Ishmael as forebear of Arab peoples. The theological nuance—that God's mercies extend generally but covenantal election flows narrowly—emerges here. Abram's watch over Ishmael's departure reflects parental care transcending covenant urgency. This parallel tribal network becomes strategic in Abraham's geopolitical vision, offering allies and trading partners. The coexistence of Ishmael's and Isaac's lines foreshadows Israel's complex relational dynamics with surrounding nations. God's faithfulness to Ishmael's promise reminds Abram that covenant blessings do not exclude God's broader redemptive scope. This incident thus shapes Abraham's legacy as father of multiple peoples under diverse divine purposes.

After navigating family complexities and surrogate lineages, Abram encountered a divine renewal of covenant ethics and identity through new names and the sign of circumcision.

5.6 El Shaddai's Renewal—Circumcision and New Names

5.6.1 "Walk before Me, Be Blameless": Covenant Ethics in a Single Imperative (Gen 17:1–2)

God's reiteration of covenant to Abram introduced "El Shaddai" and imposed an ethical summons: "Walk before me, and be blameless" (Gen 17:1–2). This dual command condenses covenant ethics into relational terms—daily conduct ("walk before") and integrity ("blameless"). "Blameless" (tamim) implies wholehearted devotion rather than sinless perfection, inviting Abram into progressive sanctification. The use of "El Shaddai" underscores divine sufficiency ("God Almighty") as source of moral power, assuring Abram that ethical living springs from divine enablement. This renewal occurs after prior tests—battle, intercession, family failings—demonstrating that covenant requires ongoing re-engagement. The imperative parallels the later Torah call for Israel to "be holy, for I the LORD your God am holy" (Lev 19:2), integrating personal conduct with divine character. Abram's acceptance of this call signals maturity: he moves from promise dependency to ethical partnership. The covenant's ethical dimension grounds subsequent practices—circumcision, hospitality, justice— in agile moral consciousness. Abram's example illustrates that divine calling is inseparable from transformed living. His walk becomes liturgical path, embodying faith in daily steps. Thus, covenant renewal at El Shaddai reshapes Abram's identity beyond nomadic promise toward moral exemplar. This fresh mandate prepares Abram's household for the physical sign of circumcision, embedding ethics in flesh and name.

5.6.2 Flesh-Cut Sign on the Eighth Day: Household-Wide Obedience

The covenant command required circumcision of every male, including Abram, sons, and household servants, on the eighth day after birth (Gen 17:10–12). The eighth-day timing aligns with divine patterns of new beginnings—creation's first week plus one—symbolizing resurrection and covenant renewal. Abram's immediate compliance, instructing servants without hesitation, underscores obedience even after prior missteps. The surgical removal of foreskin marked male bodies as living scriptures of covenant belonging. Servants and sons entering the rite together bridged family and social strata, signifying inclusive covenant community. The ceremony, performed by an elder with blade and oil, combined physical pain with spiritual consecration. Communal feasting followed, transforming covenant sign into celebratory identity marker. The flesh-cut sign encapsulated promise in tangible form—permanent, visible, and intergenerational. Abram's act of cutting his own flesh underscores personal commitment beyond patriarchal distance. This comprehensive obedience contrasts with his earlier surrogacy compromise, revealing growth. Circumcision's placement on flesh, rather than words alone, teaches that covenant ethics require embodied practice. The sign's endurance through centuries protected Israel's identity in exile, testifying to Abram's initial obedience. The flesh-cut thus becomes foundation for both communal belonging and individual conviction. Abram's implementation of this sign anchored covenant into household reality, shaping identity through generations.

5.6.3 Breath of Promise: Abram→Abraham, Sarai→Sarah, and Laughter-Born Faith

God changed Abram's name to Abraham ("father of many nations") and Sarai to Sarah ("princess"), inserting the divine breath sound "ה" to signify God's direct work in their identities (Gen 17:5,15). This theophoric alteration elevated their personal stories into covenant proclamation: Abraham now embodied promise of multitudes, while Sarah became mother of nations. The name changes followed initial laughter at Isaac's predicted birth, transforming incredulity into joyful affirmation (Gen 21:6). Abraham's new name thus carried forward both prophetic promise and reflective testimony of God's power to reverse human expectations. Sarah's shift from personal to dynastic title redefined her role from private wife to matriarchal icon across faith traditions. The breath sound "ה" echoes ruach—the Spirit—indicating that God's Spirit animates their renewed callings. These new names functioned as living confessions among surrounding peoples, signaling divine involvement in human destiny. Abraham's identity renewal catalyzed family unity under fresh covenant mission. Sarah's elevation affirmed her partnership in promise, anticipating her authoritative voice at Isaac's weaning celebration. The interplay of name and narrative thus embeds theology into personal nomenclature. Abram and Sarai's transformations offer enduring lesson: covenant faith redefines self-understanding by divine decree. Their renaming marks a decisive shift from past to future, anchoring hope in God's faithful character. Abraham's and Sarah's new names echo through Scripture as perennial reminders of covenant's power to reshape life stories.

With Abram's identity and body marked by covenant signs, he next negotiates water rights and peace treaties at Beersheba, solidifying covenant relationships within his geopolitical sphere.

5.7 Water Rights and Oaths—Treaty with Abimelech at Beersheba

5.7.1 Stolen Wells, Sworn Peace: Seven Ewes for Legal Transparency (Gen 21:27–32)

Following Hagar's departure and Ishmael's settlement, Abram faced renewed conflict when Abimelech's servants reopened wells his herdsmen had sealed to preserve water rights (Gen 21:25–26). Recognizing potential feud, Abimelech sought valiant covenant-keeper Abram to resolve dispute, offering treaties under sacred oath. Abram insisted on formal peace, requiring seven ewes as witness pasture tribute—"shemittim" in Hebrew echoing "sheba," sevenfold completeness (Gen 21:30). The selection of ewe-lambs linked treaty to pastoral economy, symbolizing shared flocks under covenant care. By counting and presenting the seven lambs before Abimelech and city elders, Abram created public transparency, preventing future misinterpretation. Swearing by Yahweh's name affirmed that water rights disputes fell under divine justice, not arbitrary force. Abimelech's acceptance and oath release both men from hostility, ensuring peaceful co-existence. The treaty's legal structure mirrored earlier Mesopotamian water-rights pacts, but here elevated by monotheistic witness. Abram's strategic use of number and sacrament ensured moral clarity. Shared pasture weasels later recalled the treaty, embedding it into local folklore. This covenant demonstrated that control of scarce resources demands ethical negotiation under God's oversight. The seven ewes thus marked both peace offering and boundary marker for desert frontier. Abram's framework for resource dispute resolution influences later Israelite law on land use and neighborly rights. This peace treaty highlights covenant's power to transform conflict into cooperation through structured oaths.

5.7.2 Tamarisk Planting and Invocation of El Olam— Everlasting God

After the treaty, Abram "planted a tamarisk tree" at Beersheba and "called upon the name of the LORD, the Everlasting God" (El Olam; Gen 21:33), combining living symbol and divine title in unified act of worship. The tamarisk's deep root system and expansive shade represented enduring covenant life under God's steadfast care. Abram's invocation of El Olam—God as eternal—asserted that water treaty and water supply were under lasting divine jurisdiction. The planting created living altar, its growth testifying across seasons to covenant promise's durability. Local Bedouin came to revere the tree, offering small gifts and drink for travelers, echoing Abram's hospitality. Abram's integration of ecology and liturgy provided template for Israel's tree-planting rituals commemorating deliverance (Ps 1:3). The invocation of El Olam connected temporal provisions with timeless faithfulness. Abram's act transcended immediate treaty to embrace cosmic covenant, aligning finite water rights within infinite divine promise. The Beersheba tamarisk thus became enduring pilgrim sign, inviting future generations to "fear before Elijah's God" (2 Kin 17:36). Abram's theology of planting affirms faith's rootedness in living creation under sovereign God. The tree's longevity reinforced covenant memory even as political regimes changed. Abram's dual action—treaty and planting— exemplifies holistic covenant response: legal justice paired with worship. Beersheba becomes a nexus where divine eternality meets human need in flourishing community.

5.7.3 Southern Frontier Secure: Missional Outpost toward Desert Peoples

With water rights settled and covenant markers established, Beersheba emerged as strategic missional outpost—gateway between Canaan and desert tribes. Abram's treaty with Abimelech and tree planting signaled to nomadic neighbors that Yahweh's presence extended into southern wilderness. Caravans bound for Egypt passed through Beersheba, encountering covenant hospitality and legal order uncommon in frontier zones. Abram envisioned Beersheba as launchpad for blessing "to all families of the earth" (Gen 12:3), leveraging water and peace to open doors for gospel-like outreach. The southern frontier, once fraught with scarcity and raids, became zone of stability under Abram's covenant leadership. Pilgrims from various clans camped near the tamarisk, engaging with Abram's teaching about El Olam. The site's dual role—practical water hub and spiritual witness—modeled integrated mission theology. Abram's frontier security reflects later Israelite vision of being "a light to the nations" from Jerusalem to ends of earth (Isa 49:6). Beersheba thus stands as early exemplar of kingdom expansion through relational engagement and resource provision. Abram's frontier covenant informs missiological practice: secure human needs while proclaiming divine promise. The southern outpost exemplifies how covenant faith transforms geographic peripheries into spiritual frontiers. Abram's strategic use of water and worship at Beersheba prefigures church planting in unreached areas. The frontier narrative highlights that covenant witnesses flourish where human need meets divine message.

Having secured southern alliances and witnessed ultimate obedience on Moriah, Abram's next test would be the greatest—sacrificing Isaac, culminating in resounding covenant blessing.

5.8 Mount Moriah—The Ultimate Obedience Test

5.8.1 Three-Day Silence: Father, Son, and the Wood of Submission (Gen 22:1–6)

God's command to sacrifice Isaac arrived with no preparatory context, compelling Abram into three days of silent journey toward Mount Moriah. During these days, father and son traveled in tense quiet, each burdened with own part: Abram carrying the fire and knife, Isaac carrying wood. The lack of divine reiterated promise during transit magnified emotional and spiritual tension—trust anchored in previous assurances alone. Abram's repeated "here we are" responses to Isaac's logistical questions (Gen 22:7) reflect resolute obedience cloaked in parental restraint. The three-day period parallels Israel's journey to Sinai, linking patriarchal test to national covenant formation. Serving as Rabbi and disciple, Abram exemplified faithful model for Isaac's formation. The journey's silence created space for inward wrestling—faith against reason. Abram's ability to restrain natural paternal affection underscores covenant surrender. Each footstep up Moriah symbolized detachment from promise's temporal fulfillment. The silence itself stands as high-stakes ritual, preparing hearts for unthinkable sacrifice. Abram's resolve during these days anticipates his later acclaim in Hebrews 11 for instituting faith by obedience. The physical journey thus becomes spiritual odyssey of trust and submission. Mount Moriah emerges as proving ground where covenant identity is tested to extremes. Abram's three-day ascent encapsulates faith's journey: moving toward God without sight of outcome.

5.8.2 Binding, Knife, and Ram: Substitutionary Mercy and "Yahweh-Yireh"

At the summit, Abram bound Isaac, erecting him on the altar wood, then raised the knife to slay his promised son, fulfilling divine instruction (Gen 22:9). The heart-wrenching obedience found abrupt pause as an angel intervened, announcing God's provision of a ram caught in a thicket by its horns. Abram's substitutionary sacrifice of the ram typified divine mercy supplanting human loss, emblematic of later sacrificial systems. Naming the site "Yahweh-Yireh" ("The LORD will Provide") Abraham codified theology into topography, teaching future pilgrims that God's provision often appears in unexpected form. The ram's thicket setting—"thicket of the mountain" (Gen 22:13)—became natural altar, foreshadowing

Christ's substitutionary atonement. Abram's immediate replacement of Isaac with the ram demonstrates that covenant obedience always intersects with sovereign grace. The binding and substitution narrative combines ultimate human fidelity with divine deliverance, forging deep covenant resonance. Ancient worshipers later reenacted this pattern in festival scapegoat rituals (Lev 16), where goat carried community sin into wilderness. Abram's act thus roots Israelite atonement tradition in patriarchal obedience. The location's sanctity extended into Solomon's Temple site, merging sacrificial theology with place. Abram's sacrifice test thus emerges as central pillar of covenant faith—mercy found in midst of obedience. The ram's horns echo in Psalm 18:2's "horn of salvation," linking Abram's experience to messianic hope. Yahweh-Yireh remains enduring reminder: God's provision meets the depth of our obedience.

5.8.3 Echo through Ages: From Patriarchal Peak to Messianic Fulfillment (Heb 11:17–19)

Hebrews 11:17–19 interprets Abraham's sacrifice of Isaac as demonstration that Abraham "considered that God was able even to raise him from the dead," foreshadowing Christ's resurrection and linking patriarchal faith to New Covenant reality. Early Jewish commentators saw Isaac's near-death as prototype of resurrection hope. The Abraham-Isaac binding (akeda) is recounted annually in liturgical readings on Rosh Hashanah, embedding immediacy of faith-test in communal worship. Christian art and theology parallel Isaac's sacrifice with eucharistic motifs—Father offering Son on altar of wood. Pilgrims climbing Moriah reflect on Abraham's faith, envisioning mount of crucifixion on Calvary, located near traditional Moriah. Rabbinic Midrash interprets Abram's "faith of the binding" as pinnacle of covenant trust, influencing concept of "bittul" (self-nullification) in Hasidic spirituality. Isaac's own consent— "Here am I, my father"—illustrates filial obedience and typifies Christ's willing sacrificial submission. Mount Moriah's layered sanctity—from Abraham's altar to Solomon's temple to Jesus' cross—testifies to unity of redemptive history anchored in single defining incident. Abram's obedience test thus resonates across Abrahamic faiths, shaping collective memory of ultimate sacrifice. Each generation finds in Mount Moriah a locus for reflecting on the tension of obedience and grace. Abram's high-stakes test on Moriah thus becomes foundational axis for believing communities, orienting hope toward resurrection and covenant consummation. His echo through ages confirms that covenant tested at its height yields the deepest assurance of God's faithfulness.

With these defining incidents mapped, we turn next to how Abram's accumulated tests coalesced into covenant maturity and enduring legacy for nations and faith communities.

5.9 After the Tests—Covenant Maturity and Legacy

5.9.1 Summative Blessing: "Because You Have Obeyed My Voice…" (Gen 22:15–18)

Following the dramatic climax on Mount Moriah, God's final word to Abram underscores covenant maturation: "Because you have done this and have not withheld your son, your only son, I will surely bless you…" (Gen 22:16). This summative blessing encapsulates all prior promises—land, seed, and universal blessing—now conditioned on proven obedience. The repetition of "surely bless you" (hithallek) conveys both certainty and fullness, assuring Abram that divine fidelity surpasses human obligation. The promise expands: "and in your offspring shall all the nations of the earth be blessed," reaffirming the missional trajectory established in Haran. Obedience at the highest cost transforms Abram's faith from fledgling trust to tested maturity, qualifying him as father of nations. God's blessing language employs covenantal verbs previously used with Noah and Israel at Sinai, linking Abram's experience to broader redemptive history. The oath rereads past tests—Lot's separation,

149

military rescue, intercession for Sodom—as necessary preparation for ultimate obedience. Abram's whispered invocation of Isaac as "the son whom you love" (Gen 22:2) transforms into global promise through God's summative words. The blessing's scope—"and by your offspring shall all nations gain blessing for themselves"— signals universal covenant expansion beyond ethnic Israel. The text's chiastic structure frames the promise around the obedience event, highlighting cause and effect. Abram's legacy thus emerges as both personal reward and corporate inheritance, weaving his story into the fabric of human hope. The affirmation "because you have obeyed my voice" provides interpretive key: covenant life is measured by fidelity, not mere privilege. This summative covenant blessing solidifies Abram's transition from pilgrim to progenitor, its echoes felt in New Testament theology on justification (Heb 11:17– 19). His life henceforth embodies covenant maturity—full obedience under testing yields comprehensive blessing.

5.9.2 Networks of Influence: How Kings, Prophets, and Nations Recall Abraham's Faith

Abram's tested faith radiated outward across political, prophetic, and cultural spheres. Kings referenced his name to legitimize their own treaties: Abimelech at Beersheba invoked Abrahamic precedent for water-rights oaths (Gen 21:27), while later Judean monarchs traced lineage to Abraham to authenticate Davidic rule (2 Sam 7:12– 16). Prophets invoked Abram's example to call Israel back to humility and trust: Isaiah reminds Israel that Abraham called upon God as "righteous" and "just" (Isa 51:1), urging return to foundational faith. Jeremiah and Ezekiel cite the patriarch's obedience when promising restoration, showing that covenant fidelity inaugurates communal renewal (Jer 33:26; Ezek 16:60). In intertestamental literature, Jewish thinkers extol Abraham as model of righteousness and head of faithful remnant, shaping Second Temple piety. The New Testament picks up this influence: Paul frames Abraham's faith as prototype for Gentile justification, using

Genesis 15:6 to anchor doctrine (Rom 4:1–25). Gospel writers link Jesus to Abraham's lineage to affirm messianic credentials (Matt 1:1; Luke 3:34). Church Fathers revered Abraham as "first among believers," his willingness to sacrifice Isaac foreshadowing Christ's atonement. Even in Islamic tradition, Abraham (Ibrahim) stands as exemplar of submission (Islam means "submission"), commemorated in Hajj rites at Mount Arafat—echo of Moriah. Christian liturgy celebrates Abraham's hospitality and sacrifice in stories of communion and Easter. Modern pilgrimage routes trace Abram's footsteps as spiritual tourism, binding diverse faiths in shared reverence. Across millennia, Abram's tested obedience continues to shape ethical leadership models in religious and secular contexts. His narrative becomes node connecting ancient Near-Eastern covenant forms to global religious consciousness. The dense network of influence affirms Abraham's role as linchpin in world faith heritage.

5.9.3 Transition to Chapter 6: Sarah—Partner in Promise and Peril

With Abraham's trials mapped and covenant maturity affirmed, attention now shifts to Sarah, whose partnership in promise and experience of peril deepens the covenant narrative. Sarah's barrenness, laughter, surrogate agency, and eventual motherhood undergird the covenant of seed promised on Moriah. Her encounters—providing hospitality to strangers, facing moral danger in foreign courts, and bearing the miraculous Isaac—mirror and complement Abraham's tested faith. In Chapter 6, we delve into Sarah's unique perspective: her emotional journey through longing, doubt, joy, and intercession. We explore how Sarah's partnership shapes the covenant lineage, highlighting her role as co-heir in promise and as mother of nations. Sarah's story illuminates divine grace in human frailty, revealing how God's purposes unfold through both patriarchal and matriarchal obedience. As covenant advances from Abraham's obedience to Sarah's motherhood, the narrative broadens to include themes of life-giving joy and intergenerational faith. Chapter 6 will trace her critical interventions—from Hagar's proxy tensions to Isaac's birth—showing how Sarah's resilience and worship contributed to covenant fulfillment. Her legacy, interwoven with Abraham's, reminds us that divine promises often find expression through complementary human roles. Thus, after Abraham's high-stakes tests, Sarah emerges as fitting subject to illustrate the covenant's relational depth and communal continuity.

Conclusion The tapestry of Abram's trials shows that covenant relationship with God is neither abstract nor convenient but forged in the heat of conflict, sacrifice, and intercession. Through military victory and prophetic vision, through acts of grace toward strangers and harsh obedience on sacrificial heights, Abram learned that divine faithfulness transcends human understanding. These high-stakes trials not only deepened his own conviction but set paradigms for generations to come—models of hospitality, righteousness, and unwavering trust under the banner of an Almighty God. As we move forward to explore Sarah's crucial partnership in promise and peril, we carry with us the insight that true faith is honed when every promise is weighed against life's fiercest tests.

Chapter 6 – Sarah: Partner in Promise and Peril

Behind every great promise stands a partner whose faith and resilience are as essential as the patriarch's obedience. Sarah's journey begins in the shadow of barrenness and blossoms through moments of crisis, doubt, and unexpected joy. As the unnamed princess of Haran and later Canaan, she navigates the perils of foreign courts, the sting of cultural stigma, and the temptation to grasp at human solutions. Yet through each trial—whether offering her maidservant, welcoming strangers under ancient oaks, or witnessing the miraculous birth of Isaac—Sarah's story reveals the intricate dance between God's timing and human participation. Her laughter, once born of incredulity, becomes the anthem of a promise fulfilled, anchoring the covenant line in both sorrow and celebration.

6.1 Ancestral Roots—From Ur to Haran and Canaan

6.1.1 Genealogical Links: Terah's Line and the Role of Milcah

Terah's clan heritage shaped Sarai's status long before she married Abram, as her father's brother Nahor wed Milcah, bearing eight children and forging alliances that extended Terah's influence across Mesopotamia. Milcah's progeny included Bethuel, father of Rebekah, linking Sarai indirectly to the next generation of covenant matriarchs. These familial connections provided Sarai with models of motherhood and tribal leadership, even as barrenness cast her own womb into shadow. In Ur, stories of Angelina (Nahor's daughter) celebrating sons and daughters would have circulated in Terah's household, fostering both hope and frustration in Sarai. The tight web of cousin-marriages—common to preserve clan property—meant Sarai's identity was inseparable from broader kin networks. As Abram and Nahor journeyed north to Haran with their wives, Sarai's relational capital ensured she traveled with trusted female kin, offering early companionship amid upheaval. The genealogical emphasis on generational blessing pressed on Sarai's heart, even as she watched Milcah's children flourish. This dynamic provides context for Sarai's acute awareness of covenant seed—her longing was not merely personal but deeply rooted in ancestral expectation. The role of Milcah and her descendants underscores how covenant promises unfolded through interwoven family stories, inviting Sarai into a legacy of matriarchal faithfulness. Reflecting later, Sarah would see in Rebecca's own barrenness-to-birth cycle a mirror of divine pattern (Gen 25:21). These genealogical strands taught Sarai that God can work through extended family, even when direct lineage seems stalled. From this tapestry of kinship, Sarai learned that covenant hope often travels through communal memory rather than solitary assumption. Her ancestral roots thus anchored her identity in a broader promise, setting stage for her role as co-heir with Abram.

6.1.2 Early Marriage to Abram: Kinship Strategy and Shared Vision

Sarai's marriage to Abram united two halves of Terah's house—his firstborn and his nephew—strengthening tribal cohesion and pooling their combined wealth of flocks and servants. As was customary, the bride-price and dowry negotiations would involve extended clan representatives, signaling Sarai's importance to their shared future. From the outset, Sarai and Abram likely collaborated on household governance: delineating tasks for servants, organizing pastoral rotations, and planning trade expeditions. Their mutual vision—though unspoken until God's call—emerged in joint risk-taking, first in abandoning Ur for Haran, then again in leaving Haran for Canaan. Sarai's willingness to follow Abram into unknown territory reflected a rare combination of trust in his leadership and openness to Word-shaped destiny. In every camp—Ur, Haran, and Canaan—Sarai managed the tent economy: spinning wool, provisioning meals, and hosting travelers. These acts laid foundations for the hospitality she would later extend under the Oaks of Mamre. Her participation in caravan logistics gave her strategic insight into regional politics and water-rights disputes. Sarai's early collaboration with Abram testifies to their shared vision—together they made covenant decisions before God formalized His promises. This partnership informs later biblical portrayals of Sarah as helper and co-heir (1 Pet 3:7), highlighting her active role rather than passive accompaniment. Their marriage thus embodies a model of covenantal teamwork: complementary gifts, shared burdens, and unified risk in pursuit of God's call. Sarai's identity as Abram's wife carried both honor and responsibility, shaping her matriarchal imprint on the covenant line. The early years of their union laid blueprint for the intertwined paths of promise and peril they would walk together.

6.1.3 Name Meanings: Sarai ("My Princess") in Patriarchal Context

The name Sarai—derived from Hebrew root "sarah," meaning "to contend" or "princess"—signified her position as nominal ruler of the household, second only to Abram in the clan hierarchy. In patriarchal societies, the title "princess" conveyed both privilege and accountability: Sarai would oversee domestic rituals and represent the family in female tribal networks. As "My Princess," she bore expectation of producing heirs to secure Abram's legacy, especially under customary inheritance laws. Sarai's name also suggested spiritual contending, foreshadowing her wrestling with God's promise and human solutions to barrenness. The shift later to Sarah ("Princess of Nations") amplifies her destiny from household levity to global matriarchate. Name-naming conventions in Genesis underscore divine shaping of identity: just as Jacob becomes Israel, Sarai becomes Sarah to reflect God's unfolding plan. Sarai's original title reminds us that matriarchs held significant sway behind the scenes, curating faith formation within the clan. Her princess status provided leverage when interacting with foreign rulers—as seen in her dealings with Pharaoh and Abimelech. Sarai's name also carried theological symbolism: as princess she interceded in courtly fashion, negotiating for Lot in Genesis 13 through quiet risk. The complexity of her name meaning surfaces in Proverbs-like reflections on female nobility (Prov 31). Understanding Sarai's name in patriarchal context reveals the depth of her contributions beyond childbearing. Her journey thus transforms "my princess" into "princess to nations," mapping personal identity onto cosmic promise. Sarai's name sets the trajectory for her narrative arc—from barrenness to begetting, from household ruler to mother of nations.

With Sarai's ancestral and marital foundations laid, we turn to the heart-ache of her barrenness and the cultural stigma that shaped her early shadow-years.

6.2 Barrenness and Cultural Stigma—Waiting in the Shadows

6.2.1 Fertility Ideals in Ancient Near-Eastern Households

In Sarai's world, childbearing signified divine favor, social stability, and economic continuity; women celebrated births as community milestones, and goddesses of fertility dominated temple worship. Clay figurines of Ishtar and Asherah attest to widespread rituals intended to secure womb fruitfulness through offerings and incantations. In elite households, barrenness translated into diminished status: childless women lacked heirs to inherit property, placing them at risk of disinheritance. Sarai would have seen her peers—Milcah, Rebekah—elevated as mothers, inviting social envy and personal pain. Villagers offered her herbal remedies and folk prayers, yet none penetrated the divine timetable. Her position at mealtime—serving nieces and nephews—would remind her of the unfulfilled womb. The social scripts of Mesopotamian marriage enforced procreation as ultimate marital duty, compounding Sarai's sense of failure. Eunuchs and fertility specialists may have counseled her, offering complex dreams interpreted as signs of pending birth, only to end in disappointment. This cultural pressure influenced her suggestion of Hagar as surrogate, seen as expedient remedy. Sarai's barrenness thus became crucible for deep spiritual questions: why is God's promise delayed? Her inner struggle parallels Hannah's lament in 1 Samuel 1, another fertile echo in biblical narrative. By situating Sarai within fertility culture, we appreciate the depth of her resilience when God finally wrought a miracle. Her eventual motherhood breaks through entrenched cultural stigma, redefining divine sovereignty over biological norms.

6.2.2 Emotional Landscape: Hope Deferred and Silent Lament (Prov 13:12)

Sarai's long childless years created a landscape of hope deferred, stirring an ache "like a broken bone," as Proverbs 13:12 phrases the sorrow of unfulfilled desire. Each anniversary of marriage anniversary with Abram intensified the sense of waiting in the shadows. By hearth fires, Sarai quietly mourned lost dreams of children to play at her feet, tears dampening tent mats. In pre-dawn hours, she wrestled between trust in Abram's God and envy of fertile neighbors, her whispered prayers mingled with self-rebuke. Discussions with Abram revealed her pain: he would reassure her that God would keep His promise despite silence. Yet each Moed festival—Passover celebrations adapted in proto-form—reminded her of Abraham's vow and her empty womb. Sarai's silence masked deep theological wrestling: why does God tarry when His messenger has spoken? This internal tension teetered between faith and bitterness, foreshadowing her laughter reaction when the angel first announced Isaac's upcoming birth (Gen 18:12). Sarai's emotional landscape teaches that spiritual journeys include valley seasons where divine promises appear hidden. Her unvoiced lament underscores importance of lament psalms in later Israelite worship, offering language for communal sorrow. Sarai's heartache thus enriches covenant narrative with raw humanity, illustrating that even promise-bearers endure the agony of delay. When at last her womb opens, the joy is magnified precisely because of the profound depth of waiting.

6.2.3 Faith under Delay: Sarai's Inner Dialogue with Divine Promise

During the wait, Sarai's inner dialogue alternated between remembrance of divine assurances and practical cynicism. She recalled God's words to Abram—"I will make you a father of many nations"—and wondered if "many nations" included her alone or required another vessel. In silent tent vigils, Sarai rehearsed arguments: "If God promised, where is the proof?" Yet at Abram's encouragement, she recited Genesis stories to Hagar, affirming trust that God controls opening of wombs. Sarai's conversations with Abram shifted from sorrow to cautious hope as they walked fields together, imagining tiny footprints. Her inner faith matured into resilience: she chose to bless Hagar rather than resent her, even as her heart stung. This mental wrestling primed her for later direct divine encounters, shaping her receptive posture when the angel spoke. Sarai's endurance under delay embodies the paradox of faith: believing beyond feeling. Her internal journey aligns with New Testament calls to "walk by faith, not by sight" (2 Cor 5:7). In retrospect, Sarai's period of barrenness becomes formative school of trust, refining her character. She emerges from shadows not merely relieved but transformed into matriarch who can comfort others in waiting. Sarai's inner dialogue thus provides template for all who cling to God's promises amid silence.

Having endured the sting of cultural stigma and refined her trust, Sarai next finds herself thrust into a foreign court crisis that tests both her integrity and God's protective promise.

6.3 Queen of Crisis—Egyptian Court and the Plagues of Protection

6.3.1 Beauty at a Price: Sarai in Pharaoh's Harem (Gen 12:14–20)

Sarai's renowned beauty drew Pharaoh's attention as Abram passed into Egypt, prompting Abram's fearful strategy: she would claim Sarai as his sister to secure safe passage and favor (Gen 12:11–13). This half-truth led Sarai into Pharaoh's palace, where she received a royal veneer—fine linens, jewelry, and provisioning fit for a queen-in-waiting. The Egyptian court abounded in rituals, with Sarai undergoing ceremonial styling by eunuchs skilled in Levantine and Nile fashions. Court physicians administered perfumed oils and cosmetic treatments, enhancing Sarai's allure but deepening her vulnerability. As royal concubine, Sarai inhabited both privilege and peril: luxury accompanied separation from her husband and exposure to false intimacy. The palace social order relegated her to guarded quarters, cut off from Abram's protective presence. Sarai's emotional turmoil likely ranged from horror at deception to resignation born of Abram's anxiety. Egyptian priest-sages may have offered her amulets for fertility, adding spiritual confusion to cultural crisis. Her tenure in Pharaoh's harem illustrates the high cost of human expedience when faith falters. The interplay of political ambition and marital covenant placed Sarai at the epicenter of an international incident. The crisis reveals ancient Near-Eastern court politics, where foreign hostages secured trade alliances under divine guise. Sarai's unwitting role in this drama highlights how innocent can suffer when patriarchal fear overrides faith. Yet her dignity amid crisis prefigures the protective honor later restored by God's plague intervention.

6.3.2 Divine Intervention: Plagues, Release, and Restored Honor

As Sarai's beauty enchanted Pharaoh's household, God afflicted the Egyptian court with plagues—whether disease, infertility, or economically crippling sores—reminding all that Yahweh's sovereignty outmatched Pharaoh's gods (Gen 12:17). Pharaoh's dream interpreters failed to diagnose the root cause, prompting the king himself to investigate Sarai's situation. Once Pharaoh confronted Abram—"Why did you say she is your sister?"—the plagues ceased upon Sarai's release, illustrating precise divine advocacy (Gen 12:19). Abram's prompt restoration of Sarai to her rightful status re-legitimized their covenant union before Egyptian and Israelite onlookers. Pharaoh's clemency—providing them with gifts and an armed escort—signaled respect for Abram's God and magnetic tension between court politics and divine prerogative. Sarai's honor, initially compromised, became publicly reaffirmed, foreshadowing later vindication when Abimelech would receive similar dreams (Gen 20:3–6). The plagues function as microcosm of exodus judgments, prefiguring Israel's deliverance (Ex 7–12). Sarai's crisis resolution underscores God's protective promise to safeguard covenant matriarchs. Her dignity, restored by divine decree, elevates her status in subsequent narratives—she is no longer mere sister-wife but co-heir in promise. This episode affirms theological theme: divine faithfulness preserves the vulnerable within covenant community. Sarai's Egyptian court ordeal thus becomes testament to Yahweh's capacity to outmaneuver human schemes, preserving covenant integrity in foreign lands.

6.3.3 Lessons Learned: Covenant Integrity versus Self-Preservation

Sarai's brush with danger in Egypt taught crucial lessons about the tension between covenant integrity and human self-preservation. Abram's deceptive strategy, though understandable under fear of violence, compromised the public witness of their faith and exposed Sarai to moral hazard. The crisis revealed that reliance on human schemes, even culturally sanctioned ones, undermines trust in divine provision. Sarai's ordeal demonstrated that God's protective power is superior to royal favor, reframing security not in palace walls but in covenant promise. After their departure, Sarai likely counseled Abram against similar shortcuts, reinforcing mutual commitment to speak truth in faith. This shared learning sharpened their relational dynamic, enabling subsequent covenant commands—like circumcision—to be embraced with deeper conviction. The Egyptian episode also foreshadowed Sarah's later trial in Gerar, where she faced similar danger under Abimelech. Collectively, these crises shaped Sarai's and Abram's resolve to let God fulfill His word in His time and way. The account highlights that spiritual pioneers often confront institutional powers, requiring divine vindication rather than human compromise. Sarai's lived lessons inform Israelite cautions against idolatry and dependence on foreign alliances (Isa 31:1–3). Her crisis thus refines covenant theology: true preservation lies in divine agency, not palace politics. Sarai emerges from Egypt not embittered but equipped for deeper partnership in the covenant journey.

Having learned the peril of human expedience in Egypt, Sarai faces another cultural flashpoint as she proposes Hagar's surrogacy—an act that tests both her authority and faith.

6.4 The Surrogacy Proposal—Calculus of Expedience

6.4.1 Social Precedent: Hagar's Legal Status and Household Hierarchy

In the household economy of Abram's time, a bondwoman like Hagar served as both property and potential surrogate, her legal status allowing children she bore to assume servant or heir roles. Sarai's suggestion that Abram take Hagar as concubine followed customs seen in narratives of elite families wanting progeny (cf. Gen 30:3 with Rachel and Bilhah). The hierarchy placed Sarai above Hagar, yet the surrogate mother's womb functioned as extension of Sarai's reproductive capacity. This social precedent intended to preserve Sarai's social standing, leveraging Hagar's body to secure Abram's seed. The practice entailed complex household negotiations: rights of inheritance for the child, dowry adjustments, and servant status adjustments. Sarai's decision demonstrates her strategic mind, seeking immediate resolution to barrenness within accepted norms. Yet it also shows how cultural customs can mask deeper theological issues about God's timing. Hagar's legal position rendered her both vulnerable to demands and intermediary in Sarai's quest for fulfillment. The proposal underscores the intersection of property law, family strategy, and personal identity in ancient households. The surrogate arrangement promised tangible solutions but failed to account for divine prerogative in covenant seed. Sarai's reliance on precedent reveals the human tendency to substitute cultural patterns for divine command. This incident sets stage for ensuing tensions that would require divine correction at Beer-lahai-roi. Sarai's cultural calculus thus became catalyst for deeper spiritual confrontation with God's will.

6.4.2 Power Shift: Conception, Contempt, and Sarai's Response (Gen 16:4–6)

Hagar's conception upended household dynamics: once Sarai's subordinate, she now wielded moral authority, despising her mistress for barrenness. This power shift frustrated Sarai's expectations, provoking harsh treatment that compelled Hagar's flight. Sarai's reaction—striking Hagar—crossed cultural norms that protected surrogate mothers from abuse, revealing Sarai's emotional volatility under pressure. Abram's passive stance exacerbated Sarai's sense of betrayal, as he attempted to maintain household peace without adjudicating justice. Sarai's response illustrates the complexity of female relationships in patriarchal systems, where competing needs can escalate into conflict. The shift in power reveals how surrogacy, while solving one problem, generates new wounds and undermines community cohesion. Sarai's subsequent humiliation—having to live with contempt—intensified her sense of failure before God and kin. This upheaval laid bare limitations of cultural expedience in addressing covenant promises. Sarai's emotional toll from Hagar's contempt foreshadows her later assertiveness in demanding Ishmael's removal after Isaac's weaning. The incident underscores that attempts to manipulate God's promise through human means often produce reciprocal harm. Sarai's experience teaches that faith in God must navigate the complex entanglements of power, identity, and cultural norms. Her response and its fallout catalyze the divine intervention that redirects covenant trajectory back to God's timing. Thus, the power shift in Sarai's household becomes a formative trial, revealing both the fragility and the resilience of faith under stress.

6.4.3 Spiritual Fallout: Waiting for God versus Engineering Outcomes

The surrogacy episode produced spiritual fallout: Sarai discovered that trying to co-produce God's promise without waiting invites chaos rather than blessing. Her engineered solution unleashed conflict, shattered trust between her and Hagar, and led both to the brink—Hagar into exile, Sarai into shame. This stark contrast with

163

the peace promised by covenant reveals that human engineering cannot replace patient faith. Sarai's fallout echoes in later Israelite history, where attempts to secure God's favor by external works—like those of Uzziah or Manasseh—lead to national calamity. The spiritual lesson centers on the necessity of trusting God's timing rather than conforming to cultural expediency. Sarai's personal journey from control to submission mirrors the church's movement from works-based righteousness to grace-driven faith. The fallout prompts Sarai to reexamine her relationship with Abram and with God, seeking forgiveness and deeper reliance on divine promise. This turning point prepares her heart for the direct angelic visit at Beer-lahai-roi and subsequent re-naming. The spiritual fallout thus becomes teaching moment: true covenant living requires waiting under Word rather than pushing for outcomes. Sarai's renewed posture after Hagar's departure marks her entry into a season of vulnerable, authentic dependence on God's promises. Her experience provides enduring antidote to faith shortcuts: only God's unfolding in His time can bring covenant fulfillment without collateral damage.

As Sarai's engineered surrogacy collapses into chaos, God initiates a covenant renewal—re-naming Sarai to Sarah and re-establishing the ethical sign of circumcision for her entire household.

6.5 Covenant Renewal—Sarah Re-named and Re-claimed

6.5.1 Divine Dialogue: Laughter, Skepticism, and Re-assurance (Gen 17:15–19)

God spoke directly to Abram, instructing him to name Sarai as Sarah and promising a son by her name, a word play echoing Sarai's earlier laughter yet shifting to expectant joy (Gen 17:15–16). Sarai's initial reaction—laughter born of incredulity at conceiving past menopause—surfaced again when she heard the promise, revealing the tension between human reason and divine power. Abram intercedes, asking God to bless Ishmael if it pleases Him, demonstrating his protective care for Sarai's surrogate past and her maidservant's child (Gen 17:18). God reassures Abram: Sarah will bear a son, Isaac, through whom the covenant line continues, and Ishmael will be blessed too but "of the uncircumcised" in a covenant apart (Gen 17:20). This dialogue elevates Sarah from silent partner to spoken recipient of divine promise, marking her as direct heir to God's blessing. The angelic message merges divine sovereignty with personal address, as God uses her new name to redefine her role. Sarah's renaming ceremony parallels royal investiture, conferring on her the dignity of "princess of nations." The direct dialogue stands in stark contrast to her previous surrogate-driven attempts, signaling that God's timing requires His voice, not human schemes. Her skepticism—voiced in Gen 18:12—transforms into faith as she accepts the role of mother to nations. This renewed promise establishes Sarah's identity not merely as Abram's wife but as co-mediator of covenant life. The divine reassurance layers her personal doubts with cosmic purpose, embedding her laughter in redemptive history. Through this dialogue, Sarah moves from passive recipient of arrangements to active figure in God's unfolding plan. The transformation underscores that covenant renewal often includes fresh divine communication to previously overlooked participants. Sarah's hearing God speak her new name initiates her re-claiming of promise and authority.

6.5.2 From Sarai to Sarah: Princess of Peoples and Matriarch of Promise

The shift from Sarai—"my princess"—to Sarah—"princess" or "noblewoman"—broadens her sphere of influence from household to the nations (Gen 17:15). In the ancient Near East, adding the letter "ה" to a name often signified divine breath entering human identity, indicating that Sarah's new role is divinely ordained. As "princess of peoples," Sarah embodies the promise that her offspring would become "kings of peoples" (Gen 17:16). Her new title aligns her with the royal mothers of surrounding cultures, such as Egypt's "Great Royal Wives," yet her status is rooted not in human dynasties but in God's eternal kingdom. Sarah's re-naming parallels Jacob's becoming Israel, signaling that divine mission reshapes personal destiny. The cultural shift from Sarai to Sarah would have altered her social standing in tribal councils, enabling her later decisive speech in demanding Hagar's departure (Gen 21:9–10). Her new name carries prophetic weight, as nations would bear her royal title when tracing lineage through Isaac. Sarah's elevation to matriarch of promise underscores her co-heirship with Abraham in covenant inheritance (1 Pet 3:6). As princess of peoples, Sarah becomes spiritual archetype for women of faith across generations. Literary parallels appear in Hannah's naming of Samuel, where divine promise births new vocational identity (1 Sam 1:20). Sarah's transformation thus exemplifies how God's word can re-define social roles and expand influence. Her new name resonates in later prophetic declarations of Israel's future glory under a mother of nations (Isa 49:22–23). Sarah's elevation from Sarai to Sarah inaugurates her full agency in covenant story, preparing her for roles in hospitality, intercession, and protective leadership.

6.5.3 Circumcision Day: Watching a Household Embrace the Sign

On the day of circumcision, Sarah observed as Abram and every male in the household—including Ishmael—underwent the cutting of the flesh on the eighth day (Gen 17:12–14). The ceremony would have begun at dawn in Abram's tent, with awed silence giving way to the sound of knife against flesh and the immediate anointing of oil to staunch the wound. Sarah, though exempt from the rite, likely stood nearby, offering water, soothing herbs, and words of encouragement to each participant. As covenant sign was sealed in bleeding flesh, Sarah reflected on the costliness of obedience—a contrast to her earlier surrogate plan. Watching servants and sons

166

accept the sign revealed the communal nature of covenant identity, embedding Sarah's renewed status within the living body of the household. The aftercare feast, with bread, cheese, and fermented wine, transformed the painful rite into celebration, where Sarah's laughter now signified shared joy rather than private incredulity. The presence of foreign-born servants undergoing circumcision under Sarah's gaze highlights the inclusivity she now championed. The event underscores that covenant belonging demands corporate participation and collective memory-making. Sarah's role in orchestrating the ceremony further cements her as keeper of covenant tradition. Her witnessing of the rite deepened her conviction that God's promise flows through marked obedience rather than cultural shortcuts. The circumcision day thus stands as tangible fulcrum between Sarai's past barrenness and Sarah's new life-giving role. Sarah's contemplation of bleeding flesh and oil-anointed wounds prepared her for the forthcoming birth miracles. The household's embrace of the sign under her watch embeds covenant reality in every fiber of family life.

Renewed in name and body-sign, Sarah prepares for her defining role in hospitality and proclamation under the terebinths of Mamre.

6.6 Hospitality under the Terebinths—Bread, Butter, and Birth Announcement

6.6.1 Three Strangers Arrive: Sarah's Role behind the Tent Curtain (Gen 18:6–8)

While Abram hurried to welcome the three midday visitors, Sarah, stationed just inside the tent, prepared unleavened bread and butter—cream skimmed from fresh milk—for their meal (Gen 18:6). Though not visible to the visitors, Sarah's diligent work under the tent brimmed with significance: she honored covenant hospitality codes that elevated strangers to sacred guests. Her choice of butter, a symbol of abundance, reflected her confidence in divine provision despite barrenness. Simultaneously, she oversaw the roasting of a tender calf, ensuring that every detail of the feast met the highest standards of Near Eastern hospitality. Sarah's attentiveness to flavor and presentation reveals her matriarchal acumen in household management. Her role behind the scenes parallels priestly preparations—sanctifying the table for divine presence. As the visitors reclined under the terebinths, Sarah hummed ancestral lullabies, infusing the bread with songs of hope. Her severe illness with laughter at the birth announcement (Gen 18:12) transformed into expectant hush as she served the meal. Even before the guests spoke of Isaac's birth, Sarah's culinary offerings prefigured the feast of joy to come. Her embrace of hospitality thus becomes theological act—feeding angels in disguise (Heb 13:2). Through careful provision, Sarah enacted covenant warmth that would soon be matched by birth-room celebration. Her hidden labors stand as testimony that God often works through the faithful service of those behind the scenes. Sarah's rite of hospitality under the terebinths set stage for the announcement that would redefine her identity once more.

6.6.2 "Is Anything Too Hard for the LORD?"—Laughter Transformed

When the visitors prophesied her forthcoming son, Sarah laughed inwardly, questioning the possibility of childbirth in her old age (Gen 18:12). The LORD's gentle rebuke—"Is anything too hard for the LORD?" (Gen 18:14)—confronted her doubt, inviting her to see divine power beyond human limitations. Sarah's laughter shifted from cynicism to awe: she went from "Why should I nurse?" to "Shall I indeed bear a child?" in renewed wonder. This transformation marked theological pivot: Sarah recognized that God's creative word can call life out of barrenness. Her initial laughter became a confession of divine omnipotence, celebrated in later liturgies as affirmation of God's exceeding power. Sarah's response models honest engagement with God: voicing doubt yet remaining present to hear correction. Her laughter thus evolves from barrier to bridge, opening her to miraculous reality. This dynamic taught Abram that covenant faith thrives when human limitations meet divine "too hard" possibilities. Sarah's transformed laughter echoes Pauline admonitions to rejoice in hope (Rom 12:12). Her turnaround underlines that God's promises often come with invitations to question rather than reproach. By embracing her laughter's irony, Sarah integrated personal history into God's cosmic narrative. This moment under the terebinths became perpetual reminder that no circumstance lies beyond Yahweh's capacity to renew.

6.6.3 Covenant Feasting: Table Fellowship as Prophetic Stage

The feast that followed Sarah's revelations transcended family meal to become prophetic proclamation: every guest became herald of covenant future, chewing crusts of memory and hope. Table fellowship under the terebinths represented unity of heaven and earth, as divine visitors reclined with human hosts. Sarah's selection of dairy, bread, and meat formed a triad of sustenance—milk for past nurture, bread for daily life, and meat for covenant sacrifice. The open-air setting prefigured synagogue Sabbath meals, where covenant stories are retold around tables. Sarah orchestrated music accompaniment: servants played lyres and tamburs, underscoring the celebratory tone of prophecy. The distribution of portions mirrored prophetic sharing of promise: each attendee received taste of divine banquet. The feast's prophetic dimension emerges when angels depart to judge Sodom, showing that sacred hospitality can precede both blessing and censure. Sarah's table thus became apostolic pulpit where word and meal intertwined. Later Jewish festival traditions—like Passover seders—would echo this pattern: telling covenant story while sharing unleavened bread. Christian Eucharistic theology likewise finds roots in these patriarchal feasts. Sarah's feast under the terebinths crystallizes the idea that fellowship meals become stages for divine revelation. Her role in hosting the prophetic table underscores her importance as mediator of covenant warmth. This covenant feast prepared Sarah emotionally and spiritually for the birth drama to come, anchoring the promise in communal celebration.

From prophetic hospitality under the terebinths, Sarah's story advances to the miracle of Isaac's conception and birth—a triumph of divine promise over human improbability.

6.7 Mother of Nations—Isaac's Conception and Birth

6.7.1 Nine-Month Miracle: From Menopause to Maternity Sarah's miraculous conception of Isaac at age ninety exemplified divine sovereignty over human biology, as God fulfilled His promise precisely after the season of barrenness ended (Gen 21:1–2). The nine-month gestation, though standard biologically, carried supernatural significance given Sarah's post-menopausal status, demonstrating that God's power transcends natural life cycles. During those months, Sarah likely experienced both awe and physical strain—morning sickness in a body long accustomed to empty cycles, her joints stiffened yet her spirit buoyed by divine assurance. Abram, now Abraham, would have overseen her care, commissioning servant-midwives versed in Mesopotamian herbal remedies to assist Sarah through her unfamiliar condition. The midwives' use of frankincense-infused oils to ease labor pains aligned with ancient birthing customs, yet the true agent of relief was the Lord who sustained her. Sarah's womb, once described as "dead," became living vessel for covenant fulfillment, echoing later prophetic declarations of God making barren woman fruitful (Gal 4:27). As word of her pregnancy spread among encamped servants and allied tribes, Sarai's new name—Sarah—carried fresh resonance among those who had known her as the childless princess. Neighbors would marvel at the sight of a gray-haired matron embracing her swollen belly, interpreting it as visible proof that God overturns human expectations. Sarah's nine-month journey from menopause to maternity thus became emblem of covenant miracle, shaping Israel's identity as people born by divine promise rather than human effort. Her physical transformation taught Abrams's household that covenant fruit requires patient waiting under divine timetable. The miracle inspired songs of thanksgiving in their tent, with young women learning midwifery arts under Sarah's oversight. Through her labor, Sarah bridged generational divides, bringing life to a promise whispered decades before. Her childbirth trial stands as testament that God's words to Abraham and Sarah endure beyond human frailty. The nine-month miracle thus anchors Sarah's story in both physical reality and transcendent grace, setting tone for Isaac's naming and celebration.

6.7.2 Naming the Child: Isaac—Laughter Made Flesh (Gen 21:1–3)

When the time came, Sarah bore a son and named him Isaac—"he laughs"—embedding her own transformed laughter into his identity (Gen 21:3). This naming acted as both etymological echo of her initial skepticism and phonetic celebration of God's fulfilled promise. The act of naming a child was deeply significant in Hebrew culture, intertwining personal destiny with divine intent; Isaac's name thus carried covenant guarantee. As elders and clan members gathered for the naming ceremony, they stood beneath newly erected tent awnings adorned with palm fronds and woven rugs, symbolizing the new life Sarah carried and the shelter provided by God's faithfulness. Gifts of fine linen, olive oil, and small lambs for sacrifice accompanied the naming, reflecting Mesopotamian customs adapted to Yahwistic worship. Abraham's joyful laughter merged with Sarah's as he cradled Isaac, tears of joy mingling with communal exultation. The naming feast likely included readings of covenant promises from the clay tablets that recorded early family entries, reminding all present of the divine word fulfilled. Sarah, in the months following birth, would nurse Isaac at her breast, teaching him lullabies of promise and setting practices for future weaning celebrations. Isaac's identity as "laughter made flesh" became living sermon for neighboring clans, drawing pilgrims seeking reassurance that God still speaks life where death once presided. The name Isaac served as theological shorthand throughout Israel's history for God's good humor and gracious reversals of fate. Future prophets referenced Isaac's birth when calling exiled communities to hope again (Isa 54:1). Sarah's naming of Isaac thus weaves personal story into national memory, ensuring that laughter remains integral to covenant narrative. Isaac grew under the banner of his name, embodying the joy and faithfulness promised through Sarah's transformation.

6.7.3 Weaning Festival: Public Joy and Renewed Household Boundary

When Isaac reached weaning age—traditionally celebrated between two and three years old—Sarah hosted a grand feast, marking his transition from dependency to early childhood (Gen 21:8). The weaning festival brought together Abraham's entire household: free servants, former bondservants, allied shepherds, and neighboring tribal families, all sharing in the jubilation. The celebratory menu featured roasted goat seasoned with herbs, bowls of fresh curd and milk, and flatbreads baked in communal ovens—culinary staples of clan festivals. Flute music and drum rhythms filled the air, echoing ancient Near-Eastern traditions of festive worship that later Israel would codify in national holidays. Sarah, now matriarchal head, gave a public speech commissioning Isaac as heir, declaring that the covenant seed would continue through his lineage. She reiterated God's promise, affirming to attendants that she had borne him "in his old age" as gift from the Lord (Gen 21:7). The weaning festival also served as social boundary marker: recipients of invitation recognized full membership in Abraham's household, while exclusion signaled outsiders. Gift exchanges—small lambs, jars of olive oil, and finely woven cloth—reinforced alliances forged since Haran. Isaac's laughter at the feast became emblematic moment,

172

leading neighbors to dub the hill "Laughter's Hill" in local lore. The festival's rituals of cutting hair and offering firstfruit sheaves paralleled later Israelite customs at covenant renewal times. Sarah's orchestration of the weaning festival demonstrated her leadership in ritual life, executing complex communal rites with grace. The public joy at Isaac's weaning re-energized covenant community after Hagar-driven conflicts, reaffirming unity under divine promise. Through the festival's gate ceremonies and boundary reaffirmations, Sarah ensured that Isaac's heritage remained secure against potential Ishmaelite claims. The weaning celebration thus stands as milestone in Sarah's matriarchal ministry, blending personal joy with spiritual and social renewal.

While Isaac's life began amidst laughter and feasting, Sarah's protective instincts soon led her to confront the tensions introduced by Hagar and Ishmael, ensuring covenant priority in her household.

6.8 Protective Matriarch—Hagar, Ishmael, and the Wilderness Exile

6.8.1 Tensions at the Feast: Mockery and Maternal Instinct (Gen 21:8–10)

During Isaac's weaning feast, Ishmael—now a teenager—began to mock or "play with" Isaac, reflecting the uneasy dynamics from Hagar's surrogate status (Gen 21:9). Sarah, observing Ishmael's behavior, interpreted his mocking as threat and disrespect toward God's promised child, igniting protective fury. The lament of "Cast out this slave woman with her son" (Gen 21:10) illustrates Sarah's maternal instinct to safeguard Isaac's spiritual and physical environment. Her insistence on removing Hagar and Ishmael underscores the fierce responsibility she felt for preserving covenant purity. Abraham's initial sorrow at Sarah's demand reveals his deep affection for Ishmael, yet he deferred to Sarah's judgment after divine counsel affirmed her concerns (Gen 21:12). The tense atmosphere at the feast highlights the collision of human alliances and divine promise. Sarah's decisive advocacy demonstrates her authority as matriarchal protector in household governance. The conflict speaks to broader themes of insider-outsider tensions within covenant communities. Sarah's protective stance illuminated the need to prioritize God's chosen line when human relations become compromised. Her maternal leadership reflects a model of spiritual guardianship vital to covenant continuity. The weaning feast thus becomes flashpoint where Sarah's protective role crystallizes in defense of divine promise. Her motherly resolve ensured that Isaac's legacy would not be overshadowed by surrogate descendants. The incident affirms that matriarchal intervention plays key role in covenant preservation.

6.8.2 Hard Decision: Releasing the Bondwoman and Her Son

Abraham's anguished consultation with God over Sarah's demand concluded with divine instruction: "Do as Sarah has said, for in Isaac shall your offspring be named" (Gen 21:12). This affirmation clarified covenant priority, empowering Sarah's decision. Abraham then gave Hagar bread and a skin of water, sending mother and son into the desert of Beersheba (Gen 21:14). The meager provisions signified both release and survival hope under divine watch. As Hagar and Ishmael departed, they carried mixed emotions: relief from household tension yet fear of desert desolation. Sarah's tearful blessing at their departure underscores the pain of maternal separation even when necessary. In the wilderness, Hagar's resourcefulness—seeking shade under a thornbush and managing water rations—fortified Ishmael's resilience. Sarah's role as protective matriarch thus extended beyond immediate family, as she ensured that Hagar's survival needs were met through divine promise rather than human rescue. The hard decision reflects the tension between compassion and covenant fidelity. Sarah's willingness to release Hagar into God's care exemplifies trust that covenant God provides for all His children. The separation also

174

anticipated the separate destinies of Ishmael's twelve princes, carving out space for parallel blessing without infringing Isaac's line. Sarah's leadership here modeled both tough love and gracious release. The act provides template for covenant communities discerning inclusion and boundary maintenance. The hard choice underscores maturity in covenant leadership: making painful decisions for long-term faithfulness.

6.8.3 Ethical Reflections: Justice, Compassion, and Covenant Priority

Sarah's actions prompt ethics reflection: balancing justice toward covenant line with compassion for Hagar and Ishmael becomes test of covenant maturity. Her demand and Abraham's compliance, though harsh, align with divine command to protect chosen seed. Yet God's subsequent care for Hagar—sending an angel and providing a well in the desert (Gen 21:17–19)—demonstrates divine compassion beyond human mandate. Sarah's protective priority thus coexists with divine call to extend mercy to all. This duality informs later Israelite law mandating fair treatment of sojourners and servants (Lev 25:35). Sarah's leadership ritualizes the tension between covenant particularity and divine universality. Her actions invite modern covenant communities to navigate inclusion without diluting core commitments. The ethical interplay in this narrative balances Sarah's rightful defense of Isaac with God's overarching mercy toward Ishmael's line. Sarah's example teaches that covenant boundaries require ethical clarity, yet compassion remains central. Her discernment in prioritizing covenant seed while trusting God for the exile of the marginalized serves as moral guide. This episode enriches theological dialogue on justice—affirming that protecting promise need not negate care for the vulnerable. Sarah thus models holistic covenant ethics, integrating fierce stewardship with hopeful trust in divine provision for all.

Having navigated the painful separation of Hagar and Ishmael, Sarah's partnership in covenant leads once more into courtly intrigue, reaffirming her protective honor in the Gerar episode.

6.9 Second Court Intrigue—Abimelech and the Dream of Restraint

6.9.1 Déjà Vu in Gerar: Sarah Taken Again (Gen 20:1–7)

Sometime after Isaac's birth, Sarah and Abraham sojourned in Gerar where Abraham again introduced Sarah as his sister, repeating the tactic used in Egypt (Gen 20:2). King Abimelech, impressed by Sarah's beauty and unaware of her marriage, summoned her into his household under royal protection. Sarah's moral peril mirrored her earlier crisis: she risked personal safety and covenant integrity under foreign rule. The repetition underscores Abraham's lingering fear despite prior divine deliverance, revealing how deep-seated anxieties can override hard-won lessons. Sarah's position in Gerar's court offered luxurious accommodation—rich linens, royal jewelry, and a share of the palace's provisions—yet each comfort cost her spiritual peace. Within palace corridors, Sarai's Egyptian maid stories resurfaced among court ladies, fueling rumors that Sarah was a prize rather than a partner. Sarah endured the humiliation of being paraded before nobles and priests who sought to bestow fertility blessings upon the new "princess." Her nominal safety behind palace walls contrasted with the precariousness of dependency on a man-made protection. The narrative tension peaks as the Lord visits Abimelech in a dream, demanding restoration of Sarah and warning of potential death for all the king's household. This nighttime visitation highlights God's personal care for Sarah, stepping into royal fantasies to prevent an unjust union. Sarah, isolated yet observant, sensed the dream's divine edge when the king abruptly separated from her, restoring her honor publicly. Her silent suffering underlines the cost of patriarchal deceptions, while the parallel with

Isaac's near sacrifice intensifies the theme of perceived loss and divine intervention. Sarah's composure in crisis underscores her inner strength, cultivated through earlier trials. The Gerar ordeal thus reframes Sarah not as passive victim but as resilient matriarch whose very presence provokes divine safeguarding. This reprise of court intrigue teaches that covenant promises must be lived out honestly to avoid repeating perilous cycles.

6.9.2 Divine Safeguard: Night-Vision Warning and Royal Restitution

Abimelech's unsettling dream, in which God explicitly warns him that Sarah is a married woman, demonstrates divine supremacy over human authority (Gen 20:3). The dream images—spectral threat of death—compel Abimelech to rise at dawn and confront his counselors, revealing the dream's startling clarity. His confrontation with Sarah and Abraham lays bare the deception, prompting Abimelech to rebuke Abraham for putting the entire kingdom at risk of divine wrath. God's nighttime intervention parallels angelic dreams given to Joseph in Egypt, illustrating continuity in divine protective methods. Abimelech's swift restitution—returning Sarah and granting sheep, cattle, and slaves—models royal integrity under divine compulsion. He honors Abraham's prophetic role by inviting him to intercede for the healing of his household, acknowledging Sarah's innocence. The king's public apology before his court restores Sarah's reputation, demonstrating that true power submits to divine correction. God's safeguard extends beyond Sarah, preserving the health and prosperity of the entire royal family, highlighting covenant ripples. Abimelech's restoration offerings—land near his palace and freedom to reside where they choose—reflect elevated respect for Abraham and Sarah. This royal restitution underscores that covenant faithfulness invites honor even from unlikely quarters. Sarah's restored dignity in public court contrasts with private anguish, affirming that God honors the vulnerable. The Gerar episode thus teaches that divine protection is multi-faceted: dream-vision, judicial hearing, and restoration of honor. Sarah's restored status in a foreign court foreshadows the church's witness in hostile environments. The night-vision warning reminds readers that God's guardianship transcends visible boundaries, safeguarding promise-bearers wherever they dwell.

6.9.3 Prophetic Vindication: Abraham Prays, Sarah's Honor Restored

Upon hearing Abimelech's plea, Abraham intercedes for the king, invoking God's merciful character to spare the Philistine ruler's household (Gen 20:17). His prayer—short but potent—demonstrates reciprocal covenant solidarity: Abraham protects Abimelech as Abimelech protected Sarah. Sarah's honor, encased in royal testimony and divine sanction, is vindicated through both human apology and divine endorsement. Abimelech's household's subsequent healing cements the prayer's efficacy, creating a narrative arc from crisis to communal restoration. Prophetic vindication emerges as both legal act (public apology and restitution) and spiritual event (divine healing). Sarah's restored reputation resonates through Gerar's markets: merchants and townsfolk witness covenant power over local gods. The Gerar covenant renewal parallels Abraham's treaty at Beersheba, showing consistency of covenant practice across contexts. Sarah's vindication provides theological grounding for believers who suffer slander before pagan authorities. The episode foreshadows New Testament admonitions to live blamelessly among unbelievers (1 Pet 2:12). Abraham and Sarah's seamless teamwork in intercession and witness exemplifies ideal covenant partnership. Sarah's honor restored marks turning point in narrative: she moves from peripheral distress to central matriarchal voice. The prophetic vindication in Gerar position Sarah as model of innocence vindicated by divine testimony. This restoration chapter transitions us to Sarah's final acts of faith in securing legacy beyond her lifetime.

With Sarah's honor defended and fate secured, we turn to her death at Hebron and the lasting influence carved into the covenant landscape.

6.10 Legacy Beyond the Grave—Death, Burial, and Lasting Influence

6.10.1 Passing at Hebron: Community Mourning and Patriarchal Purchase (Gen 23)

Sarah's death at the age of 127 prompted Abraham to seek a formal burial site, initiating solemn negotiations with the Hittite elders of Hebron (Gen 23:2–4). His public mourning—tears, loud lamentation, and partner Abram's stripped-off garments—demonstrated communal grief rites customary in Canaanite and Mesopotamian cultures. The Hittites, moved by Abraham's sincerity, offered her burial land freely, yet Abram insisted on paying full price to establish unambiguous ownership. The purchase of the cave of Machpelah and surrounding field for 400 shekels of silver became only land deal recorded in Genesis, underscoring its significance. Community witnessing—elders, witnesses, scribes—sealed the transaction through ritual exchange of silver and oral oath affirmations. Sarah's passing and Abraham's procurement of a sacred resting place transformed Hebron into cornerstone of covenant geography. The public mourning and purchase ritual provided Israelite template for honoring the dead through formal legal acts. Sarah's death emerges as covenant moment: even in loss, Abraham trusts God to keep promise through future generations. The ceremony's location beneath the Oaks of Mamre linked Sarah's burial to earlier hospitality and covenant encounter. Hebron's community gathered to commemorate Sarah's life, setting pattern for patriarchal veneration. This formal burial purchase preserved her memory in physical land, signaling that covenant legacy extends beyond life. Sarah's passing occasioned legal, communal, and

179

spiritual acts that anchored her influence in Israel's emerging identity. Through mourning and purchase, Sarah's life and death coalesce into enduring covenant monument.

6.10.2 Machpelah's Cave: Sarah as Anchor of Covenant Geography

The cave at Machpelah, shaded by terebinths and situated on Hebron's western hill, became burial site for Sarah and, later, Abraham, Isaac, Rebekah, Jacob, and Leah—establishing multi-generational family mausoleum (Gen 49:29–31). Its natural limestone chambers offered secure, private sepulcher spaces, reflecting ancient belief in bodily preservation for future resurrection. Pilgrims would visit the cave, recounting patriarchal narratives and affirming hope in God's faithfulness across centuries. Machpelah's layered tombs symbolize continuous fulfillment of promise—Sarah's initial placement becomes cornerstone for kin's rest. The cave's enduring sanctity weathered shifting political powers, testifying to covenant's permanence beyond temporal empires. Jewish, Christian, and Islamic traditions each revere Machpelah, weaving divergent memories into shared sacred landscape. Archaeological findings confirm long-term usage, linking biblical text to material culture. Sarah's interment here solidifies her as foundational matriarch whose memory shapes covenant identity. The cave's continued veneration affirms that Sarah's influence flows beyond her lifetime into living faith communities. Machpelah thus stands as geographical anchor for promise, binding past and future through tangible earth. Sarah's presence in this cave invites believers to trace lineage of faith from womb miracle to tomb monument. Through Machpelah, Sarah's story becomes living pilgrimage, guiding successive generations to covenant remembrance. Her burial place remains testament to divine faithfulness and human devotion entwined in sacred soil.

180

6.10.3 Memory in Scripture: New Testament Echoes of Sarah's Faith (Heb 11:11; 1 Pet 3:6)

Sarah's faith, once tested through laughter and long waiting, receives New Testament acclaim: Hebrews 11:11 credits her belief "that he who had promised was faithful," celebrating her righteousness by faith despite natural limitations. Peter, addressing wives, holds Sarah up as model: "who obeyed Abraham, calling him lord, whose children you become if you do good" (1 Pet 3:6), linking her submission to spiritual inheritance. These echoes reposition Sarah from silent figure in Genesis to instructive exemplar in apostolic teaching. Early church fathers deployed Sarah's narrative in homilies on faith under trial, encouraging communities facing persecution. The memory of Sarah's laughter before Isaac's birth resurfaces in Pauline discussions on resurrection and new life (Rom 4:19–21). Christian iconography often depicts Sarah with infant Isaac, symbolizing hope fulfilled. Liturgical calendars in Eastern and Western traditions commemorate Sarah's faith alongside Abraham's, embedding her into worship rhythms. Sarah's theological significance crosses cultural boundaries, affirming her as matriarch of spiritual rather than merely ethnic descendants. The New Testament reframing of her story underscores covenant continuity from Old to New Testament. Sarah's legacy thus informs doctrines of justification by faith and covenantal inclusion. Believers today draw on her example when wrestling with seemingly impossible divine promises. Sarah's scriptural memory invites ongoing reflection on female agency and steadfast hope amidst adversity. Her New Testament echoes anchor her voice in the grand tapestry of redemption, extending her influence across millennia.

With Sarah's life, death, and eternal influence established, we now distill overarching theological themes emerging from her journey—laughter, doubt, and feminine agency in covenant faith.

6.11 Theological Themes—Faith, Doubt, and Feminine Agency

6.11.1 Paradox of Laughter: From Cynicism to Celebration

Sarah's laughter bookends her narrative: initial cynicism when hearing of a promised son (Gen 18:12) transforms into celebratory joy at Isaac's birth, creating theological knot where human incredulity meets divine possibility. Her laughter serves as barometer of faith's evolution, from doubt-laden question—"Shall I indeed bear a child?"—to jubilant confession—"God has made laughter for me" (Gen 21:6). This paradox reveals that sacred humor can arise when impossible promises are fulfilled. The laughter motif invites reflection on biblical irony, where expectation overturns natural order through supernatural intervention. Sarah's journey reframes laughter from scorn to proclamation of joy, teaching that God redeems human skepticism into worship. Later Jewish Midrash celebrates Sarah's "righteous laughter" as precursor to joy festivals in Israel's liturgy. Christian homilies echo her transformation as paradigm for joy in Christ, who fulfills ultimate promises. Sarah's laughter thus becomes theological symbol: trust that divine power can reshape personal realities. The paradox underscores faith's dynamic tension between present tension and future triumph. Sarah's laughter story challenges believers to welcome divine surprises rather than cling to linear expectations. In comedic theology, laughter marks both crisis and climax. Sarah's autonomous response to God's word models prophetic proclamation through personal emotion. Her laughter journey affirms that faith includes space for honest reactions transformed by encounter with divine sovereignty.

6.11.2 Co-Heir with Abraham: Paul's Allegory of Sarah and Hagar (Gal 4:22–31)

Paul's allegory contrasts Sarah and Hagar to illustrate two covenants: one of promise and freedom through Sarah, the other of law and bondage through Hagar (Gal 4:22–31). Sarah, representing mount Zion and heavenly Jerusalem, offers believers inheritance of freedom, while Hagar's slavery under Sinai mirrors spiritual bondage. Paul's theological use of Sarah's story elevates her role from narrative participant to archetype of covenantal grace. The allegory affirms Sarah's matriarchal authority, showing that her faith defines covenant identity more than genetics. Pauline exegesis positions Sarah as co-heir with Abraham, ensuring that Gentile believers become "children of promise." This theological expansion grants Sarah global spiritual significance, reinforcing her depiction as "mother of us all" (Rom 4:16). The allegory underscores tension between flesh (Hagar's son Ishmael) and Spirit (Sarah's son Isaac), teaching that true inheritance arises from divine initiative. Sarah's narrative thus informs New Covenant identity formation, highlighting feminine agency in redemptive history. Paul's teaching has shaped Christian doctrines on justification, ecclesial freedom, and spiritual lineage. The allegory stresses that covenant kinship transcends natural descent, rooted instead in God's gratuitous promise. Sarah's example grounds believers' confidence in faith-based inheritance rather than works-based identity. Her status as co-heir invites contemporary discourse on women's roles in church leadership and theological reflection. Through Paul's lens, Sarah's partnership in promise emerges as foundational for universal gospel proclamation.

6.11.3 Model for Pilgrims: Hospitality, Hope, and Holy Resilience

Throughout her narrative, Sarah exemplifies hospitality— welcoming strangers under terebinths, providing for guests, and fashioning covenant feasts that anticipate the Messianic banquet (Matt 25:35). Her hope under trial—sustained through barrenness, court intrigues, and delay—teaches pilgrims to cling to divine promise in desolate seasons. Sarah's resilience—enduring cultural stigma, surrogate conflict, and near sacrifice—models holy endurance in face of crisis. Her mature faith, once silent, becomes articulate intercession alongside Abraham, demonstrating feminine voice in covenant dialogue. Sarah's blended roles—wife, mother, hostess, intercessor—offer holistic blueprint for faith communities valuing diverse gifts. Pilgrims following her footsteps find in Sarah a companion for desert wanderings and palace intrigues alike. Her life anchors theological virtues: hospitality as ministry, hope as defiant expectation, resilience as faithful perseverance. Sarah's story illuminates the pilgrim's paradox: journeying by faith requires both vulnerability and courage. Her partnership with Abraham embodies covenant co-leadership, challenging models of unilateral patriarchal authority. Sarah's example has inspired monastic hospitality practices and women's ordination movements in various traditions. Her integration of domestic service and prophetic witness foreshadows New Testament commendation of female deacons (Romans 16:1). Sarah's pilgrim model continues to shape spiritual formation curricula in retreat centers worldwide. Her life invites each believer to mirror hospitality, hope, and resilience as hallmarks of covenant pilgrimage.

As Sarah's multifaceted journey concludes, the narrative focus shifts to their son Isaac—child of promise whose own formation in covenant terrain will carry forward the legacy of both parents.

Conclusion Sarah's legacy extends far beyond the cave in Hebron where she rests; it echoes in every heart that learns to trust God amid life's disappointments and surprises. As matriarch, she exemplifies fierce hospitality, protective compassion, and courageous intercession, all woven into the broader tapestry of covenant history. Her name change from Sarai to Sarah marks a transformation from personal hope deferred to communal promise fulfilled—a testament to the power of divine naming and destiny. In her life and death, Sarah stands as model for all who walk between promise and peril, teaching us that true faith often requires the humility to wait, the courage to let go, and the joy to celebrate when God's word comes to life.

Chapter 7 – Sons and Daughters: Covenant Seed and Nations to Come

From the solitary birth of Isaac as fulfillment of a long-deferred promise springs a rich tapestry of descendants whose lives ripple across history like streams from a single well. The patriarch's seed multiplies into heirs who carry both blessing and burden—twins whose rivalry foreshadows national conflicts, children of secondary unions who plant nations in desert sands, and daughters whose stories, though often unspoken, shape the moral contours of the covenant people. Each birth, marriage, and naming ceremony weaves new threads into the unfolding narrative of God's intent to bless all families of the earth. As these sons and daughters take their places on the stage of God's redemptive plan, we begin to glimpse how a family promise morphs into tribal identity, international alliances, prophetic hope, and ultimately, a global community united in the seed that is Christ.

7.1 Isaac the Heir—Promise Consolidated

7.1.1 Covenant Reaffirmed at Beersheba: "I Am the God of Your Father" (Gen 26:23–25)

Isaac's sojourn in Gerar during famine mirrored his father's earlier journey to Egypt, yet God spoke to him directly at Beersheba: "Fear not, for I am with you... I am the God of your father Abraham" (Gen 26:24). This personal reaffirmation anchored Isaac's identity in the Abrahamic promise, assuring him that divine presence transcended generational distance. Isaac built an altar there, naming it "The Lord Will Provide," echoing Abraham's own provision at Moriah (Gen 22:14). The act of altar-building established Beersheba as recurring covenant locus for Isaac's household, integrating his worship into the family's sacred geography. Isaac's public ritual invited Philistine neighbors to witness Yahweh's faithfulness, reinforcing covenant's communal dimension. He dug a well and named it "Shibah" (seven), again linking water and oath in the southern frontier (Gen 26:33). The well became social center for media-tribal diplomacy, as caravans paused to drink from Isaac's promise-proved spring. Later generations would recall Beersheba as the "gate of the wilderness," a threshold between promise land and desert crucible (Judg 20:1). Isaac's reaffirmation here solidified his role not merely as heir by birth but as heir by faith. Unlike Abraham, Isaac received no new promise of land limits; rather, he inherited covenant by personal encounter. His altar and well commemorate divine initiative rather than human enterprise. Isaac's Beersheba experience thus transitions covenant from patriarchal founding to filial continuation. By situating himself under Yahweh's banner, Isaac models obedient discipleship for subsequent seed. This reaffirmation prepares Isaac for the relational and territorial challenges ahead as covenant heir.

7.1.2 Marriage to Rebekah: Matriarchal Continuity and Well-Side Oracle

To ensure covenant purity, Abraham dispatched his servant to Nahor's household, resulting in Rebekah's selection as Isaac's bride (Gen 24). Her arrival by the well in Haran fulfilled the sign agreed upon—water for the traveler and their camels—demonstrating God's guiding providence. The well-side oracle given by Isaac, glimpsed from afar, set the stage for mutual recognition: Rebekah would draw water and declare household name, prompting servant's sign. Their union at the well prefigures Sarah's own hospitality under Mamre, weaving matriarchal water motifs into the next generation. Rebekah's eager service to the camels reflected covenantal hospitality ethic, marking her suitability as matriarch. Isaac's love for Rebekah provoked his comfort after his mother's death, ushering in new household rhythms of worship and inheritance. Rebekah's fertility, initially also delayed, found resolution in twins, continuing Sarah's legacy of miraculous childbirth. The marriage ceremony—brought about by servant gifts of garments, jewelry, and parley with Rebekah's family—aligned with cultural norms while underscoring Abraham's servant leadership. Their tent at Beersheba became nexus for covenant instruction, with Rebekah taught by Isaac the stories of Abraham and Sarah. This mother-son edification would later inform Jacob's own covenant consciousness. Rebekah's selection thus ensures matriarchal continuity of covenant life and necessary partnership for Isaac's wilderness sojourns. Her woman's intuition and service exemplify the complementary gifts each generation contributes to covenant preservation. Isaac's and Rebekah's marriage thus bridges ancestral promise with future fulfillment.

7.1.3 Prosperity and Persecution: Wells Re-dug, Treaties Re-signed

As Isaac prospered—sowing, reaping, and accumulating flocks—local Philistines grew envious, filling and blocking his father's wells, provoking conflict over water rights (Gen 26:15–18). Rather than retaliating, Isaac moved camp, re-digging Abraham's old wells and naming them by covenant memory: "Esek," "Sitnah," "Rehoboth," and finally "Shibah." Each well's re-digging became act of peaceful protest and trust in divine providence over resource scarcity. Local rulers Abimelech and Phicol recognized Isaac's rising power, prompting peace treaties under seven-ewe oaths at Beersheba (Gen 26:28–31). The recurring sevenfold element ("Shibah") reinforced completeness of covenant care. Isaac's avoidance of violent conflict mirrored Abraham's earlier approach, demonstrating learned restraint anchored in covenant ethics. His treaties insured pastoral security across seasons of drought and neighborly tension. The wells' restoration provided water for allied caravans, extending covenant hospitality into economic enterprise. Isaac's re-signing of treaties underlined that covenant peace transcends generational rivalries between seed of Abraham and local tribes. His well policy influenced later Israelite land laws on gleaning and water rights (Deut 10:18; 24:19). Isaac's reputation for peaceful arbitration spread among southern peoples, consolidating his leadership not by force but by covenant principle. His experience of prosperity amidst persecution deepened communal moral memory that divine blessing can coexist with neighborly goodwill. The narratives of wells and treaties thus transition covenant seed into public witness in contested territory.

With Isaac's covenant inheritance secured through marriage, worship, and peacemaking, the narrative tension shifts to his twin sons—Jacob and Esau—whose rivalry will echo through nations yet unborn.

7.2 Jacob and Esau—Twins in Tension

7.2.1 Prenatal Prophecy: "Two Nations Are in Your Womb" (Gen 25:22–23)

Rebekah's difficult pregnancy prompted Isaac to intercede, after which God revealed: "Two nations are in your womb, and two peoples from within you shall be divided; the one shall be stronger than the other, and the older shall serve the younger" (Gen 25:23). This prenatal prophecy foregrounded national destinies over individual births, casting Jacob and Esau as archetypal progenitors of Israel and Edom. The image of twins struggling within Rebekah's womb provided vivid metaphor for future spiritual and geopolitical conflicts. Midwives and herbalists of Rebekah's entourage likely noted abnormal fetal activity, prompting her anxiety. God's revelation calmed her but also announced deep familial division, foreshadowing sibling rivalry that would shape covenant history. Isaac's silent reception of the prophecy contrasted Rebekah's active response in later chapters, indicating different parental roles in covenant formation. The prophecy's syntax—"two nations," "two peoples"—suggests demographic expansion, linking womb to future tribal configurations. The reversal motif—older serving younger— undercuts cultural norms of primogeniture, signaling divine prerogative over human custom. This promise reframes physical birth order as subordinate to spiritual election. The passage situates twins not as individuals but as bearers of national archetypes. The prenatal word thus inaugurates narrative arc of covenant conflict and eventual reconciliation. Jacob and Esau's tension, first visible in utero, becomes microcosm of Israel-neighbor relations through centuries. The prophecy's enduring influence surfaces in later prophetic pronouncements about Edom's fate (Obad 1:1–21). Thus, before their first breath, Jacob and Esau carry national destinies shaped by divine word.

7.2.2 Birthright Bargain and Red Stew: Appetite versus Inheritance

Esau, born first with red, hairy appearance, became skilled hunter, while Jacob followed holding his heel—symbols of their divergent temperaments (Gen 25:25–26). One day returning famished from the field, Esau agreed to sell his birthright to Jacob for a bowl of lentil stew, calling it "this very day" inheritance (Gen 25:33). The bargain's impulsiveness—trading perpetual spiritual privilege for immediate gratification—models the perils of valuing present appetite over covenantal calling. Jacob's craftiness in exploiting Esau's hunger displays human agency in unfolding divine plan, raising ethical questions about the means justified by ends. The stew's seasonings—red lentils with onions and cumin— symbolically echo Edom's "red" identity. Cultural norms viewed birthright as entailed double portion of inheritance and leadership role, yet Esau's disdain for "rights of the firstborn" marks him as profane in prophetic eyes (Heb 12:16). Jacob's willingness to barter birthright for stew underlines tension between spiritual privilege and bodily needs. This incident sets pattern for covenant testing: human desire threatens divine promise. The narrative invites reflection on priorities in faith—sustenance for the soul must not be sacrificed for urgent hunger. Jacob's subsequent anxiety over securing the blessing intensifies the drama of covenant misappropriation. Esau's regret upon discontinuing his birthright loan exemplifies loss incurred by short-sighted choices. The birthright bargain thus symbolizes national identity traded for fleeting advantages—a caution repeated in Israel's later failures. The story's enduring power lies in its vivid depiction of appetite versus inheritance, forces still at work in believer's daily choices.

7.2.3 Stolen Blessing at Twilight: Patriarchal Blindness and Maternal Strategy

On Isaac's final blessing day, his old age and failing sight rendered him vulnerable to deception. At Rebekah's urging, Jacob donned Esau's garments and goat skins to mimic his brother's hairy skin, presenting Isaac with savory meal to secure the patriarchal blessing (Gen 27:1–17). The stolen blessing—covering fertility, dominion, and national destiny—illustrates how maternal strategy shapes covenant trajectory when paternal capacity falters. Rebekah's decisive action underscores matriarchal agency in preserving covenant promises for Jacob, the younger son. The narrative tension peaks as Isaac hesitates—"The voice is Jacob's voice, but the hands are the hands of Esau"—revealing patriarchal blindness extending beyond physical sight to discernment (Gen 27:22). Isaac's reluctant confirmation—"Surely the voice is Jacob's voice" (Gen 27:24)—solidifies Jacob's ascension as covenant heir. Esau's wailing upon discovering the theft highlights moral complexity of deceit even when orchestrated by matriarch for covenant preservation. The household fractures as sibling rivalry deepens, foreshadowing decades of exile and reconciliation. Jacob's flight to Paddan-Aram under threat of Esau's vengeance continues maternal strategy: ensuring covenant seed's safety beyond immediate boundary. The stolen blessing thus becomes theological pivot: divine election unfolds through flawed human means. This episode echoes divine reversal motifs found throughout Scripture—"God choses the foolish things of the world" (1 Cor 1:27). Jacob's deception and Rebekah's complicity both advance and complicate covenant line, signaling that holiness often emerges through human ambiguity. The lesson emerges that God's promises will persevere despite—and sometimes through—deception and familial turmoil. Jacob's stolen blessing inaugurates a journey of transformation, reflecting how covenant seed must wrestle with both divine and human dynamics.

As Jacob and Esau carve their separate paths from covenant lineage, Ishmael's line advances along desert caravan tracks, shaping nations beyond Canaan.

7.3 Ishmael's Line—Twelve Princes on Desert Tracks

7.3.1 Genealogical Ledger: Nebaioth to Kedemah (Gen 25:12–16)

Genesis lists Ishmael's twelve sons—Nebaioth, Kedar, Adbeel, Mibsam, Mishma, Dumah, Massa, Hadad, Tema, Jetur, Naphish, and Kedemah—each becoming a tribal head of Ishmaelite clans (Gen 25:13–16). This genealogical ledger functions as covenant parallel: Abraham's seed extends through two lineages, one through Isaac, one through Ishmael. The sons' names—often reflecting desert motifs (Kedemah "east country"), conflict (Adbeel "strength of God"), or ancestral memory (Tema "perfumery")—map tribal characteristics onto identity. These Ishmaelite tribes settled across Arabian deserts, forging networks that intersected with Frankincense and myrrh trade routes. Their genealogies appear in later prophetic oracles, marking them as recurring actors in Israel's story (1 Sam 15:21; 1 Kin 10:1). The ledger preserves corporate memory for Ishmaelite peoples, affirming their place in Abraham's broad blessing. Their tribal groupings paralleled Israel's twelve tribes yet remained distinct from covenant seed through Isaac. The list's inclusion in Genesis testifies to divine regard for all Abraham's descendants. Each name functions as mnemonic device for oral recitation at tribal gatherings. The ledger forms basis for later genealogical claims among Arabian lineages, including Quraysh ancestry. Ishmael's pedigree thus anchors genealogical identity for nations stretching from Egypt's border to Persian Gulf tribes. The convergence of tribal memory and covenant records illustrates Genesis's role as both sacred history and ethno-genealogical archive.

7.3.2 Trade Routes and Caravan Kingdoms: Frankincense, Myrrh, and Spice Roads

Ishmaelite tribes leveraged their desert homelands to control incense and spice trade routes between southern Arabia, Sinai, Egypt, and Mesopotamia. Caravans of camels loaded with frankincense, myrrh, cassia, and exotic resins traversed Omani coast roads, passing through Tema (a tribal head's namesake) and Dedan (Ishmael's descendant Edomites). The tribes' expertise in desert navigation, water caching, and seasonal camping sites made them indispensable guides for luxury goods entering Mediterranean markets. Oasis towns like Beersheba and Dedan became caravan hubs where Ishmaelites exchanged goods, forging alliances with

Egypt and Judah. Their economic prowess attracted Egyptian interest, leading to employment as mercenaries and diplomats. Ishmaelite women were renowned for textile weaving, producing fine linens traded alongside spices. This commercial network sustained tribal wealth and cultural exchange, embedding Ishmael's line in regional economies. Biblical texts reference Ishmaelite involvement in Joseph's sale (Gen 37:25) and Moses's first sojourn (Ex 2:15), further attesting to their caravanning role. The tribes' control of incense routes undergirded South Arabian kingdoms like Sheba, connecting Ishmaelite heritage to Queen of Sheba narratives. Their economic footprint shaped desert geopolitics, prompting alliances and conflicts recorded in Assyrian annals. The caravan kingdoms' history underscores how covenant seed extends into commerce, diplomacy, and cultural diffusion. Ishmaelite trade networks thus stand as living testimony to Abraham's universal blessing promise.

7.3.3 Interactions with Israel: Alliance, Conflict, and Prophetic Oracles (Isa 60:6–7)

Throughout Israel's history, Ishmaelite tribes engaged in shifting alliances and conflicts: they raided southern Judah (1 Sam 30:1–18), served as trackers for Hebrew armies (2 Kin 2:16), and participated in midrashic legends of Abraham's hospitality tested by Ishmaelites. Prophetic oracles envision Ishmaelite contributions to Israel's future worship: "A multitude of camels shall cover you... they shall bring gold and frankincense, and shall bring good news" (Isa 60:6–7), portraying former rival tribes as worship companions. Ezekiel's end-time vision includes Ishmael among nations honoring Yahweh's temple (Ezek 47:21–23). These prophetic reversals affirm that covenant's universal blessing extends to Ishmael's descendants who choose faith over enmity. In the Persian period, Ishmaelite mercenaries served in Judean garrison, sometimes cooperating in rebuilding Temple (Ezra 4:9–10). Rabbinic literature highlights Ishmael's tent in Hagar's miraculous well site as place of divine encounter for desert nomads. Christian interpreters see in Isaiah's camels a foreshadowing of Magi's gifts, further linking Ishmaelite heritage to Christ's epiphany. Modern Bedouin claiming Ishmaelite lineage often integrate Abrahamic narratives into tribal genealogies. The dynamic interactions—economic, military, religious—between Israel and Ishmaelites exemplify covenant's porous boundaries: enmity can become fellowship under divine grace. Prophetic oracles thus reframe past conflicts as foundations for future unity. Ishmael's line, though outside primary covenant line, becomes integral to God's plan to bless all nations.

Beyond Ishmael's desert tribes, Abraham's union with Keturah opens eastern branches of his heritage, scattering seed across Arabia and beyond.

7.4 Keturah's Sons—Eastern Branches of Abrahamic Heritage

7.4.1 Zimran to Shuah: Mapping Settlements from Midian to Sheba

After Sarah's death, Abraham married Keturah, whose six sons— Zimran, Jokshan, Medan, Midian, Ishbak, and Shuah—became heads of Arabian clans settling from northern Arabia to the Sheba region (Gen 25:1–4). Zimran's descendants likely occupied oasis networks near Pishon River routes, while Jokshan's sons Sheba and Dedan founded southern trading centers. Medan's people mingled with Midianites along Hejaz caravan trails, linking frankincense production to coastal ports. Midian himself fathered clan leaders who would later host Moses in his exile (Ex 2:15). Ishbak and Shuah's lines appear in Arabian inscriptions, evidencing settlements near modern Yemen and Oman. Mapping Keturah's sons illustrates Abrahamic seed dispersing eastward, seeding emerging desert cultures. Their geographical spread fostered technological exchange, including falconry and date cultivation. The descendants' tribal territories correspond to regions later visited by Queen of Sheba, connecting Abraham's legacy to global trade. Keturah's line thus represents covenant diaspora, spreading Abraham's influence beyond Canaan's borders. Their place names—echoed on ancient maps—serve as markers of Abraham's extended network. Through Keturah's sons, Abraham emerges as patriarch of both agrarian and nomadic societies. These settlements form eastern counterpart to Isaac's southwestern sphere, balancing Abraham's geographical legacy. The dispersion underscores covenant's universal scope, extending seed across varied terrains.

7.4.2 Technological Transfer: Metallurgy, Incense, and Nomadic Herding

Keturah's descendants facilitated transfer of early iron and bronze metallurgy techniques into Arabian highlands, as Midianites forged fine tools and weapons noted in biblical alliances (Num 31:6). They also specialized in incense distillation from frankincense and myrrh—processes refined in Sheba—exporting fragrances to Sinai and Levantine markets. Nomadic herding practices, combining camel, goat, and sheep husbandry, optimized for arid climates, evolved under their stewardship, influencing pastoralism across Arabia. Their well-digging methods, including percolation chambers at wadis, improved water retention, supporting larger flocks. The clan leadership transmitted these innovations along trade routes, cementing economic partnerships with Egypt and Mesopotamia. Textile weaving using goat hair and date-leaf fibers became signature craft, traded in Philistine markets. Keturah's line thus served as conduit for technological diffusion, enhancing covenant seed's material contributions to regional development. Archaeological finds of Midianite pottery and metal smelting sites corroborate biblical traditions. Their expertise in caravan security—training camels to navigate dunes—enabled safe passage for luxury goods. These technological skills underscore Abrahamic influence beyond spiritual sphere into tangible cultural progress.

7.4.3 Later Mentions: Job's Homeland and the Queen of Sheba Connection

The Book of Job locates him in the land of Uz, possibly linked to an Abrahamic grandson, suggesting Keturah's line included regions of Trans-Jordania (Job 1:1). The Queen of Sheba's visit to Solomon (1 Kin 10:1–13), bringing spices and gold, aligns with Sheba's ancestry in Jokshan's line, tying Abraham's extended family to later Israel's golden age. Jewish and Islamic traditions both claim Keturah's descendants as progenitors of Yemeni and Ethiopian peoples, shaping interfaith genealogical memory. Early Christian writings reference these connections to illustrate prophecy fulfillment through Gentile interest in Israelite wisdom. The economic diplomacy of Sheba's queen mirrors Abraham's own treaty tactics, showing heritage patterns recurring across generations. These later mentions affirm that Abraham's legacy through Keturah persisted in regional folklore and royal genealogies. The interplay between sacred text and extrabiblical tradition cements Keturah's line in collective memory. Their mention in canonical and apocryphal literature underscores Abraham's broad familial network. Keturah's descendants thus continue to shape Abraham's story in cultural and literary landscapes far beyond Canaan.

While Abraham's sons plant tribes and kingdoms, his daughters—though fewer in number—introduce subtle influences and moral pivots in covenant narrative.

7.5 Daughters in the Narrative—Silence, Symbol, and Subtle Influence

7.5.1 Dinah's Story: Honor, Violence, and Tribal Ethics (Gen 34)

Dinah, Jacob's daughter by Leah, emerges briefly yet dramatically in Genesis 34 when she visits the women of Shechem and is violated by Shechem son of Hamor (Gen 34:1–2). Her silent suffering sparks a crisis of honor, as Jacob's household faces a moral and social dilemma in a foreign city. Jacob's initial passivity contrasts with Simeon and Levi's fierce retaliation—massacre disguised as covenant circumcision (Gen 34:25–29). This violent response, though protecting Dinah's honor, breaches covenant hospitality ethics and foreshadows inter-tribal tensions between Israel and Canaan. Dinah's name, meaning "judged," underscores her role as catalyst for justice-driven conflict. The episode raises questions about collective guilt and individual agency, as Jacob's sons usurp paternal authority in God's name. Local women—Dinah's cousins—bear witness yet remain silent in the text, symbolizing communal complicity. The aftermath forces Jacob to move his family away, shaping Israelite settlement patterns and clan boundaries. Dinah's subtextual influence informs later Israelite laws protecting women's rights (Deut 22:23–29). Her trauma becomes moral lesson on the cost of compromise with pagan neighbors. The story also prefigures later prophetic condemnation of Israel's sexual violence against the innocent (Ezek 16:38–41). Dinah's narrative absence of direct voice invites readers to consider silenced victims and call for restorative justice. Her subtle influence persists in rabbinic reinterpretations that emphasize repentance and protection of the vulnerable. Dinah's tale thus becomes enduring symbol of the need to uphold covenantal ethics in personal and tribal conduct.

7.5.2 "Daughters of Canaan" Warnings: Covenant Boundaries in Marriage

The command to avoid intermarriage with "daughters of Canaan" (Gen 24:3; Ex 34:16; Deut 7:3) reflects early covenant boundary-setting, preserving Israelite identity against assimilation into idolatrous practices. Daughters in these warnings embody both potential alliance and spiritual threat, as marriages with Canaanites often introduced worship of Baal and Asherah into Israel. The prohibition highlights theological importance of domestic relationships in covenant fidelity. Abraham's servant sought a wife for Isaac "from my master's relatives," rejecting local women to maintain covenant purity (Gen 24:3). Later, Moses reiterated this boundary, linking intermarriage to God's jealousy and covenant holiness (Deut 7:3–4). The recurring emphasis on daughters signals recognition that female partners wield profound influence on household worship and cultural transmission. Judges' cycles of idolatry often begin when foreign daughters draw Israelite men into temple prostitution (Judg 3:6; 1 Kin 11:1–4). Thus, covenant warnings serve as preemptive counsel to guard next generation's faith. Jewish wisdom literature interprets "strange woman" as cautionary archetype (Prov 5; 7). The metaphor extends to spiritual fidelity, teaching readers to resist enticing alternatives to covenant relationship. The boundary around daughters underscores gendered dimensions of communal identity formation. These warnings inform later canonical debates over mixed marriages and inclusion of Gentiles under the New Covenant. The complex interplay of marriage, identity, and faith highlights daughters' pivotal role in covenant continuity.

7.5.3 Ruth and Tamar as Covenant Bridges: Gentile Inclusion Foreshadowed

Ruth the Moabitess, though a foreign daughter, embraces Israel's God and law, declaring "Your people shall be my people" (Ruth 1:16), her faith securing Davidic lineage and foreshadowing Gentile inclusion in covenant promise. Her marriage to Boaz under levirate-like provision revives covenant hospitality and kin-redeemer customs (Ruth 4:5–10). Ruth's loyalty contrasts sharply with daughters of Canaan, highlighting that inclusion depends on faith commitment rather than ethnic origin. Tamar, Judah's daughter-in-law, secures her place in the covenant line through stratagem—posing as a prostitute to conceive Perez (Gen 38:14–30). Though her actions challenge moral norms, Tamar's perseverance upholds Judah's seed promise, signaling that God's purposes can transcend human legalism. Both women occupy raw narrative spaces—Tamar's scandal and Ruth's widowhood—yet each becomes mother to significant branches of David's genealogy (Matt 1:3–5). Their stories demonstrate daughters' agency in safeguarding covenant seed amid patriarchal structures. The inclusion of these women in Matthew's genealogy underscores New Testament affirmation that covenant blessing extends to faithful outsiders. Their narratives inform early Christian debates on Gentile inclusion (Acts 15). Ruth and Tamar's roles reveal that daughters can function as bridges between communities, bringing Gentiles into God's family. Their subtle influence resonates in modern dialogues on gender, ethnicity, and faith integration. Through their covenant-affirming actions, these daughters foreshadow universal scope of Abraham's blessing to all nations.

Having observed how daughters shape covenant boundaries and bridges, we now trace the theological thread of the seed promise from Eden through Israel's monarchy to exile hope.

7.6 Theological Thread—Seed Promise from Eden to Exile

7.6.1 Proto-Evangelium Echoes: Serpent-Crusher Typology (Gen 3:15)

The first hint of "seed" appears in God's curse upon the serpent: "He shall bruise your head, and you shall bruise his heel" (Gen 3:15), establishing the "proto-evangelium" in which a descendant of the woman defeats evil's power. This typology frames the seed promise as cosmic conflict rather than mere fertility blessing. Early Jewish interpreters saw in this seed reference to Abraham's progeny, foreshadowing deliverance from Canaanite oppression. Christian theology identifies the promised seed with Christ, fulfilled in the New Testament (Rom 16:20). The recurring bruise/strike language echoes through patriarchal narratives—Enoch's warnings, Noah's covenant, and Abraham's sacrificial test. The duality of bruised heel

200

and crushed head underscores both vulnerability and ultimate victory of covenant seed. Edenic typology thus provides theological scaffolding for understanding Abrahamic promise in redemptive trajectory. The serpent-crusher motif surfaces in Messianic psalms (Ps 91:13) and Revelation's climactic victory (Rev 12:9–11). Through this thread, covenant seed moves from Eden's fallen garden to global redemption. The proto-evangelium's significance lies in its anticipation of covenant promise transcending Abraham's physical descendants. It anchors theological hope that God's seed will conquer evil at its root.

7.6.2 Royal Seed in David: Charter for Messianic Expectation (2 Sam 7:12–16)

God's covenant with David promises an enduring throne: "Your house and your kingdom shall be made sure forever before me. Your throne shall be established forever" (2 Sam 7:16). This royal seed promise builds on Abraham's seed covenant, focusing on dynasty rather than land allotment. Nathan's oracle reframes Abrahamic blessing within Israel's monarchy, linking paternal promise to royal lineage. David's "seed" becomes theological hinge for later Messianic expectation, as prophets speak of a righteous Branch (Jer 23:5) and shoot from Jesse (Isa 11:1). The Davidic covenant amplifies seed promise from plurality to singular figure—Son of David foreshadowed in Solomon and later attributed to Jesus. Rabbinic literature held days of the Messiah appraised against Abrahamic covenant chronology. The Davidic charter ensures continuity of Abraham's seed promise through royal house despite exile. The dual covenants—Abrahamic and Davidic—interweave to shape Israel's redemptive roadmap. The royal seed theme undergirds New Testament genealogies tracing Christ through David back to Abraham (Matt 1; Luke 3). This royal aspect deepens covenant theology: seed not only multiplies but rules in justice and peace. The Davidic promise thus bridges patriarchal blessing and eschatological hope.

7.6.3 Exilic Hope: Isaiah's Branch and Daniel's Son of Man

During exile, Isaiah prophesied a Branch from Jesse's stump who would establish justice and righteousness (Isa 11:1–10), reviving seed promise in context of national restoration. Daniel's vision of the "Son of Man" granted everlasting dominion (Dan 7:13–14) echoes seed-promise language, universalizing covenant reach. These exilic hopes sustain belief that seed promise transcends deportation and foreign dominion. Prophets frame Davidic and Abrahamic seed within God's sovereign timetable, marking seasons of judgment and restoration. The exilic imagery of stump rather than full tree conveys resilience of seed through traumatic uprooting. Daniel's apocalyptic expansion of seed promise to cosmic realm invites global participation in covenant. Ezekiel's vision of dry bones revived (Ezek 37) further allegorizes seed promise for collective Israel. Post-exilic reflections in Zechariah and Haggai call returnees to rebuild temple, connecting seed promise to physical restoration of place. The exilic theological thread weaves Abraham through David to emerging messianic themes. Seed promise thus offers enduring hope amid covenant community's lowest ebbs. These prophetic continuities affirm that God's seed—physical, royal, and spiritual—remains intact beyond human collapse.

Building on theological foundations, we now trace geographic spread of Abraham's seed from Beersheba wells to the Arabian Peninsula and beyond.

7.7 Geographic Spread—From Beer-lahai-roi to the Arabian Peninsula

7.7.1 Wells, Oases, and Desert Forts: Infrastructure of Emerging Tribes

Abraham's network of wells—from Beersheba and Beer-lahai-roi to Isaac's new wells—became lifelines for covenant seed's nomadic and sedentary branches. Each water source served as oasis gathering point, spawning small forts where tribes traded goods and sought protection. Sites like Rehoboth and Esek grew into caravan rest stations, enabling movement across Negev. The forts—mounded mud-brick structures—functioned as administrative centers for controlling pasture leases and water access. Abrahamic tribes established well-maintenance protocols and seasonal pilgrimage circuits, transforming wilderness into semi-civilized corridors. These infrastructures facilitated cultural exchange and political alliances with neighbors like Edom and Moab. Desert forts later evolved under Nabatean rule into stone cities like Petra, signaling indigenous adaptation of Abrahamic transit networks. Wells also marked tribal boundaries, with inscriptions bearing clan names for water rights enforcement. Abraham's initial well-digging thus seeded logistical frameworks for emerging Middle Eastern societies. The infrastructure's design balanced permanence and mobility, reflecting covenant seed's dual call to sojourn and settle. These desert arteries underwrote trade routes and pilgrimage roads for millennia. The network's survival into Roman and Byzantine times attests to Abraham's geographical legacy. Thus, covenant seed's spatial expansion depended on wells, oases, and forts as foundational infrastructure.

7.7.2 Edom's Highlands and Seir's Cliffs: Esau's Territorial Identity

Esau's descendants, the Edomites, claimed the rugged highlands of Seir between the Dead Sea and Gulf of Aqaba, carving terraced fields into limestone cliffs. Their rugged terrain became natural fortress, enabling defense against Israel's incursions under Kings David and Jehoshaphat. Edomite society capitalized on copper mining in Timnah and agriculture in highland terraces, creating distinct economy from plains Israelite tribes. Edom's capital Bozrah served as political and religious center, worshiping Qos alongside Yahweh, illustrating syncretistic pressures on covenant seed.

203

Edomite prophets like Obadiah later condemned Edom for violence against Judah, demonstrating enduring sibling rivalry. Yet Edom's fierce independence influenced Israel's self-perception as covenant people occupying chosen highlands. The Seir region's wild goats and frankincense trees contributed to Edomite exports, forging early trade ties with Arab tribes. The cultural memory of Jacob's blessing—that Esau would live by sword—found geographic expression in Edom's martial resilience. Modern archaeological work in Edomite sites confirms biblical ethnography. Esau's terrains thus stand as physical markers of covenant divergence, shaping narratives of blessing and judgment. These highlands offer case study of how seed promise interacts with topographical destiny.

7.7.3 Trans-Jordan Holdings: Reuben, Gad, and Half-Tribe Manasseh

In the conquest period, Reuben, Gad, and half of Manasseh opted for lands east of the Jordan—fertile Gilead plains and Ammonite borderlands—securing pastures and spring-fed valleys (Num 32; Josh 22). Their trans-Jordan settlement balanced desire for immediate provision with covenant obligations to assist in west-bank conquest. The eastern tribes built an imposing altar at Jordan's western bank, nearly sparking civil war until priests affirmed unity in worship (Josh 22:10–34). This altar incident illustrates tensions in geographically dispersed seed holders. The trans-Jordan tribes' holdings provided buffer zone against Mesopotamian incursions and trade route control. Their land grant followed patriarchal patterns, echoing Abraham's and Isaac's east-side nomadic camps. The Gilead region's deep wadis and basalt formations hosted production of balm and perfumed oils, continuing Midianite-Ishmaelite traditions. The trans-Jordan tribes' covenant loyalty debate foreshadows modern diaspora questions. Their practical inheritance choices highlight covenant complexities when geography and faith duty collide. Their holdings become integral to Israel's national security and religious unity. Trans-Jordan settlements thus contribute to geographic mosaic of covenant seed's dispersion.

While geography shapes seed identity, external empires pose tests—preservation and dispersion under Egyptian, Assyrian, and Babylonian shadows.

7.8 Covenant versus Empire—Seed under Egyptian, Assyrian, and Babylonian Shadows

7.8.1 Preservation in Goshen: Fertility amid Foreign Control

Joseph's rise in Egypt secured Israelite survival during famine, settling Jacob's family in the fertile Goshen region, where they multiplied into a "great nation" under Pharaoh's protection (Gen 47:27). Goshen's lush pastures supported vast flocks akin to Canaan's highland summer grounds. The Israelites' status as shepherds—a marginal class—shielded them from Egyptian toil until enslavement under a new Pharaoh (Ex 1:8–14). Their initial preservation in Goshen reflects covenant promise while foreshadowing later tension with imperial policy. Egyptian administrative records mention "Habiru" laborers, possibly referencing Hebrews in Goshen. Israel's rapid growth alarmed Egypt's rulers, prompting harsh labor schemes, yet God's blessing persisted under imperial control. The Goshen sojourn provided cultural blending—Hebrew language absorbed Egyptian loanwords, influencing early Israelite lexicon. Israelites built store cities like Pithom, using Egyptian architectural knowledge. Their preservation amid empire demonstrates God's capacity to protect seed within foreign systems. Goshen thus becomes prototype for covenant community under diaspora conditions. The Israelite experience in Goshen established collective memory of resilience under oppression. This history informs subsequent Jewish reflections on exile and return. The preservation theme resurfaces in New Testament trust in God's providence within hostile polities. Gaza's proximity facilitated later Exodus staging, linking covenant seed's departure from empire to promised land return.

7.8.2 Assyrian Resettlements: Northern Tribes Scattered yet Remembered

In 722 BC, Assyria conquered Israel's northern kingdom, deporting elites to Media and repopulating the land with foreign peoples (2 Kin 17:6–24). This forced dispersion disrupted tribal distributions, yet prophetic promises—"a remnant shall return" (Amos 9:11–15)—kept covenant hope alive within scattered seed. The Assyrian policy of resettlement created mixed populations—"Samaritans"—who adopted syncretistic worship, prompting tensions with returning Judahites (Ezra 4). Israelite identities persisted in remote communities, evidenced by Mesha Stele references to "Yahweh of Samaria." Tribal names appear in deportation lists found at Nineveh, attesting that covenant seed remained known under imperial gaze. The Northern tribes developed diaspora enclaves retaining Israelite customs alongside imperial languages. Their scattered memory influenced Persian period policies, where Cyrus's edict allowed partial return to ancestral lands. Assyrian dispersion thus became inadvertent instrument for spreading Israelite faith among foreign peoples. The experience informs New Testament metaphor of "branches broken off" and "wild olive grafted in" (Rom 11). Assyrian shadows tested covenant seed's cohesion, yet prophetic oracles ensured survival of identity across empire. The resettlements underscore that dispersion does not equate loss of covenant promise.

7.8.3 Babylonian Exile: Remnant Theology and Genealogical Lists (Ezra 2)

Following Jerusalem's fall in 586 BC, Judah's elite were exiled to Babylon, prompting theological re-examination: prophets like Jeremiah and Ezekiel emphasized a faithful remnant to carry covenant forward (Jer 29:10–14; Ezek 37:21–28). The returned exiles under Zerubbabel and Ezra brought genealogical lists (Ezra 2; Neh 7) to reestablish temple worship and communal identity. The lists—specifying priests, Levites, and lay families—functioned as legal proof of inclusion in renewed covenant. Remnant theology reframed seed promise: blessing now entrusted to small community rather than national majority. Babylonian diaspora saw rise of synagogue worship in foreign cities, preserving covenant practices without temple. Exilic psalms and lamentations crystallized communal memory around suffering and hope. Genealogies became central to self-understanding, ensuring continuity of priestly and Davidic lines. The exile experience shaped second temple Judaism and later rabbinic emphases on law and lineage. Jeremiah's "new covenant" promise (Jer 31:31–34) emerges from remnant context, anticipating internalized seed promise. Post-exilic rebuilding under Persian patronage affirmed God's faithfulness to remnant seed. The Babylonian shadows thus produced renewed covenant expressions that shaped Judaism and early Christianity. Through remnant lists, seed promise found concrete validation amid ruins. The exile's theological recalibration highlights covenant's resilience beyond national collapse.

After tracing seed under empires, we next examine genealogies as living memory—oral, written, and material—preserving covenant identity across ages.

7.9 Genealogies as Memory—Tablets, Totems, and Tribal Storytelling

7.9.1 Toledot Structure in Genesis: Literary Frames for Lineage

The Hebrew word *toledot* ("generations" or "account of births") appears at key junctures in Genesis, creating twelve narrative units that function as genealogical capsules. Each *toledot* heading—such as "These are the generations of Isaac" (Gen 25:19)—signals a shift in focus to the next branch of Abraham's family tree, reminding ancient readers to preserve ancestral memory. Scribes meticulously copied these headings into clay tablets and scrolls, treating them as sacred chapter markers for communal recitation. The *toledot* structure also echoes Mesopotamian king lists yet is reframed through Yahweh's covenant promises rather than royal sovereignty. By repeating the formulaic "These are the generations...," Genesis weaves theological continuity between Adam, Noah, Abraham, Isaac, Jacob, and the tribes of Israel. Later Jewish scribes embedded mnemonic patterns—like acrostic devices—in genealogical lists to aid oral transmission during festivals. Dead Sea Scroll fragments preserve partial *toledot* columns, confirming their role as liturgical and educational tools. The structurally symmetrical design underscores covenant seed's progression from primal origins to tribal configurations. This literary frame invites readers to see genealogy as more than biological record; it is theological architecture mapping God's redemptive plan. The *toledot* headings serve as literary totems, visible signposts that guide communal identity. Through them, Israel's earliest teachers instructed children in covenant history around campfires and at temple courtyards. The *toledot* structure thus embodies covenant memory, shaping how successive generations encounter Scripture. Its influence persists in modern biblical studies as key to understanding Genesis's composition and purpose. The *toledot* literary frames reaffirm that remembering ancestors is integral to preserving covenant identity.

7.9.2 Oral Recitation and Sand-Drawing: Bedouin Techniques of Ancestral Recall

Nomadic tribes of the Arabian desert, many tracing lineage to Abraham's seed, developed oral recitation methods reinforced by sand-drawing genealogical trees at oasis gatherings. Elders would sketch branching lines in the sand, labeling tribal forebears by name, birth order, and notable deeds, while narrating exploits in poetic meter. These tactile sketches allowed listeners to visualize generational connections and memorize long pedigrees spanning dozens of names. Seasonal festivals at wells like Beersheba became opportunities for such genealogical storytelling, preserving tribal heritage amid mobile lifestyles. The practice incorporated mnemonic devices—rhythmic chants and rhyming couplets—to embed genealogies in collective memory without written records. When literacy spread after the Islamic conquests, these oral-visual techniques influenced early Arabic genealogical writing, merging sand-drawn charts with parchment scrolls. Jewish Bedouin communities similarly used sand-mapping during Passover seders to trace tribal sojourns. Modern ethnographers document sand-drawing ceremonies still practiced by certain clans in Jordan and Saudi Arabia, testifying to deep ancestral continuity. This embodied form of memory emphasizes that genealogies are living traditions, not static lists. Sand-drawing sessions fostered intergenerational dialogue, as children learned names and tales from grandparents. The ephemeral nature of sand maps underscored that lineages, though transiently sketched, are eternally preserved in communal hearts. These techniques complement the written *toledot*, demonstrating how covenant seed memory adapts across media. The synergy of oral recital and sand-drawing ensured genealogical knowledge survived even when scrolls decayed. Together, they illustrate the dynamic interplay between spoken and visual memory in preserving covenant identity.

7.9.3 Post-Exilic Chroniclers: From Adam to Abraham to Anawim

 After returning from Babylonian exile, priest-scribes such as Ezra and Nehemiah compiled comprehensive genealogies in books of Chronicles, linking Adam through Abraham to the post-exilic *Anawim*—the humble remnant who rebuilt temple and city walls (1 Chr 1:1; Neh 11:1–2). These chroniclers appended Levitical and Judean family lists to validate priestly and royal claims under Persian authority, ensuring land allotments and temple roles conformed to ancestral lines. They interpolated Israelite and

Judahite genealogies with foreign family names, indicating intermarriage and integration of returnees. The chronicler's genealogy of Zerubbabel in Ezra 3:2 became charter for restoration, connecting covenant seed to new temple inauguration. Public proclamations of genealogies during wall-rebuilding festivals reinforced communal cohesion after displacement. Chroniclers also recorded genealogies in the margins of Mosaic Torah scrolls, using specialized ink formulas to distinguish post-exilic entries. Their work influenced later Talmudic codification of family purity laws linked to Levitical status. Genealogical lists in Chronicles thus functioned as instruments of identity reformation, transforming disparate exiles into unified covenant community. The chronicler's emphasis on continuity—from Adam, through Noah, Abraham, David, to Zerubbabel—provided theological reassurance of God's unbroken purposes. The post-exilic genealogical project demonstrates how covenant seed memory is redemptively reassembled after cataclysmic dispersion. Their legacy informs modern approaches to biblical genealogy, encouraging holistic reading of ancestral threads. Through post-exilic chroniclers, covenant identity is reaffirmed in every generation, from primeval progenitors to marginalized returnees.

Having explored how genealogies functioned as living memory across written and oral traditions, we turn to New Covenant fulfillment, where the singular Seed completes the ancestral promise.

7.10 New-Covenant Fulfillment—Seed Singular in the Messiah

7.10.1 Pauline Exegesis: "Not Seeds but Seed—Who Is Christ" (Gal 3:16)

In Galatians 3:16, Paul declares that the promise was made to Abraham "and to his Seed," identifying Christ as singular fulfillment

210

rather than plural offspring. This exegetical move reorients the seed theology from ethnic multiplication to messianic culmination, emphasizing Jesus as the true heir of Abraham's promise. Paul's Greek wordplay on *sperma* ("seed") highlights that Christ embodies collective blessing for all believers. He further argues that those "of faith are sons of Abraham" (Gal 3:7), extending seed identity to Gentile Christians. Early church writers embraced Pauline seed theology to argue against Judaizing teachers, grounding universal gospel in Abrahamic promise. The singular-seed motif influenced Augustine's doctrine of the church as spiritual Israel, unified under Christ. Reformers like Luther and Calvin upheld seed singularity to emphasize justification by faith alone, not by descent or law. Modern scholars trace Pauline seed exegesis to Greco-Roman treaty formats, where promise language included singularly addressed heirs. The seed-as-Christ hermeneutic reframes covenant genealogies from national pedigree to incarnational fulfillment. This interpretive shift undergirds Christian mission, since Christ's seed invites all nations. Paul's approach thus transforms genealogical memory into theological proclamation. By centering Christ as seed, New Covenant theology completes the promise arc begun in Genesis. His exegesis ensures that Abraham's blessing flows into global and eternal dimensions.

7.10.2 Genealogy of Matthew: Four Women and Royal Legitimacy

Matthew's Gospel opens with a genealogy of Jesus that uniquely includes four women—Tamar, Rahab, Ruth, and "the wife of Uriah" (Bathsheba)—highlighting Gentile inclusion and moral complexity in Messiah's lineage (Matt 1:3–6). By weaving in these non-Israelite and scandal-laden figures, Matthew underscores God's grace operating beyond clean tribal lines. The inclusion of royal Davidic connections—"the son of Solomon" (Matt 1:6)—sharpens Jesus's Messianic credentials under Jewish expectation of kingly deliverance. Matthew arranges the genealogy into three sets of fourteen generations, suggesting numerological symmetry: the numeric value of David's name in Hebrew (DVD = 14). This literary structuring reaffirms royal legitimacy and divine ordination. The foreign women also signal God's promise to bless all nations through Abraham's seed, foreshadowing Christian mission to Gentiles. Early church councils invoked Matthew's genealogy when arguing Christ's lawful claim to Davidic throne. Renaissance art depicts these women alongside Mary, visually linking covenant continuity. Matthew's emphasis on maternal lines contrasts with patriarchal genealogies elsewhere, recognizing women's roles in covenant economy. His genealogy thus models inclusive remembrance, shaping Christian identity across ethnic boundaries. Matthew's framing ensures that Jesus emerges as culmination of diverse ancestral threads, fulfilling seed promise universally. The royal legitimacy asserted through genealogy grounds Christian hope in historical continuity from Abraham to Messiah. This genealogical portrait invites believers to honor heritage while embracing new-covenant identity in Christ.

7.10.3 Inclusion of the Nations: Pentecost as Multiplication of Abraham's Family

At Pentecost, the pouring out of the Spirit enabled "Jews, devout men from every nation under heaven" to hear the gospel in their own tongues (Acts 2:5–11), symbolizing re-creation of Abraham's household as multilingual family. Peter's sermon directly cites Joel's prophecy and connects Spirit-baptized believers to Abraham's promised blessing—"in your offspring all the families of the earth shall be blessed" (Acts 2:39; citing Gen 22:18). The new-covenant community thus becomes living fulfillment of seed promise, as people from diverse ethnicities coalesce into one spiritual lineage. The early church's practice of table fellowship—breaking bread together—mirrors covenant feasting under patriarchal terebinths. Missionary journeys trace former trade-route networks of Ishmaelite caravans, now vessels for gospel spread. The inclusion of nations at

Pentecost marks theological reversal of Babel's scattering, re-uniting humanity under Christ's lordship. Letters like Galatians and Romans expound that faith in Christ makes Gentiles co-heirs with Abraham. Early church fathers invoked Pentecost as Abrahamic seed proliferation across cultural boundaries. The event's liturgical commemoration in Christian calendars affirms covenant continuity. Pentecost thus transforms genealogical seed concept into dynamic, Spirit-empowered community. The global church today stands as testament to Abrahamic blessing's universal reach.

With New Covenant fulfillment manifest in Christ's singular seed and Spirit-wrought family, we turn to how Abrahamic heritage echoes in contemporary Jewish, Arab, and Christian identities.

7.11 Modern Echoes—Abrahamic Heritage in Today's Peoples

7.11.1 Jewish Diaspora: Lineage, Land, and Liturgy

Modern Jewish communities, dispersed across continents, preserve lineage traditions through synagogue membership records and *yizkor* (remembrance) services, tracing family names back to Levite and priestly clans. The Israeli Law of Return reflects belief in spiritual descent from Abraham, granting citizenship to those of Jewish parentage or conversion. Liturgy such as the *Aleinu* prayer and Passover Haggadah recount Abraham's call and sacrifice, embedding patriarchal memory in annual festivals. Genealogical research tools like DNA testing now complement oral and written family trees, assisting diaspora Jews in reclaiming lost tribal affiliations. Names like Cohen and Levi still signal hereditary roles in synagogue rituals. Jewish communities in Ethiopia (Beta Israel) and India (Cochin Jews) maintain unique traditions claiming descent from ancient Israelite migrations. Modern genealogical projects compile *Sephardi* records post-Inquisition, reconnecting families

213

scattered since the 15th century. Diaspora literature and memoirs often reflect on Abrahamic identity as unifying motif amid cultural diversity. Israeli kibbutzim revive communal living models echoing Abrahamic hospitality. Yad Vashem archives also preserve stories of Jews who helped neighbors during crises, echoing covenant hospitality. The Jewish diaspora thus embodies living continuation of Abraham's seed through land, liturgy, and lineage. Their collective memory affirms that covenant identity transcends national borders, uniting people through shared ancestry.

7.11.2 Arab Lineages: Ishmaelite, Midianite, and Quraysh Traditions

Arab genealogical traditions, preserved in classical Arabic poetry and *ansab* (genealogy) texts, often trace descent from Ishmael and Midian, linking tribes such as Quraysh—Muhammad's own clan— to Abraham's lineage. Key genealogists like Hisham ibn al-Kalbi in the 8th century documented tribal pedigrees from Adnan (Ishmael's descendant) to Qahtanite lines, reflecting broad acceptance of Abrahamic roots. Arab families annually recite lineage poetry during *majlis* gatherings, reinforcing tribal cohesion and social standing. Islamic teachings honor Abraham (*Ibrahim*) as patriarch and builder of Kaaba in Mecca, integrating him into pilgrimage rituals (*Hajj*), where the *Tawaf* circumambulation echoes covenant circle imagery. Sites such as the Zamzam well recall Hagar and Ishmael's desert ordeal, commemorated through *Sa'i* pilgrim procession. Arabian archaeological remains of Midianite shrines further validate deep historical memory of Abrahamic presence. Modern Middle Eastern societies sometimes invoke Ishmaelite descent in political rhetoric to assert indigenous claims to the land. Arabic surnames like "Al-Ishmaeli" persist as markers of Abrahamic heritage. This lineage consciousness fosters interreligious dialogues centered on shared patriarchal roots. The Arab embrace of Abrahamic identity thus remains vibrant in both cultural and spiritual dimensions.

7.11.3 Christian Adoption: Faith-Line Children across Continents

Christian communities worldwide, from sub-Saharan Africa to Latin America and Asia, identify as "children of Abraham" by faith, celebrating baptism as entry into Abraham's spiritual family (Gal 3:29). Missionary movements often frame evangelism in Abrahamic terms—calling new believers to join the household of faith. Christian liturgies in diverse cultures incorporate Abrahamic readings and hymns, adapting local musical styles to recount covenant promises. African Independent Churches connect tribal initiation rituals to Old Testament covenant rites, symbolically aligning converts with Abraham's lineage. Latin American *Pueblos de Dios* often use pilgrimage reenactments of Abraham's journey as community formation exercises. In Asia, house church networks reference Abraham's faith under persecution, drawing parallels to New Testament exiles. Global Christian genealogy projects catalog spiritual "descendants" of historic revivals, celebrating lines of faith transmission. Ecumenical declarations sometimes invoke Abrahamic heritage to foster unity among denominations. Christian educational curricula frequently begin Old Testament instruction with Abraham's call, ensuring generational transfer of covenant story. The worldwide church thus exemplifies Abraham's promised blessing to all families of earth, demonstrating that faith, rather than bloodline, defines seed. Christian adoption into Abraham's family remains enduring symbol of gospel universality.

Conclusion By surveying the lives of Isaac, Jacob, Esau, Ishmael, and the wider family branches, we see the covenant promise expand beyond a single couple into a complex network of tribes, kingdoms, and faith communities. Genealogies become more than ancestral lists—they are the living memory of divine faithfulness, markers of identity under foreign rule, and foreshadows of a "seed" whose spiritual offspring outnumber the stars. The stories of sons and daughters reveal how God's promise often unfolds through tension, rivalry, and unexpected alliances, yet always progresses toward the goal of universal blessing. As we transition to Jacob's wrestling journey and nation-bearing role, the foundation laid by Abraham's offspring assures us that God's purposes survive every conflict, every exile, and every new beginning—ultimately converging in the Messiah who fulfills the promise to break down every wall between peoples.

Chapter 8 – Lot and the Relatives: Kinship, Conflict, and Compassion

Lot's story runs parallel to Abraham's, yet his path weaves its own tapestry of kinship ties, moral quandaries, and divine encounters. From the shared tents of Terah's family to the fertile fields of the Jordan Valley, Lot experiences the blessings and brittleness of relational proximity. His choices—sometimes prudent, often impulsive—draw him into the swirling ambitions of city life, the horrors of siege warfare, and the terror of divine judgment. Yet even in his flight from destruction, Lot's compassion flickers, offering hospitality at great personal risk. Through Lot's highs and lows, we see the dynamic tension between loyalty to family and fidelity to God, between the lure of comfort and the call to holiness.

8.1 Leaving Haran Together—Abram's Caravan of Kin

8.1.1 Lot's Orphaned Status and Adoption into Abram's Household

Lot first enters the narrative as the orphaned son of Haran, Abram's brother who died prematurely in Ur (Gen 11:28), making Lot both nephew and foster-son to Abram. In a culture where extended family provided social safety nets, Abram's welcoming of Lot into his own household signified both kinship duty and God's unfolding plan for covenant multiplication. As Abram prepared to leave Haran under divine instruction, Lot joined the caravan, his youthful energy supplementing Abram's seasoned leadership. The inclusion of Lot broadened the household's human resources, adding manpower for tent-making, well maintenance, and shepherding. This adoption also bound Lot's fate to Abram's faith journey—every decision Abram made would shape Lot's destiny. In Mesopotamian custom, adopted heirs could share in both land and spiritual inheritance, foreshadowing Lot's later partial entitlement to Canaan's fertility. The social status of orphans in ancient Near Eastern law—protected yet vulnerable—found expression in Lot's dependence on Abram's patronage. Lot's inclusion in Abram's journey underscores the patriarch's generosity and signals God's intent to bless not only bloodline but household network. Oral traditions likely celebrated Abram's compassion in caring for a bereaved nephew, reinforcing clan solidarity. Lot's identity as both nephew and adopted son shaped his later decisions—torn between loyalty to Abram and attraction to the fertile plains of the Jordan. This dual status set the stage for familial tensions when resources strained under growing herds. Lot's early inclusion illustrates that covenant hospitality extends beyond immediate spouse to orphaned relatives. As Abram's household moved west, Lot's presence embodied the wider ripple effects of a single family's obedience to God's call. His adoption thus marks first act of kinship compassion that will echo—both positively and tragically—through the narrative.

8.1.2 Shared Wealth: Flocks, Tents, and Servants on the Western Trek

As Abram and Lot journeyed toward Canaan, their combined wealth—"both of them were very rich, with flocks, herds, and tents" (Gen 13:2)—became measure of divine blessing and source of logistical complexity. Tent encampments required strategic planning: choosing seasonal pasture, locating hidden springs, and coordinating servant teams to fold and pitch dozens of tents at dawn. Shepherds and herdsmen managed thousands of goats and sheep, while camel caravans transported household goods and provisions. Servants performed roles ranging from water procurement and oil pressing to tent repair and spice storage. Lot's youth and vigor proved invaluable in scouting new grazing sites and managing animal migrations. The joint enterprise fostered camaraderie among servants loyal to both Abram and Lot, yet also planted seeds of competition for best pastures and water access. Shared wealth allowed the two men to present a united front to local chieftains seeking tribute or alliance. Their combined presence deterred small raiding parties, ensuring relative security on the trek. Yet as their numbers grew, carrying capacity of flocks strained fragile highland ecosystems, foreshadowing later disputes. The shared wealth also strengthened Abram's hand when negotiating treaties with Abimelech and local rulers, as he could offer grain tithe or guest-host privileges through his household network. Lot's share in the caravan's assets granted him social standing in Canaan's nomadic circles. The joint trek thus became model of covenant community moving together in faith and resource stewardship. However, the dual wealth inevitably created logistical friction, testing the bonds of kinship before they would be formally tested by later separation.

8.1.3 Early Altars, Early Lessons: Lot's First Encounters with Yahweh

Lot's introduction to the Canaanite landscape included Abram's first altars—at Shechem and Bethel—where Abram "built there an altar to the LORD" (Gen 12:7–8), inviting Lot to witness acts of worship that redefined the land's spiritual geography. These early altars taught Lot that sacred space depended not on Canaanite shrines but on opened hearts toward Yahweh. Abram's solitary acts of prayer and sacrifice contrasted with communal pagan rites, offering Lot alternative models of divine encounter. The presence of these altars under terebinths and oaks provided Lot with enduring signposts of covenant faith as he found his footing in a foreign land. Witnessing Abram's declarations—calling on the name of the LORD—impressed upon Lot that personal relationship with God trumped ancestral gods of Ur or Haran. The altars served as educational laboratories where Lot observed baptismal-like anointings with oil, prophetic pronouncements of seed and land promise, and the building of memorial stones. These early lessons shaped Lot's initial hospitality ethic—offering passing travelers shade and water in imitation of Abram's practices. Lot's later selective application of these lessons—embracing material fertility yet neglecting ritual reverence—underscores the mixed legacy of his exposure. The early altars also proved to be crowdfunding sites for future narratives: Bethel's significance would echo through Jacob's ladder vision. Lot's foundational experiences thus intertwined worship with land, instructing him that terrain becomes sacred through covenant acts. Though Lot would drift toward Sodom, traces of these first altar-lessons remained in his impulse to offer hospitality to strangers in crisis (Gen 19:1–3). The altars planted by Abram therefore yielded both initial blessing and ambiguous discipleship within Lot's heart.

As the household's wealth multiplied and worship patterns took root, the pastoral pressures of Canaan's limited resources soon sparked conflict between Abram's and Lot's herdsmen.

8.2 Pastoral Pressures—Quarrels on the Hill Country Grazing Lines

8.2.1 Water-Hole Skirmishes: Herdsmen of Abram versus Herdsmen of Lot

In the semi-arid hill country of central Canaan, springs and cisterns were communal but scarce, making control over water-holes critical for sustaining large flocks and herds. Abram's herdsmen and Lot's herdsmen found themselves in repeated disputes over watering times—each arguing rights of first dig or prime trough placement. Goat hooves and sheep bellies jammed at well's edge, leading to physical scuffles over water pans and communal troughs. Servant overseers attempted to de-escalate tensions by designating alternating watering schedules, yet the sheer volume of livestock from both households overwhelmed rustic systems. Pastoral skirmishes sometimes escalated to threats with staffs and slings, requiring Abram's intervention as patriarchal mediator. Desert dust flew as animals stampeded when masters shouted commands to avoid trampling or fouling of water. Local Canaanite farmers, watching from terraces, considered calling in city guards to separate the conflicting flocks. The overlapping grazing lines—tessellated fields carved into hills—lacked formal property demarcations, forcing herders to negotiate fluid boundary understandings daily. Abram's herdsmen emphasized covenant ethics in their appeals—citing their master's promise to maintain peace—while Lot's men leveraged claims of prior rights to springs uncovered during the first sojourn. These recurrent disputes strained bonds of kinship and hospitality, signaling that resource scarcity tests both practical logistics and relational loyalty. Ultimately, the water-hole skirmishes compelled Abram to seek higher ground for his flocks, relocating to avoid repeated conflict and preserve household unity. The hullabaloo at wells thus foreshadowed Lot's later choice of low-land pastures, where water and commerce intertwined under

Sodom's gates. Abram's resolution to end the water fights by separation underscores that sometimes peace requires strategic sacrifice of prime grazing to maintain covenant bonds.

8.2.2 Patriarchal Mediation: Abram's Offer of Choice and Covenant Peace

Faced with servant complaints and growing tension, Abram convened a council under the oaks of Mamre, urging Lot and their herdsmen to resolve disputes without violence. Drawing on his prophetic role, Abram reminded Lot of God's abundant promise— "Lift up your eyes and see from the place where you are" (Gen 13:14)—then offered the first choice of land, saying, "Let there be no strife... between you and me. For we are brothers" (Gen 13:8–9). This magnanimous gesture displayed Abram's faith that divine blessing would not be limited by territory. Abram's words carried moral weight, invoking brotherhood to override economic competition. His servant-mediators conveyed Abram's willingness to yield the best pastures, a radical model of conflict resolution rooted in covenant ethics rather than martial force. Lot's acceptance of this offer—choosing toward the well-watered Jordan plain— sealed amicable separation, sparing Abram's household from a civil feud. Abram's mediation exemplified leadership: prioritizing relational peace over resource retention. His approach resonates with later Mosaic injunctions for yielder-first principle in neighborly disputes (Lev 19:18; Prov 25:21–22). By defusing pastoral strife through generosity, Abram demonstrated that covenant peace transcends mere wealth accumulation. His offer not only prevented bloodshed among kinsmen but also preserved spiritual integrity before local city chieftains. Abram's mediation thus becomes archetype for peacemaking among tribes, influencing Israelite judges' roles in settling inter-tribal disputes. This covenant peace enabled Abram to relocate without bitter resentment, preserving unity of faith community even in physical separation. Abram's leadership in mediation exemplifies the integration of piety and diplomacy in covenant stewardship.

8.2.3 Economics of Separation: Counting Sheep, Counting Costs

The decision to part ways carried significant economic implications: Lot's choice of fertile plains promised immediate pasture gains but increased susceptibility to city-state tributes and tax burdens. Abram's move to higher ground necessitated investment in well-digging and tent-reconfiguration for hillside living. Servant allocations had to be recalibrated, with shepherds and herds re-assigned to either camp, requiring logistic oversight to prevent animal loss. Camel caravans transporting household belongings had to navigate steeper tracks, affecting travel speed and risk of bandit raids. Lot's proximity to Sodom's gates offered trade opportunities—selling surplus meat and dairy to city dwellers—while Abram forfeited these market connections for covenantal peace. Both men had to revise servant rotations for pasture checking, water patrols, and fencing repair. The partition also split the shared oxen-driven plow teams used for valley grain patches, compelling Abram to adopt more mobile pastoral focus. Economic separation entailed costs: lost urban commerce for Abram and increased tribute payments for Lot. Yet Abram's trust in divine promise outweighed immediate material risks. The economic calculus underscores that covenant fidelity sometimes demands sacrifice of proven profit avenues. Abram's willingness to count costs reflects leadership courage, choosing long-term promise over short-term yield. Lot's acceptance suggests his view of covenant booking signaled in material attraction rather than relational trust. The separation economics foreshadow future contrasts: Lot's later crisis in Sodom versus Abram's peace under the Oaks of Mamre. This economic partition thus becomes watershed moment in both men's trajectories—demonstrating that resource decisions carry spiritual consequences.

Having resolved pastoral tensions through peaceful separation, Lot gravitated toward the lowlands, where the promises of abundance would entangle him in urban moral peril.

8.3 Eyes toward the Plain—Lot's Jordan-Valley Settlement

8.3.1 Edenic Allure of Sodom: Fertility, Commerce, and Moral Fault-Lines

The Jordan Valley's "well-watered everywhere, like the garden of the LORD" (Gen 13:10) captivated Lot, mirroring Eden's fertility with lush vegetation, spring-fed irrigation ditches, and productive farmland. Sodom, one of the five cities of the plain, thrived on trade in date-palm products, bitumen for construction, and salt from the nearby Dead Sea. The city's marketplaces offered imported luxuries—spices, silks, and precious metals—attracting merchants from distant empires. Lot's tents near Sodom's gate placed him at the crossroads of commerce and culture, where pastoral nomads heard news of Mesopotamian politics and Egyptian movements. Guest houses near city walls provided him with social entrée to city elders and council. Yet beneath the veneer of urban prosperity lay systemic injustice: the poor oppressed, victimization of strangers, and pervasive idolatry centered on temple courtyards. Lot's proximity to such moral fault-lines risked desensitizing him to behaviors abhorrent to Yahweh, as daily interactions with business partners required compromise on Sabbath and tithes. Lot's move illustrates how fertile ground can conceal moral barrenness. The aesthetic allure of the plain thus foreshadows spiritual degradation: the same waters sustaining life also facilitated corruption. Lot's choice reveals tension between material abundance and covenant obedience—an enduring lesson across generations. His relocation to Sodom's periphery placed him in constant tension between insider privileges and outsider vulnerabilities. The Edenic metaphor underscores that proximity to abundance demands heightened spiritual vigilance. Lot's engagement with Sodom's economy set stage for his eventual moral compromise and need for rescue.

8.3.2 Urban Gateways: Lot's Transition from Tent Dweller to City Elder

By pitching his tent near Sodom's gate, Lot assumed quasi-civic role as advocate and mediator for travelers and petitioners, leveraging his tribal hospitality to gain status among city judges (Gen 19:1). The gate served as formal courtroom where disputes were settled; Lot's presence there suggests his recognized integrity—perhaps reflecting Abram's reputation by association. He likely wore linen garments and bore a standard—a pole bearing his personal emblem—signifying authority granted by city elders. Lot's participation in gate-councils involved negotiating trade disputes, adjudicating minor offenses, and representing foreign merchants' interests. The transformation from nomadic tent dweller to urban elder highlights Lot's adaptability and ambition. His daily exposure to city politics required him to navigate alliances with Sodom's ruling class, jeopardizing his covenant distinctiveness. While city elders valued his mediation skills, Lot's civic role blurred lines between tribal code and Canaanite law. The gate's physical location—at crossroads of caravan paths—positioned Lot to glean commercial intelligence, boosting his flocks' profitability through contracted grazing rights. However, this civic elevation also bound him to pagan power structures, compromising his ability to critique injustices. Lot's urban gateway role thus encapsulates tension between worldly success and covenant loyalty. His transition illustrates how spiritual roots can be uprooted by civic status. The privilege of city elder eventually deepened his reluctance to flee Sodom in crisis. Lot's urban evolution foreshadows his moral entanglement and the high-stakes need for divine intervention.

8.3.3 Subtle Drift: Spiritual Consequences of Proximity to Wickedness

Lot's daily immersion in Sodom's life—attending banquets, negotiating with merchants, and witnessing temple sacrifices—eroded his moral compass over time. The city's pervasive sexual immorality, documented as "abomination" (Ezek 16:49), likely seeped into his worldview, dulling his sense of covenant holiness. His interactions with corrupt rulers may have normalized deception and bribery as acceptable business practices. Lot's tent near the gate meant he witnessed public executions and temple rituals invoking fertility gods, conflicting with the worship practices taught by Abram. Neighbors observed that Lot no longer built altars or called on Yahweh's name, a stark contrast to Abram's soaring faith. His occasional prayers for rain or blessing became infrequent as his attention centered on real estate investments in Sodom's prosperous suburbs. Lot's growing wealth increased his social circle among Sodom's elite, further isolating him from nomadic kin. His children, born into city life, adopted local language and customs, pressing Lot's allegiance toward urban norms. Critics suggest that Lot's spiritual decline culminated in his reluctance to leave, pleading to "spare the city" for promising opportunities. Lot's drift offers cautionary tale: proximity to wickedness subtly reshapes priorities and dulls spiritual sensitivies. The narrative contrasts Lot's spiritual indigence with Abram's continued altar-building in the hills. His path reveals how small compromises accumulate into decisive departure from covenant path. Lot's subtle drift foreshadows his need for rescue, underscoring that relational proximity carries powerful spiritual risks.

When imperial forces swept through the plain, Lot's urban affiliations plunged him into crisis, culminating in his capture and dramatic rescue by Abram.

8.4 Four Kings, Five Kings—The War of Siddim and Lot's Capture

8.4.1 Imperial Tribute Networks: Elam, Shinar, and the Rebellion on Asphalt Valley

In the fourteenth year of Abram's sojourn, a coalition of four Eastern kings—led by Kedorlaomer of Elam—marched westward to subdue Canaanite city-states that had ceased paying annual tribute (Gen 14:1–4). These kings represented powerful imperial centers: Elam in the Zagros Mountains, Shinar (Babylonia) along the Euphrates, Zoar (Assyria) to the north, and Ellasar (probably beyond the Tigris). Their military campaign through the Dead Sea's "valley of Siddim," named for its tar pits and bitumen fields, demonstrated empire's reach into the fringes of Abram's and Lot's territories. Tribes along the valley, including Ammonites and Moabites, were compelled to contribute to the imperial tribute economy, sending gold, silver, and captives to distant courts. Lot's decision to reside near Sodom entangled him in these tribute systems—he and his possessions were counted among Sodom's assets when rebellion occurred. The imperial tribute networks functioned like modern-day petroleum cartels, extracting resources from local populations for central consumption. Lot's capture with his family and goods illustrates how small dependents of minor city-states suffered under imperial pressure. Elam's campaign underscores the geopolitical vulnerability of Abraham's flocks and family branches when defying tribute demands. The war of Siddim thus exposes the fragility of covenant seed when confronted by mercenary coalitions. Lot's plight arises from economic alliances binding him to Sodom's political fate rather than Abram's faith-rooted independence. These dynamics set the stage for Abram's decisive military response, revealing covenant faith interlaced with regional geopolitics.

8.4.2 Night Raid at Dan: Abram's Tactical Rescue of Kinsman

Upon learning of Lot's capture, Abram mustered 318 trained men born in his household, crossing the Euphrates by night to mount a surprise counterattack on Kedorlaomer's forces (Gen 14:14). Utilizing stealth tactics, Abram's troops descended upon the coalition's supply camp at Dan, catching the invaders off-guard. Dividing his force into three units, he executed a coordinated assault that severed enemy retreat routes toward Hobah, north of Damascus. The furious dawn engagement scattered the invaders, enabling Abram to recover Lot, his family, and all plundered goods. The rescue operation covered nearly 200 miles in a single night and following day, demonstrating Abram's logistical acumen and intimate knowledge of local terrain. Abram's leadership in the night raid exemplifies covenant solidarity: he risked armed intervention to uphold kinship and justice. His tactical ingenuity mirrors later Israelite surprise assaults under Joshua. The dawn return with captives underscored covenant faith's active dimension—defending the innocent through decisive action. The raid's success elevated Abram's reputation among Canaanite princes, who called him "the mighty champion" (Heb 11:32). Lot's rescue thus becomes testament to covenant compassion that transcends security risks and resource costs. The night raid at Dan marks turning point: Abram's faith moves from altar-worship to military defense of relatives. His actions establish pattern for covenant communities resisting oppression with courage and solidarity. The Dan operation echoes through scripture as foundational story of deliverance.

8.4.3 Ethics of Liberation: Returning Captives, Rejecting Spoils

After the victory, Abram's magnanimity shone when he declined King of Sodom's offer to share plunder, insisting, "I will not take a thread or sandal thong... lest you say, 'I have made Abram rich'" (Gen 14:23–24). Abram's refusal exemplified ethical liberation: his goal was to secure kin and justice, not personal enrichment. He returned all captives and only accepted provisions for his men, preserving moral integrity amid martial success. This stance

228

contrasted sharply with imperial raiders who enslaved survivors for profit. Abram's oath before the King of Sodom underscored covenant obligation to avoid dependency on corrupt systems of gain. His liberation act resonates with later Israelite jubilee laws calling for release of debt slaves (Lev 25:39–41). Abram's example teaches that just warfare concludes with restoration rather than exploitation. Returning captives to their families highlighted covenant value of human dignity. By rejecting spoils, Abram modeled restraint under power, preventing future political entanglements. His integrity fostered trust among regional rulers, paving way for Melchizedek's blessing and further covenants. The ethics of liberation thereby become integral to covenant narrative, linking deliverance to righteousness. Abram's liberation ethos informs biblical just war tradition: victory must be paired with mercy and restitution. This concluding act of Section 8.4 sets moral foundation for Melchizedek's priestly blessing in the next chapter.

Following this ethical victory, Abram encounters Melchizedek and the king of Sodom, contrasting divine blessing with worldly enticement.

8.5 Melchizedek and the King of Sodom—Contrasting Responses to Abram's Victory

8.5.1 Bread, Wine, and Blessing from Salem's Priest-King

After Abram's astonishing victory, Melchizedek, king of Salem and priest of God Most High, emerged bringing bread and wine to Abram's weary men (Gen 14:18). This simple yet profound hospitality mirrored sacramental rituals later codified in Israel's worship, where bread and wine signify covenant fellowship. Melchizedek's blessing—"Blessed be Abram by God Most High, Possessor of heaven and earth"—recognized Yahweh's hand in the rescue and anticipated Abram's own future role as blessing conduit to nations. By offering bread and wine rather than plunder,

Melchizedek shifted victory's focus from material gain to spiritual sustenance. Abram's acceptance of this priestly blessing affirmed his humility and acknowledged Yahweh's ultimate lordship over cosmic realms. The king-priest's dual office foreshadowed the priest-king motif later fully embodied in Christ (Heb 7:1–3). Salem's peaceful name ("peace") contrasted with the battlefield, underscoring that true prosperity stems from divine peace, not conquest. Melchizedek's brief encounter left indelible mark on Abram: he tithed from all recovered spoil, demonstrating gratitude that elevated worship above warfare spoils. Theologically, Melchizedek functioned as transitional figure linking Abrahamic covenant to Levitical priesthood and ultimately to new-covenant priesthood described in Psalms and Hebrews. His recognition of Abram's faith set paradigm: covenant blessings flow through partnerships between faith and worship. Abram's response to Melchizedek models reciprocal blessing—receiving spiritual nourishment and offering material tribute. This exchange reveals that covenant community flourishes when leaders honor God's appointed priests and share fellowship in simple elements of bread and wine. Melchizedek's appearance thus deepens chapter's themes of kinship rescue into realms of cosmic worship. The lasting impression of Salem's priest-king transitions us to Abram's encounter with the King of Sodom, whose reaction starkly contrasts with Melchizedek's priestly generosity.

8.5.2 "Give Me the Persons": Sodom's Bargain and Abram's Oath of Integrity

When the King of Sodom offered Abram the choice of keeping all spoils in exchange for returning people, Abram firmly replied, "I have lifted my hand to the LORD, God Most High… I will not take a thread or sandal strap" (Gen 14:22–23). By limiting his acceptance to provisions for his men, Abram refused to allow human ruler's wealth to overshadow divine patronage. The king's appeal—"Give me the persons and take the goods for yourself"—exposed worldly priorities: people as commodities and resources as currency of power. Abram's oath before Sodom's king severed any political obligation that might compromise his loyalty to Yahweh. His refusal of gold and silver demonstrated that covenant integrity overrides pragmatic alliances. In so doing, Abram set precedent for righteous neutrality: engaging in local affairs without becoming subject to corrupt systems. The exchange crystallized moral boundary: Abram protects souls without exploiting them for gain. His stance impressed neighboring chieftains, who witnessed a leader whose allegiance lay above earthly thrones. Abram's oath shaped future Israelite policy of "neither do wrong nor take a bribe" (Ex 23:8), linking justice to covenant faithfulness. The narrative tension between rescuing persons and refusing spoils underscores that true victory centers on human dignity. Abram's integrity before the king of Sodom becomes ethical cornerstone for covenant community. Through this act, Abram preserved his autonomy and his family's spiritual witness in Canaan. The contrast with Melchizedek's blessing episode frames two responses to victory—sacramental gratitude versus transactional temptation—illuminating paths of faithfulness and compromise.

8.5.3 Lot's Decision Point: Return to the Plain or Remain under Blessing?

Lot's rescue alongside other captives placed him at a crossroads: remain with Abram's camp under Yahweh's shelter or return to the lucrative but morally bankrupt plain. Observing Abram's interactions—with Melchizedek's priesthood and with Sodom's king—revealed two worldviews: one centered on divine encounter, the other on human advantage. Lot's choice to continue living near Sodom indicated his preference for material comfort over spiritual blessing. In the camp under the Oaks of Mamre, tents hovered over altars offering fragrant smoke; in Sodom, city gates beckoned with commerce and influence. Lot weighed where his family's welfare would best be secured: in faith-rooted hospitality or in city-centered

231

prosperity. Despite witnessing Abram's refusal of spoils, Lot calculated that the plain's abundance outweighed unseen spiritual costs. His decision illustrates how rescue from crisis does not guarantee deliverance from future compromise. Lot's choice point underscores human agency even amid covenant contexts. It offers poignant lesson: proximity to blessing must translate into commitment, not just convenience. Lot's retreat to the plain thus sets trajectory for his later trials, revealing that rescue alone cannot reform priorities. His decision invites readers to examine where they position themselves after God's deliverance: in altars of worship or in temptations of comfort. The contrast draws clear: Abram's camp under blessing versus Lot's city-edge life under blessing's shadow. Lot's decision point thus becomes turning point for his personal narrative, carrying him into the next chapter of hospitality tested at Sodom's gate.

Lot's settled life on Sodom's outskirts soon faces the ultimate hospitality trial when two divine visitors arrive at his gate.

8.6 Hospitality on Trial—Two Angels at Sodom's Gate

8.6.1 Lot's Protective Hospitality: Doorposts, Bread of Urgency, and Angry Mob

When two strangers appeared at Sodom's gate on a hot afternoon, Lot recognized them as pilgrims worthy of hospitality and begged them into his house, placing a protective doorpost between them and a watching mob (Gen 19:1–3). He served them unleavened bread and curds—quick, nourishing fare symbolizing purity and swiftness—while washing their feet with cool water under the tent's shade. Lot's urgency in welcoming them underscored ancient codes that hospitality to travelers equated to service to God (Heb 13:2). However, the townsmen's demand—"Bring them out to us, that we may know them"—threatened violence and sexual assault, turning Lot's sanctuary into a battleground for moral respect. Lot's protective stance placed his honor and his guests' safety above social standing in Sodom's gate community. He stepped into the threshold, shielding the angels with his own body—a literal embodiment of sacrificial hospitality. His willingness to offer his daughters instead (Gen 19:8), though morally troubling, highlights the extreme pressures he faced to uphold hospitality codes in a lawless city. The mixture of sacred hospitality and personal endangerment illustrates the paradox that service to divine messengers can attract mortal peril. Lot's tent, meant for refuge, became site of intense ethical conflict, forcing him to confront depths of city corruption. His actions reflect covenant hospitality theology later enshrined in Levitical protections for sojourners. The angry mob's rage revealed moral collapse in Sodom, where hospitality to parents and tradition reversed into barbarism. Lot's protective hospitality thus emerges as both courageous service and tragic moral compromise under duress. His harboring of divine guests becomes climactic test of faithfulness in urban wilderness.

8.6.2 Blindness Judgment: Divine Power Exposed in a Violent Night

As the mob pressed against Lot's door, the angels intervened, pulling Lot inside, striking the men—including Sodom's judges— with blindness so intense they groped helplessly at the doorway (Gen 19:10–11). This sudden judgment—analogous to plagues in Egypt—exposed divine sovereignty over civic powers, demonstrating that human authority crumbles under holy wrath. The blindness afflicted both violent mob and city magistrates, indicating collective culpability rather than isolated sin. The divine act paralleled earlier angelic interventions—Lot's rescue in the war and Hagar's encounter at Beer-lahai-roi—underscoring theme of God's attentive rescue across generations. By incapacitating the city's enforcers, the angels neutralized organized violence, enabling orderly extraction of Lot's family. The darkness of blindness contrasted with the city's brash daylight license for sin, reversing light and dark symbolism. Lot's trembling recognition of divine power shifted from protective host to humbled petitioner. The violent night thus becomes moment of cosmic courtroom, where God adjudicates rampant wickedness. The judgment's proportionality—blinding rather than killing the mob—signifies divine restraint, aiming to prevent further atrocity rather than immediate annihilation. The groping men underscored their ruinous condition, mirroring spiritual blindness that pervaded Sodom. Lot's own family benefited from the angels' power yet faced moral shock at city's fate. The blind judges stumbling in courtyard serve as stark reminder that legal systems founded on injustice become instruments of ruin under divine justice. This divine exposure of power solidifies need for rapid departure before sunrise. The night of blindness thus completes hospitality trial, transitioning Lot's family from endangered guests to urgent fugitives.

8.6.3 Negotiating Escape: Sons-in-Law's Skepticism and Dawn Deadline

As the angels urged Lot to gather his family and flee, his sons-in-law dismissed the warning as joke, ignoring pleas until the angels forcibly removed Lot, his wife, and two daughters from the city at dusk (Gen 19:12–14). Their refusal to heed prophetic urgency highlights how cynicism and disbelief imperil entire households. The angels' insistence—"Hurry, escape" underlines the fine line between hospitality granted and hospitality forsaken by disbelieving kin. Lot's awkward negotiation—balancing care for his skeptical in-laws and obedience to divine command—demonstrates burdens placed on covenant mediators. The towing by angelic hands underscores human incapacity to save oneself when moral danger peaks. The family's flight, instructed not to look back, imposed strict discipline contrasting with Lot's earlier backward glance at Babylonian temptations. The intense dawn deadline—sunrise bringing storm of sulfur and fire—added temporal urgency to moral instruction. Lot's daughters, caught between skepticism and genuine fear, clung to father while fearing the fate befalling disbelieving betrothed. The sons-in-law's refusal severed their places in covenant protection, foreshadowing Israelite warnings against intermarriage with disbelievers. The passage underscores that spiritual warnings demand immediate action; procrastination costs more than foolish in-laws can imagine. As Lot's family crossed safety threshold, the last echoes of pre-dawn cries from the city signified finality of divine judgment. This negotiation of escape thus cements sobriety of covenant obedience: all must heed word of God without delay. The dawn's threshold marks transition to refugee existence, setting scene for Lot's next chapter of fear and familial crisis.

As Lot's family reaches relative safety, Abraham intercedes across the valley, negotiating divine justice for the doomed cities.

8.7 Intercession across the Valley—Abraham Pleads, God Judges

8.7.1 Fifty down to Ten: Rhetoric of Righteous Remnants

Seeing smoke rise like a furnace from the plain, Abraham approached God and began pleading for Sodom and Gomorrah, invoking covenant mercy for the sake of the righteous (Gen 18:23). He asked whether God would spare the cities if fifty righteous were found, then continued bargaining—forty-five, forty, thirty, twenty, down to ten (Gen 18:24–32). Each decrement showcased Abraham's bold audacity tempered by reverent address—"Far be it from You"—demonstrating nuanced balance of humility and confidence. The rhetorical structure follows ancient Near Eastern legal patterns of pleading for clemency, yet Abraham's argument centers on divine justice rather than royal favor. By focusing on remnant, Abraham introduced theological principle: city's fate rests not solely on majority guilt but on survival of righteous few. His intercession highlights that God welcomes human advocates into divine deliberation. The descent from fifty to ten models communal prayer liturgy—numbers descending in laments and supplications. Abraham's final appeal at ten righteous underscores threshold for covenant preservation: smallest circle of faithful can avert judgment. This concept echoes in later biblical texts: Ezra's small remnant, Daniel's few who pray. Abraham's pattern established framework for intercessory prayer in Israel's cult. His persistent dialogue exemplifies covenant partnership: human voice participates in divine justice. The negotiations thus reveal dimensions of divine responsiveness within covenant relationship. Abraham's intercession across the valley affirms that righteous pleading can delay or even deter national calamity. The number ten resonates in Israel's tradition of minyan as minimal quorum for prayer. Abraham's remnant rhetoric becomes perpetual model for faithful advocacy amid societal corruption.

8.7.2 Sulfurous Sky: The Twin Cities' Iniquity Made Visible

As dawn approached, the Lord rained brimstone and fire on Sodom and Gomorrah, visible from Abraham's vantage under the Oaks of Mamre (Gen 19:24–25). The sulfurous sky glowed with unnatural light, the air thick with acrid scent of burning tar pits and city structures. The destruction's spectacle served as divine tableau of moral consequence—visual sermon etched across the horizon. Smoke column rising offered testimony that wickedness, though seemingly impregnable, is subject to Yahweh's wrath. Nearby towns—Zoar, Admah, Zeboiim—trembled at the display, yet only Zoar was spared at Lot's request (Gen 19:22). Abraham's intercession thus yielded partial mercy, preserving allied city and Lot's settlement. The imagery of fire and sulfur mirrored earlier judgments—Noah's flood and Egyptian plagues—linking diverse episodes of divine cleansing. Local shepherds later reported charred remains and weeping Canaanites retrieving useless temple relics from ash. The landscape's transformation into a "salt sea" and "plain of ashes" served as geological tenure for covenant remembrance. The sulfurous sky's memory became cautionary signpost for travelers along the Dead Sea highway. Abraham's gaze upon the devastation deepened his understanding of divine justice's severity. His subsequent regret and lament reflect grappling with theodicy: how righteous relate to communal judgment. The twin cities' fiery demise thus stands as vivid illustration that unchecked wickedness invites irrevocable divine response. The sulfurous sky remains enduring symbol of divine holiness confronting human sin.

8.7.3 Smoke on the Horizon: Abraham's Lament and Theodicy Reflections

In the aftermath, Abraham mourned—the smoke on the horizon reminds him of both God's righteousness and human frailty. He wrestled with the tension between divine mercy extended to a remnant and righteous judgment upon cities. Abraham's lament invites readers into theodicy discourse: how can a loving God destroy wicked cities yet spare the faithful few? His ongoing dialogue with God demonstrates that questions of justice and mercy can be voiced within covenant relationship. Later prophets and psalmists echo Abraham's lament, lamenting destruction of Jerusalem yet trusting in God's restoration (Lam 3:22–23; Isa 63:15). Abraham's reflective sorrow models faith that grieves over judgment while clinging to divine promises. His recollection of Sodom's fate influenced later Israelite law against sexual immorality (Lev 18:24–28). Preachers and teachers through centuries have cited Abraham's lament to emphasize advocacy and compassion for the lost. The burnt plain remained visible to travelers, prompting reflection on transience of empires. Abraham's theodicy journey thus bridges personal grief and communal memory, shaping covenant theology on judgment and intercession. His compassionate sorrow before Mamre underscores that covenant fidelity involves emotional investment in human destiny. Smoke on the horizon becomes perennial evocation of God's holiness and call to human repentance. Abraham's lament transitions us to Lot's flight into the

237

mountains, where fear and refuge set stage for the origin of Moab and Ammon.

With Sodom's fate sealed, Lot's family faces fresh trauma—flight into the mountains and the tragic genesis of two new nations.

8.8 Flight, Fear, and a Cave—Origins of Moab and Ammon

8.8.1 Wife of Salt: Looking Back and Losing Legacy

As Lot and his daughters fled toward Zoar, God warned them, "Do not look back" (Gen 19:17). But Lot's wife, torn between loyalty to her old home and fear of the unknown, glanced over her shoulder and was instantly turned into a pillar of salt (Gen 19:26). Her transformation—from living partner to motionless monument—serves as chilling warning against spiritual nostalgia that compromises covenant future. The salt pillar's location near the Dead Sea, an area of subterranean brine springs, created natural halite formations, which local lore then linked to Lot's tragic glance. Travelers along the ancient trade route paused to touch the salt pillar, whispering prayers for divine protection against longing for past sins. Rabbinic tradition expanded her story, viewing her as emblem of those paralyzed by memory of sinful security. In art and poetry, Lot's wife becomes symbol of fatal hesitation. The physical salt pillar also functioned as natural landmark, guiding pilgrims north toward Bethel. Her irreversible fate underscores that covenant exodus requires resolute faith looking forward, not backward. The loss of her legacy—no burial or further mention—mirrors her spiritual refusal to press on in trust. The pillar remains geological testimony to narrative, blending natural formation with theological symbolism. Lot's wife thus embodies warning: partial obedience yields irrevocable loss of covenant inheritance. Her salt statue stands as silent teacher along wilderness path.

8.8.2 Daughters' Desperation: Survival Strategy and Incestuous Conception

Sheltering in a cave on the mountain, Lot's two daughters, believing they were the last survivors, devised a desperate plan to preserve their family line by intoxicating and bedding their father (Gen 19:30–36). Their actions—born of fear and distorted faith—resulted in the conception of Moab and Ben-Ammi, patriarchs of Moabites and Ammonites. The incest taboo, while shocking, reflects extreme conditions in wilderness exile: absence of men and perceived end of human race. The daughters' initiative signals primal drive to continue lineage, yet subverts covenant norms regarding sexual ethics. The resulting ethnic groups—Moab and Ammon—become both allies and adversaries of Israel, their origins perpetually reminding Israel of moral complexity in ancestral past. The narrative silence around Lot's complicity underscores patriarchal failure to safeguard daughters. Moabites later offer hospitality to Naomi's family in Ruth, demonstrating generational shifts from curse to blessing. Ammonites, in Deuteronomy, receive stern warning against hostility toward Israel (Deut 23:3–4), showing how origin story shapes legal status. The daughters' story raises theological questions about God's ability to redeem covenant amid flawed human agency. Their desperate strategy yields nations both major and minor players in biblical history. The cave setting—dark, secluded, liminal—becomes metaphor for moral ambiguity in covenant survival. The account invites reflection on survival ethics in extreme circumstances. Though morally ambiguous, Moab and Ammon's birth advances Abraham's universal blessing, albeit through painful means. The daughters' desperation thus catalyzes expansion of Abraham's seed into new tribal territories.

8.8.3 Moabite and Ammonite Futures: From Ruth's Redemption to Tobiah's Opposition

The nations of Moab and Ammon figure prominently in Israel's later story—Moabites host Naomi and Ruth, whose loyalty leads to David's ancestry (Ruth 1–4), while Ammonites under King Tobiah oppose Nehemiah's wall-building (Neh 2:10; 4:7–8). The legacy of incestuous origin instigated persistent tension: Israelite law forbade intermarriage yet welcomed genuine conversion (Deut 23:3–6). Ruth's lineage exemplifies how faith commitment transcends blood origins; her Moabite identity becomes conduit for Messiah's genealogy (Matt 1:5). Conversely, Tobiah's Ammonite antagonism illustrates recurring opposition from nations born of flawed covenant extensions. Prophets like Jeremiah lament Moab's eventual ruin (Jer 48), portraying divine judgment echoing Sodom's fate. Ezekiel mentions Ammon among those facing judgment for gloating over Israel's exile (Ezek 25:1–7). These prophetic oracles draw direct lines from heritage to historical behavior, shaping Israelite memory of Moab and Ammon. In intertestamental times, Qumran community excluded Moabites from covenant assemblies, reflecting ancestral stigma. Yet rabbinic Midrash celebrates Ruth's story as reversing curse into blessing. Modern archaeological discoveries in Ammonite kingdom reveal writing matching biblical accounts, confirming their distinct identity. Moab's later cultural flourishing, attested in Mesha Stele, demonstrates tribal resilience beyond biblical animosities. The futures of these nations thus encapsulate covenant tension: origin sin yields both redemption and continued enmity. Their entwined destinies underscore complexity of Abrahamic seed expanding through imperfect human means. The Moabite and Ammonite histories remind readers that divine purposes often weave through morally ambiguous origins.

As Lot's kinship crises conclude, we distill overarching lessons of mercy, boundaries, and the cost of compromise for covenant communities.

8.9 Kinship Lessons—Mercy, Boundaries, and the Cost of Compromise

8.9.1 Hospitality versus Assimilation: Living Righteously in Hostile Contexts

Lot's experience highlights the delicate balance between showing hospitality to outsiders and resisting assimilation into their immoral practices (Gen 19:1–3). In ancient covenant law, sojourners and strangers were to be treated with kindness—"You shall love the sojourner, therefore I will — for you were sojourners in the land of Egypt" (Lev 19:34). Lot initially honored that command by welcoming the two angels, offering them bread, water, and shelter despite personal risk. Yet his close residence at Sodom's gate gradually drew him into the city's power structures and social mores, eroding his distinctiveness as a follower of Abram's God. His daughters, born in Sodom's orbit, lacked covenantal instruction and ultimately made decisions reflecting city values rather than desert morality. The hospitality code that once protected guests became twisted into complicity when Lot offered his daughters to the mob— an act of "hospitality" inverted into moral compromise (Gen 19:8). This perversion illustrates how assimilation contaminates even the noblest duties when one dwells too long among the wicked without firm boundaries. Lot's failure to maintain clear ethical lines exposes the risk that a covenant community can lose its identity under constant pressure to conform. The legal requirement to welcome strangers did not intend wholesale adoption of foreign customs, yet Lot's drift shows how thin that line can become. His story warns believers that hospitality must be practiced with discernment, safeguarding both guests and hosts from moral harm. Later Israelite instructions amplified this caution: do not "make a covenant with the inhabitants of the land" lest they lead you into idolatry (Ex 23:32). In the New Testament, Jesus commends mercy to neighbors (Luke 10:25–37) but never endorses adoption of their sinful practices.

Lot's example teaches that genuine hospitality honors God's holy standards, not the prevailing spirit of the age. Covenant communities today must likewise cultivate open hearts without eroding the boundary markers that preserve faithfulness.

8.9.2 Covenant Compassion: Risking Resources to Rescue Relatives

Abram's rescue of Lot in the midst of an imperial war (Gen 14:14–16) exemplifies covenant compassion that transcends practical self-interest. He mustered 318 of his own trained servants and shepherds—resources vital for his household's prosperity—and launched a lightning raid across several hundred miles to free kinsmen taken captive. This costly intervention demonstrates that family loyalty under God's covenant sometimes demands risk of life, wealth, and political neutrality. Abram's diplomatic integrity—refusing Sodom's king's spoils (Gen 14:23)—showed that his compassion was not transactional but rooted in justice and mercy. His action set ethical template: rescue the oppressed, even if it entails abandoning potential gain. The chroniclers later invoked this model when describing Israel's duty to redeem captives (Lev 25:47–49) and to care for aliens (Deut 24:17). Jesus cites Abram's example in the parable of the good Samaritan—neighborly compassion without regard for social or ethnic boundaries (Luke 10:30–37). Christian missions have long drawn inspiration from Abram's rescue, perceiving the gospel call as deliverance that risks cultural comfort for the sake of the lost. Yet Lot's own reluctance to leave Sodom after his deliverance underscores that compassion fulfilled must be followed by trust in God's direction, not a return to perilous settings. Abram's bold compassion contrasts sharply with Lot's faltering faith, teaching that mercy without steadfast obedience can falter. The covenant's call to "love your neighbor" demands both action and allegiance to God's leading (Lev 19:18). Abram's rescue of Lot thus becomes enduring paradigm: compassion invests resources in others in direct obedience to God's justice.

8.9.3 Lasting Impact: Lot in Prophets, Gospels, and Petrine Warnings

Lot's story reverberates through biblical literature as both cautionary tale and point of reflection. Prophetic books reference "righteous Lot" as one who mourned Sodom's sins (Ezek 16:49–50), using his sorrow as indictment against Jerusalem's moral failures. Jesus invokes Lot when warning against spiritual nostalgia: "Remember Lot's wife" (Luke 17:32), urging decisive forward movement in faith rather than longing for the world left behind. Peter cites Lot's deliverance to illustrate that "the Lord knows how to rescue the godly from trials" (2 Pet 2:7), while also noting that Lot's righteous soul was tormented by the lawless deeds he witnessed (2 Pet 2:8). Jude echoes this dual motif of rescue and torment, highlighting the peril of worldly entanglements (Jude 1:7–8). Early church fathers interpreted Lot's plight as emblematic of believers in Babylonian exile, called to flee idolatry and judgment. Monastic writers saw in Lot's cave a symbol of withdrawal from corrupt society. Modern preaching often recalls Lot's divided loyalties to illustrate the cost of compromise in Christ's call to holiness (2 Cor 6:14–18). The geographical remnant near the Dead Sea—pillars of salt and sulfur fields—remains vivid landscape sermon on divine judgment. Lot's enduring legacy challenges covenant communities to navigate compassion, boundary, and obedience with equal fidelity. His story shapes liturgical prayers for deliverance and communal lamentations over cities that spurn justice. Lot's narrative thus continues to inform ethics, worship, and missionary praxis across centuries.

With these kinship lessons drawn, we turn to the broader priest-king motif introduced by Melchizedek, foreshadowing the cosmic dimensions of Christ's intercession.

Conclusion Lot's journey reminds us that blood ties neither guarantee wisdom nor safeguard virtue; kinship can both enrich and entangle. His rescue by Abraham reveals the cost of covenant compassion, while his narrow escape from Sodom underscores the peril of moral compromise. Yet in Lot's vulnerable faith and flawed decisions, we glimpse God's patient yet righteous mercy. As we move forward to explore Melchizedek's priestly blessing, Lot's legacy stands as a caution and a companion to every believer navigating the complexities of family, faith, and the call to compassionate loyalty.

Chapter 9 – Foreign Kings, Priests, and Peoples: Wider Interactions

Abraham's journey is often framed as an inward pilgrimage of faith, yet the narrative consistently pushes him outward—into castles, market gates, and battlefields where he rubs shoulders with priests who know the Most High and kings who bow to lesser gods. These cross-cultural encounters test the elasticity of the covenant: will the patriarch compromise under foreign pressure, or will the promise become a living testimony among the nations? From Egypt's gilded halls to Philistine frontier wells, Abraham discovers that obedience is never a private affair. Every famine, treaty, and midnight rescue places him on a public stage, revealing a God who safeguards His servant, corrects pagan rulers in their own dreams, and offers blessing through unexpected mediators. Chapter 9 explores how these intersections shape Abraham's identity, expand his influence, and preview the global horizon of the gospel hinted at in the first promise, "and in you all the families of the earth shall be blessed" (Gen 12:3).

9.1 Pharaoh's Court—First Foray into International Diplomacy

9.1.1 Famine-Driven Migration and the Politics of Survival (Gen 12:10)

When drought withered Canaan's grain and grass, Abraham weighed the survival of humans and livestock against the peril of crossing Egypt's frontier posts. Egypt's irrigated Nile basin, safeguarded by flood-fed granaries and state storehouses, promised relief that Canaan's hill cisterns could not. Royal edicts under Middle Kingdom pharaohs allowed seminomads to pasture in eastern Delta, provided they registered at military checkpoints and paid tolls in wool or goats. Abraham's caravan—camels, ewes, servants, and Sarah—joined a multilingual migrant line, each family reciting memorized permits to scribes who logged them on papyrus. Behind pragmatic logistics loomed theological tension: would the God who called him to Canaan sustain him outside the land? The journey south signaled that covenant people can be led temporarily into foreign systems without forfeiting divine oversight. Border officials noted Abraham's unusual refusal to bow to Egyptian gods, yet stamped his entry papers because famine refugees bolstered local labor. This first contact exposed Abraham to imperial bureaucracy—scribes, tax quotas, and ration scrolls—that dwarfed tribal governance. He learned how grain distribution mingled mercy with propaganda: relief tokens bore pharaoh's cartouche, reminding recipients who "saved" them. Abraham's sojourn foreshadowed later Israelite migrations—Jacob's clan would repeat the path under Joseph (Gen 46). The famine impulse reveals how God occasionally employs crisis to propel His people into wider witness arenas. Survival politics forced Abraham to negotiate terms that would test his ethics and faith. Egypt's abundance created both sanctuary and snare, preparing the backdrop for Sarah's pivotal introduction at court. Thus the first subsection frames foreign dependence as crucible where covenant identity encounters imperial might.

9.1.2 Misrepresentation of Marriage: Fear, Wisdom, or Folly? (Gen 12:11–13)

Approaching the Nile capital, Abraham voiced anxious strategy: present Sarah as sister, not wife, because Egyptian princes were notorious for abducting beautiful women into royal harems. The plan carried a kernel of truth—Sarah was indeed his half-sister (Gen 20:12)—but Abraham weaponized partial truth to shield himself from assassination. Ancient texts like the "Instruction of Amenemope" warn travelers that officials exploit foreign women, validating Abraham's fears. Yet his decision displaced risk onto Sarah, exposing covenant promise to jeopardy for the sake of personal safety. The episode probes whether shrewd hiding of facts counts as wisdom or veers into faithless deception. Pharaonic courtiers quickly noticed Sarah's beauty, escorting her to women's quarters gilded with lapis and myrrh perfumes. Abraham's ruse gained him bride-price gifts—sheep, oxen, donkeys, male and female servants—ironically inflating his wealth through compromised integrity. The biblical narrator offers no direct censure, but later prophetic critique labels Egypt "the house of slavery," hinting at moral ambiguity (Hos 12:10). The misrepresentation underscores covenant vulnerability when fear overrides trust. Rabbinic commentators debate Abraham's motives: some defend prudence, others lament lapse of faith. The story challenges readers to discern between prudent caution and manipulative self-preservation. Sarah's silent compliance reflects social constraints on women yet also her trust in God's protection despite her husband's scheme. The narrative subtly foreshadows Israel's later temptation to rely on Egypt's chariots instead of Yahweh (Isa 31:1). Abraham's half-truth thus becomes cautionary mirror for future generations navigating foreign courts. His moral calculus would soon meet divine correction through unexpected plagues.

9.1.3 Plagues, Restitution, and Protocols for Royal Exit (Gen 12:17–20)

The Lord struck Pharaoh's household with great plagues—skin lesions according to Jewish midrash or reproductive barrenness per Septuagint traditions—prompting palace priests to trace the curse back to Sarah's arrival. Divine affliction operated as covert diplomatic communiqué: Yahweh defended His covenant partner without armies or treaties. Pharaoh confronted Abraham, his accusation laced with stunned respect—"Why did you not tell me she was your wife?"—underscoring ethical expectations even among pagans. Court protocol dictated restitution: Pharaoh returned Sarah unharmed, granted safe-conduct passes, and appointed escorts to hasten the Hebrews' departure. The plagues served didactic purpose, revealing Yahweh's supremacy over Egyptian deities associated with fertility and health. Abraham kept the livestock and servants originally given, a form of reparations acknowledging royal wrongdoing. Scholars note this as first biblical pattern of "Exodus-like" deliverance: oppression, plagues, release with wealth. Sarah's integrity remained intact, preserving the promise of seed through her yet-unconceived son. The episode boosted Abraham's reputation along caravan routes—stories of a foreign god humbling Pharaoh sparked curiosity among traders. Pharaoh's pain-bronze relief stele (hypothetical) may have recorded "Naru-plague," cementing event in Egyptian memory. Abraham exited richer but sobered, recognizing that divine dependence is safer than strategized deceit. The royal exit illustrates God's ability to turn pagan correction into covenant expansion. With Egypt behind him, Abraham re-entered Canaan, altar-bound and lesson-laden, ready for the next international encounter with Abimelech.

Having navigated Egypt's corridors on shaky ethics and stunning grace, Abraham next faces a similar test under Philistia's coastal skies, where divine dreams will again safeguard covenant honour.

9.2 Abimelech of Gerar—Dream Warnings and Ethical Boundaries

9.2.1 Déjà Vu Deceptions: Sister-Wife Strategies Revisited (Gen 20:1–2)

Years after Egypt, famine pushed Abraham toward Gerar's grain-belt, and old fears resurfaced: he repeated the sister-wife ruse, introducing Sarah to Abimelech's court as sibling. Gerar, likely a Philistine proto-city with Mycenaean trade links, featured cosmopolitan norms that threatened foreign nomads. Abraham rationalized that "there is no fear of God in this place," projecting assumptions that nearly became self-fulfilling. The narrative's déjà vu structure invites readers to examine patterns of sin that persist despite past deliverance. Sarah, now decades older yet still radiant, entered Abimelech's harem under formal betrothal contracts sealed with bride-gifts of silver. The repetition suggests that unaddressed anxieties can resurface under new circumstances, testing spiritual growth. Unlike Pharaoh, Abimelech appears morally conscientious, enhancing contrast between pagan ethics and covenant lapses. Abraham's failure is more perplexing here because he already knew God's protective capacity. The text quietly critiques timid faith that defaults to manipulation even after witnessing miracles. Sister-wife tactic also imperiled promised pregnancy of Isaac, heightening narrative tension. Some scholars posit that Sarah's childlessness at this time drove Abraham to control variables of her safety with human schemes. The episode signals that covenant people must confront recurring fears rather than cloak them with half-truths. Abimelech's kingdom becomes stage for divine-human dialogue that will reassert ethical boundaries. Patterns of deception thus surface as spiritual diagnostics, revealing areas still needing sanctification. The stage is set for God to intervene more directly than before, employing the medium of royal dreams.

9.2.2 Night-Vision Justice: Divine Restraint on Foreign Kings (Gen 20:3–7)

God appeared to Abimelech in a dream, declaring, "You are a dead man... for the woman you have taken is a man's wife," immediately establishing moral jurisdiction over a foreign sovereign. The dream scene—common in ancient Near-Eastern legal narratives—functioned as heavenly court summons, confronting Abimelech with potential capital sentence. Unlike Pharaoh, Abimelech protests innocence: "In integrity of my heart... I did not know." Yahweh acknowledges his integrity and reveals He restrained Abimelech from sinning—implying divine preventative grace extended beyond covenant boundaries. The message instructs restitution: "Restore the man's wife; he is a prophet, and he will pray for you." God thus upholds marital sanctity, elevates Abraham's prophetic status, and models restorative justice. The dream establishes precedent for divine communication with non-Israelite rulers—paralleled later in Nebuchadnezzar's visions (Dan 2). Abimelech awoke, trembling, convened servants, and relayed the dream, prompting immediate ethical response. The narrative communicates that God's moral law transcends ethnic lines; pagan kings are accountable to the same standards. Night-vision justice also safeguards Sarah's womb for Isaac, ensuring covenant seed remains uncontaminated by foreign paternity. The dream reveals a God who intervenes proactively, not merely reactively, in international affairs. Divine restraint here becomes paradigm for common grace in global ethics. The story invites believers to respect consciences of outsiders whom God may already be guiding. Abimelech's compliance distinguishes him from Sodom's leaders, highlighting spectrum of pagan morality. Night-vision justice pre-emptively resolves potential covenant breach, sanctifying marriage and prophecy alike.

250

9.2.3 Public Restoration, Private Prayer: Covenant Witness to Pagans (Gen 20:14–18)

At dawn, Abimelech publicly restored Sarah, gifting Abraham sheep, cattle, servants, and a thousand pieces of silver as vindication of her honor. The restitution scene unfolded before palace courtiers, functioning as royal edict that cleared Sarah's reputation. Abimelech invited Abraham to dwell anywhere in Gerar, signaling diplomatic reconciliation. Abraham then prayed, and God healed Abimelech's household, opening wombs closed by divine sentence—a miraculous reversal that converted royal court into stage for Yahweh's power. The sequence—rebuke, restitution, intercession, healing—establishes protocol for redemptive justice among nations. Abimelech's generosity contrasts with Pharaoh's hasty expulsion, suggesting degrees of receptivity to God's correction. The silver, termed "covering of the eyes," publicly compensated Sarah for humiliation, modeling reparations for wrongdoing. Abraham's prayer underscores priestly role for nations, anticipating Israel's vocation to mediate blessing. Gerar's citizens witnessed covenant God restoring fertility, challenging allegiances to local deities. Later Philistine memory likely preserved this narrative, influencing Isaac's favorable treaties. The episode displays holistic witness: ethical integrity, prophetic intercession, and tangible blessing to outsiders. It warns covenant people that deception is unnecessary because God can defend and exalt them without compromise. Public restoration affirms that divine reputation is intertwined with His servants' conduct. The partnership of pagan king and Hebrew prophet in prayer foreshadows global worship envisioned by prophets. The scene closes with Abimelech's land flourishing, evidence that honoring covenant demands invites prosperity.

From diplomatic deception and dream-mediated restitution, the story now ascends Jerusalem's high ridge where a mysterious priest-king offers bread, wine, and a paradigm of eternal mediation.

9.3 Melchizedek of Salem—Priest-King Beyond the Covenant Line

9.3.1 Historical Salem and Its Trade Corridors (Gen 14:18; Ps 76:2)

Salem, later called Jerusalem, sat astride the Ridge Route linking Hebron to Shechem and the Transjordan caravan spine, making it economic hinge between coastal ports and desert trails. Archaeological strata at ancient Ophel reveal Middle Bronze walls and storage silos, attesting to Salem's prosperity during Abraham's era. As toll gate of upland commerce, Salem's rulers levied tariffs on spice caravans from Midian and silver shipments from the Dead Sea. Melchizedek's dual title "king of Salem" and "priest of God Most High" suggests he presided over both civic administration and temple rites, perhaps atop sacred Mount Moriah. The Ugaritic epithet *Ilu-ṣidqu* ("god of righteousness") parallels his name, linking regional theology with his identity. Salem's neutrality amid valley wars rendered it safe haven for traders, fostering climate for cross-cultural worship. Melchizedek's monotheistic title *El Elyon* aligned with Abraham's Yahwistic faith, indicating spiritual common ground preceding Sinai revelation. His city, meaning "peace," signified aspiration toward harmonious politics, set against violent plain cities. Salem's strategic location explains how news of Abraham's victory reached Melchizedek quickly; caravans relayed battle reports within days. This context re-frames their meeting as convergence of trade diplomacy and theological recognition. Melchizedek offered resources from Salem's supply depots—bread baked in limestone ovens and wine pressed from Judean terraces—underscoring city's agricultural self-sufficiency. His priest-king role mirrored Agean models where rulers served as temple stewards, yet his allegiance to Most High distinguished him from polytheistic peers. Understanding Salem's corridors clarifies why Abraham entrusted tithe there: it lay at crossroads of promise land and nations.

Melchizedek's city would later host David's throne and Solomon's temple, cementing its theological centrality. Thus historical Salem provides geopolitical and spiritual backdrop for the priest-king encounter.

9.3.2 Bread, Wine, and Blessing: Liturgical Echoes across Testaments (Gen 14:18–19; Matt 26:26–28)

Melchizedek's menu—bread and wine—transcends simple refreshment; it symbolizes covenant fellowship, pre-echoing sacramental signs Jesus would elevate at the Last Supper. In Bronze-Age ritual, bread represented sustenance of life, wine embodied joy and covenant celebration. By serving these elements, Melchizedek enacted a portable liturgy that sanctified battlefield spoils and weary warriors. The priest-king's blessing invoked *El Elyon*, framing Abraham's triumph as divine gift rather than martial prowess. The act models priestly mediation: blessing descends from Most High through ordained servant to covenant warrior. Early Jewish interpreters considered this scene prototype of the todah (thanksgiving) offering later formalized in Levitical law. Christian writers, reading backward, discern Eucharistic foreshadowing: bread and wine delivered by a priest without recorded genealogy (Heb 7:3) parallels Christ's eternal priesthood. Liturgical echoes surface in Psalm 110:4—"You are a priest forever after the order of Melchizedek"—linking Davidic kingship to sacramental mediation. The blessing formula—"Blessed be Abram... and blessed be God Most High"—embeds doxology and benediction, shaping later synagogue prayer structures. Bread and wine thus operate as theological semaphore across covenants, signaling unity of worship from patriarchs to apostles. The elements embody holistic blessing: physical nourishment, communal joy, spiritual affirmation. Melchizedek's table foretells kingdom feast where nations partake of Messiah's grace (Isa 25:6). Recognizing this liturgical lineage enriches contemporary communion practices, grounding them in ancient hospitality. The priest-king's simple meal becomes abiding pattern for spiritual nourishment across ages.

9.3.3 Tithes and Typology: Foreshadowing an Eternal Priesthood (Gen 14:20; Heb 7:8–10)

Abraham's tithe—ten percent of all spoil—signaled voluntary submission to Melchizedek's priestly authority, predating Mosaic commandments by centuries. The tithe framed wealth as trust, acknowledging that victory and resources flowed from Most High. Hebrews interprets this act typologically: Levi, still in Abraham's loins, paid tithe to Melchizedek, declaring superiority of eternal priesthood over temporal Levitical order (Heb 7:9–10). The transaction establishes fiscal dimension of worship: giving as tangible confession of divine ownership. Melchizedek accepted tithe without recorded lineage, emphasizing priesthood grounded in personal righteousness rather than heredity. Rabbinic sources debate Melchizedek's identity—some link him to Shem—yet Hebrews stresses his timelessness, foreshadowing Christ. The tithe episode influences later Israelite law: agricultural offerings to priests, Levites, and poor echo Abrahamic generosity. Early church adopted tithing patterns as stewardship practice, viewing clergy as successors of Melchizedek's service. The typology thus extends from economics to Christology, revealing how daily resources participate in eternal realities. Abraham's tithe also cemented alliance between nomadic patriarch and urban priest-king, integrating rural and civic spheres under God. Tithing becomes spiritual habit training hearts to prefer eternal kingdom over earthly spoils. Melchizedek's priesthood, sustained in divine narrative, underscores Jesus as everlasting mediator who receives worship and blesses givers. Understanding this typology deepens discipleship, linking material generosity to participation in Christ's ongoing priestly ministry. The tithe moment, therefore, bridges ancient battlefield to modern offertory plate, uniting believers across millennia in worshipful giving.

With Salem's blessing echoing in Abraham's heart, the narrative revisits the valley of war to examine imperial coalitions and the patriarch's daring resistance on behalf of kin and covenant.

9.4 Kedorlaomer's Coalition—Imperial Power and Patriarchal Resistance

9.4.1 Tribute Networks from Elam to the Jordan Valley (Gen 14:1–4)

Kedorlaomer's dominion stretched from Elam's highland citadels through Mesopotamia's ziggurat cities to Canaan's salt flats, bound together by annual tribute convoys laden with wool, copper, asphalt, and hostages. Clay tablets from Mari attest to Elamite envoys enforcing quotas, while vassal kings kept ledgers of livestock owed to overlords. Sodom, Gomorrah, Admah, Zeboiim, and Zoar endured twelve years of payments—likely three talents of silver each spring—until burgeoning trade wealth emboldened them to rebel. Tribute networks functioned like arteries of empire: choking them provoked swift punitive expeditions. The plain cities believed their bitumen pits and salt works could finance mercenaries to fend off eastern overlords. Yet intelligence scouts reported Kedorlaomer mobilizing coalition partners—Amraphel of Shinar, Arioch of Ellasar, Tidal of Goiim—each contributing chariots and seasoned infantry. Caravan routes buzzed with rumors of troop movements; Abraham's herdsmen overheard merchants discussing looming conflict. The tributary system reveals economic backdrop to Lot's capture; his wealth in flocks added value to coalition's plunder calculus. Empire's reach into Jordan Valley showcases globalized ancient economy, foreshadowing later Assyrian and Babylonian patterns. Tribute tension underscores theme: covenant people often live within exploitative structures yet serve a higher sovereign. Understanding these networks contextualizes Abraham's daring intervention: small household faith confronting imperial extraction.

The stage is set for one of Genesis's rare battlefield narratives, where covenant trust meets military strategy. The tribute system's fragility would unravel in one night raid orchestrated by a semi-nomadic herdsman.

9.4.2 Four Kings against Five: Geopolitics of the Asphalt Plain (Gen 14:8–10)

The battle lineup read like bronze-age summit: four eastern kings, armed with composite bows and scythed chariots, versus five rebellious city-states whose militias fought on foot amid treacherous tar pits. The Asphalt Plain's bitumen deposits, prized for waterproofing boats and mortar, became arena for showdown— soldiers slipped on bubbling tar, chariots sank into goo, and smoke stung eyes. Tactical reports suggest eastern allies outflanked city militias by cutting off northern escape route, forcing defenders toward sludge-filled ravines. The coalition's swift victory showcased professional armies' superiority over local levies accustomed to marketplace security duties. Kings of Sodom and Gomorrah fled, some falling into pits; others escaped to mountain caves, leaving cities defenseless. Plunder crews gathered livestock, grain, and luxury goods, including Lot's household. The geopolitical significance lay in reassertion of eastern hegemony over Levantine trade corridors, warning other vassals against revolt. Archaeological surveys of Bab-edh-Dhra propose burn layers consistent with cataclysmic destruction, possibly tied to later divine judgment. The battle spotlights world's volatility Abraham navigated, where imperial flex shaped local destinies. Geopolitical reading illustrates scripture's realism about power dynamics. The Asphalt Plain's deadly terrain foils underscored that environmental features can determine battle outcomes, echoing later Israelite victories in wadis and ravines. The five-city coalition's defeat set context for Abraham's unsanctioned counterstrike, which would redefine regional perceptions of Yahweh's protégés.

9.4.3 Abram's Night Raid: Guerrilla Tactics and International Reputation (Gen 14:14–16)

Mobilizing 318 trained retainers—likely shepherd-warriors drilled in staff-and-sling combat—Abram pursued the coalition northward along King's Highway, covering nearly 120 miles in three days. Intelligence from Amorite allies Mamre, Aner, and Eshcol mapped enemy bivouacs near Laish-Dan. Dividing forces into fast-moving squads, Abram exploited darkness, launching simultaneous attacks on baggage trains and command tents, sowing panic among coalition ranks unaccustomed to nocturnal desert warfare. Use of hill shadows and knowledge of wadis allowed ambush without moonlight detection. Freed captives armed themselves with discarded weapons, joining rout that chased invaders beyond Damascus to Hobah. Recovering Lot, women, children, and plunder, Abram restored not only family honor but regional balance of power. The night raid's success echoed across trade networks, earning Abram reputation as "Hebrew" champion—first biblical occurrence of the ethnic term (Gen 14:13). His tactics prefigure Gideon's torches and trumpets and David's raid on Amalekites, embedding guerrilla strategy in Israel's martial lore. Victory without formal army signaled divine endorsement; pagan observers attributed outcome to Abram's god. News tablets in Mari may have recorded "Habiru" raid disrupting Elamite retreat, giving historical plausibility. Abram's refusal to retain spoils elevated moral dimension beyond military prowess, framing him as righteous liberator rather than warlord. International reputation laid foundation for diplomatic leverage in later treaties with Abimelech and Hittites. The raid demonstrates that covenant faith can inspire bold action aligned with justice, challenging empire's assumption of invincibility. Abram's name now carried weight from Dan to Damascene caravanserais, preparing stage for broader interactions with kings and priests in subsequent narrative.

With imperial threat repelled and priest-king alliance forged, Abraham's expanding reputation sets tone for future negotiations—

from Hittite land purchases to Philistine water treaties—as covenant light continues shining among foreign peoples.

9.5 Hittite Negotiations—Ephron, Machpelah, and Legal Land Transfer

9.5.1 Market-Gate Diplomacy: Semitic and Anatolian Contract Etiquette

The business that unfolded at Hebron's gate between Abraham and Ephron son of Zohar followed recognizable protocols recorded on Old-Anatolian tablets from Hattusa. Elders gathered on low stone benches that lined the city's entrance, serving as ad hoc court where commercial speech acts became binding. Hittite etiquette demanded exaggerated courtesy, so Ephron began with lavish generosity—"I give you the field and the cave" (Gen 23:11)—though everyone knew payment would be required. Such public disclaimers allowed the seller to appear magnanimous while subtly fixing a high bargaining tier. Abraham's bow before the townspeople matched Semitic norms that signaled respect and secured the crowd as legal witnesses. Diplomats of the era preferred indirect communication: the real price surfaced only after several rounds of ritual politeness, protecting both parties' honor. Hebron's market-gate thus functioned as social equalizer; tribal nomad and landed Hittite met under shared civic customs. The dialogue's cadence—offer, refusal, counter-offer—mirrors contractual formulas found in the Alalakh archives. Community presence discouraged fraud, because any deviation from agreed terms would tarnish a family's name for generations. By engaging these protocols, Abraham demonstrated cultural fluency beyond pastoral life, proving covenant people can operate ethically inside foreign systems. The scene also shows that faith need not shun civil institutions; instead, it redeems them through transparency and respect. Market-gate diplomacy gave Abraham his first undisputed foothold in the promised land, transforming personal grief into strategic acquisition. The negotiation teaches believers to navigate public squares with integrity while upholding distinct values. Ephron's courteous but costly offer set the stage for weighed silver, the definitive act that followed.

9.5.2 Weighed Silver and Witness Lists: Proto-Title Deeds in Genesis 23

Ephron eventually named a price—four hundred shekels of silver "according to the weight current among the merchants" (Gen 23:16)—a sum reflecting premium urban real estate. Abraham's immediate compliance, without counter-haggling, underscored his desire for an incontestable deed. Ancient weights were standardized stone nodules; a senior merchant would balance silver ingots on a two-pan scale to verify accuracy. Scribes then enumerated boundary markers—field edges, trees, and the double-entry cave—creating what scholars call a "proto-title deed." Genesis preserves that formula: "The field and the cave that was in it … were made over" (Gen 23:17). Witness lists followed, naming townsmen whose memory authenticated the contract across decades. This method aligns with Hittite land grants where boundary oaks and standing stones ensured perpetual recognition. Silver's weight, rather than coinage, prevented debasement, guaranteeing that payment value could not later be disputed. Legal permanence mattered because Abraham sought burial ground for multiple generations; the cave would hold Sarah, himself, Isaac, Rebekah, Jacob, and Leah. By purchasing land rather than receiving it as gift, Abraham avoided future claims that his presence remained contingent on local goodwill. The text's lawyer-like precision invites readers to appreciate God's concern for meticulous justice in familial matters. Proto-title deeds foreshadow Mosaic property laws that protect both buyer and seller (Lev 25:14–17). The meticulous record stands as earliest biblical example of covenant people engaging written or oral contracts, countering the myth that faith dismisses bureaucracy.

Silver weighed and witnesses arrayed, Abraham secured a lasting anchor for promise geography. That lawful permanence paves the way for Hebron's evolving identity as multicultural memorial.

9.5.3 Hebron as Multicultural Memorial: Tomb of the Patriarchs through the Ages

From Bronze-Age burial site to Herodian basilica to present-day mosque-synagogue complex, Machpelah illustrates how one transaction reverberated through millennia. Jewish pilgrims in David's time revered the cave, and Hebron briefly served as Israel's first capital (2 Sam 2:1–4). Herod encased the cave with Cyclopean limestone walls, adding Hellenistic colonnades that still frame modern worship spaces. Byzantine Christians later built a basilica over the tomb, inscribing Greek mosaics that honored Abraham as "Friend of God." Islamic tradition equally venerates Ibrahim; the 7th-century Caliph Omar preserved the site, integrating it into Ummah heritage. Crusaders alternated stewardship with Ayyubids, layering Gothic arches beside Mamluk minarets. Today, Jewish and Muslim services occur side-by-side, separated by partition yet united over a purchase oath older than both religions. The multicultural layers testify that land legitimately acquired under righteous terms can host diverse descendants in relative, if fragile, coexistence. Abraham's measured silver thus bought more than soil; it purchased an intersection where three faiths confront shared ancestry. The tomb challenges violent exclusion by standing as legal proof of peaceful transaction. Its continued use underscores promise continuity: the dead await resurrection in soil lawfully redeemed. Machpelah's witness invites modern peacemakers to honor ancient covenants of respect as blueprint for contemporary land disputes. The memorial's resonance transitions naturally into Abraham's later negotiations with Philistine neighbors over wells—another arena where property, peace, and worship intertwine.

Having secured a burial plot through scrupulous diplomacy, Abraham next confronts coastal nomads whose quest for water threatens daily survival and calls for innovative treaty-making.

9.6 Philistine Encounters—Well Disputes and Tamarisk Treaties

9.6.1 Seaside Nomads: Early Philistines before the Sea Peoples' Arrival

Genesis labels Abimelech a "Philistine," though archaeology indicates the full Sea Peoples' influx peaked later; early Philistines likely comprised Aegean traders mingled with local Canaanites in Gerar's coastal plain. Their mud-brick forts protected barley fields benefiting from Mediterranean dew. As semi-nomads, they respected water rights yet aggressively expanded pasture zones during drought. Gerar's rulers maintained small militias, supplementing defense with charioteer vassals from inland valleys. The Philistines prized iron tools and possessed rudimentary blacksmith skill sets that impressed Abraham's bronze-age servants. Cultural protocols demanded guest-gift exchanges: Philistine chiefs offered fish, linen, and purple dye, expecting reciprocal livestock offerings. Religious life revolved around Dagon shrines where grain sacrifices appeased fertility gods. Abraham's presence as Yahweh-worshiper introduced monotheistic dissonance into this polytheistic milieu. The Philistines were shrewd political operators, balancing coastal trade with inland diplomacy to secure caravan tariffs. Their early interaction with Abraham laid groundwork for later Philistine-Israelite relations under Samson and David. Recognizing these proto-Philistines helps readers appreciate that Abraham navigated fluid ethnic identities, requiring adaptable peacemaking. Water scarcity accentuated tensions—wells bridged nomadic and agrarian economies, making them flashpoints of power. In this context, the Beersheba disputes emerged, testing covenant ethics on resource sharing. Understanding Philistine social dynamics underscores significance of tamarisk treaty that soon followed.

9.6.2 Stolen Springs at Beersheba: Conflict-Resolution Rituals (Gen 21:25–31)

Abraham accused Abimelech's servants of seizing a well he had dug at Beersheba, a strategic oasis on the edge of Negev. Wells required arduous labor—cutting through caliche layers and lining shafts with stone—so theft amounted to economic sabotage. Ancient Near-Eastern law codes, such as Eshnunna, levied heavy fines for water tampering, indicating seriousness. Abimelech protested ignorance, opening space for ritual resolution rather than retaliatory violence. Abraham set aside seven ewe lambs, symbolically transferring ownership; Abimelech accepted, swearing that the well belonged to Abraham. The number seven (*sheva*) resonated with "Beersheba" ("well of seven" or "well of oath"), preserving agreement's memory in place-name. Witnessing servants slaughtered a peace offering; their shared meal sealed covenant, paralleling parity treaties found in Hittite archives. This livestock-for-water exchange demonstrates creative conflict resolution: material tokens plus public oath satisfied honor cultures on both sides. The ritual avoided blood feud, replacing cycles of retaliation with covenant cooperation. Legal anthropologists note that gifting valuables to the offended party transforms perceived theft into consensual transfer, restoring social equilibrium. Beersheba treaty foreshadowed Israelite water ethics—including laws about freeing blocked springs (Prov 5:15). The event proved that spiritual people need not shun practical negotiation; they can sanctify it through oath invoking "the God of Abraham." Wells turned from points of contention to monuments of peace, readying soil for tree-planting ceremony and divine worship.

9.6.3 El Olam Invocation: Planting Trees, Planting Peace (Gen 21:33)

After covenanting with Abimelech, Abraham planted a tamarisk tree at Beersheba and "called there on the name of the LORD, the Everlasting God" (*El Olam*). Tamarisks, salt-tolerant and deep-rooted, symbolized permanence in arid zones—living witnesses to oaths. Their feathery canopies emitted cooling moisture, providing hospitality to shepherds for generations. By linking treaty to worship, Abraham fused horizontal peace with vertical praise. The invocation of *El Olam* identified Yahweh as time-transcendent guarantor of agreements, elevating the treaty above temporal politics. Medieval Jewish commentators observed that tamarisk branches served later as sukkah roofing, integrating peacemaking into festival memory. Archaeology at Tel Beersheba reveals cultic platforms and Iron-Age altar stones repurposed, hinting that the site retained sacred import. Abraham's act pioneered environmental peacemaking; tree planting offset grazing disputes by marking communal rest area. The tamarisk's longevity reminded Philistines and Hebrews alike of covenant obligations, reducing future vandalism risk. Worship around the tree modeled integrative faith: ecological care, social harmony, and theological proclamation interwove. The title *El Olam* reappears in Isaiah's praise, linking patriarchal worship to prophetic hope (Isa 40:28). Through this simple arbor rite, Beersheba became spiritual hinge connecting desert nomads and coastal traders in shared reverence for the Everlasting God. The peace established here prepared Abraham's household to engage broader Canaanite society without losing identity.

With water rights secured and worship trees flourishing, the patriarch's daily life among diverse Canaanite villages offers further lessons on commerce, festivals, and spiritual vigilance.

9.7 Canaanite Neighbors—Daily Commerce, Seasonal Alliances, Subtle Risks

9.7.1 Barley Markets and Bride-Price Exchanges in Highland Villages

Each spring, Canaanite highlanders hosted barley markets where nomads like Abraham traded wool, cheese, and leather for grain, wine, and bronze tools. Colorful market days featured reed-pipe music and dancing girls from Hazor, blending business with festival. Barley, the first grain to ripen, served as local currency; prices fluctuated with rainfall reports from coastal merchants. Bride-price negotiations often coincided with markets: fathers displayed dowry items—spindles, oil jars—to entice alliances. Abraham observed these customs when later arranging Isaac's marriage, preferring kin ties to endogamy with local clans (Gen 24:3). Market exchanges forged seasonal alliances; tribes honored protection pacts for caravan transit through village lands. Elders sealed deals with salted bread, symbolizing covenant fidelity. Yet markets also exposed patriarchal households to idol trinkets and fertility amulets sold by Baal prophets. Economics intertwined with religion; grain vendors invoked Asherah's blessing over harvest, prompting Abraham to maintain separate worship spaces. The bustling bazaars taught him pricing strategies and metrics of inflation, informing later livestock valuations. While trading, Abraham modeled fair weights, reflecting divine hatred of false balances (Prov 11:1). Barley markets thus offered both sustenance and subtle tests of covenant distinctness. Interactions here shaped community reputation, influencing whether villages welcomed or wary of Abraham's encampments. Understanding these rhythms helps readers grasp ordinary faithfulness amid mundane commerce.

9.7.2 Hospitality Codes versus Baal Cult Seductions

Canaanite hospitality paralleled Abrahamic values—guests received water, bread, and story-sharing by hearth. However, hilltop shrines integrated hospitality with Baal worship; visitors were invited to fertility feasts involving wine-libations and ritual intimacy with cultic prostitutes (Hos 4:14). These seductive rites blurred social lines; covenant sojourners risked erosion of monotheism through repeated participation. Abraham's household had to differentiate between legitimate neighborly meals and idolatrous banquets. Servants carried portable altars to maintain Yahwistic worship, setting them outside village gates to avoid syncretism. Abraham reinforced Sabbath-like rest days, refusing to join planting festivals dedicated to Baal Hadad. The tension between receiving kindness and resisting compromise sharpened ethical discernment; Israelites later formalized this boundary in Deuteronomy's warnings not to "inquire after their gods" (Deut 12:30). The patriarch's vigilance cultivated a culture of critical hospitality—open hand without open conscience. Local families respected Abraham's principles, though some mocked the abstention, labeling his camp "people of the hidden God." By graciously sharing water yet declining temple wine, Abraham modeled a third way between isolation and assimilation. His example prepared later generations for exile contexts where eating royal food risked idolatry (Dan 1:8). Hospitality codes thus served as arena for subtle spiritual warfare. Balancing neighborly love with covenant loyalty became daily exercise in wisdom.

9.7.3 Living Distinct Yet Connected: Lessons for Resident Aliens

Abraham identified himself to Hethites as "sojourner and foreigner among you" (Gen 23:4), capturing paradox of covenant life: resident aliens entrusted with blessing land they do not fully own. The status afforded certain protections—immunity from military conscription—but imposed limitations on political voice. Abraham navigated local councils through gift-giving and mutual defense pledges while preserving autonomy. He taught his household bilingual skills—Amorite and Hurrian—enhancing trade and witness. Distinct dietary practices, such as draining blood from slaughtered animals, raised curiosity, opening door for theological conversations. Abraham refrained from land disputes, trusting promise timing, thereby diffusing jealousy and showcasing reliance on divine providence. His camp's evening psalms drifted across valleys; villagers listened to singular worship unaccompanied by idol images. The lifestyle embodied Jeremiah's later exhortation to "seek the welfare of the city" even in diaspora (Jer 29:7). By paying fair wages to Canaanite day-laborers, Abraham demonstrated social justice anchored in God's character. Festivals celebrated at his altars invited neighbors to observe sacrifice without participating in idolatry. These rhythms forged reputation of integrity, laying groundwork for Rahab-type conversions in future narratives. Living distinct yet connected preserved covenant identity while extending relational bridges. The lessons gleaned prepare readers to explore Abraham's missional undercurrents—blessing the nations begins with daily neighborliness that refuses both isolationism and compromise.

Grounded in practical neighbor love, Abraham's story now broadens to theological vision: the patriarch as prototype missionary, called to bless every family under heaven.

9.8 Blessing the Nations—Missionary Undercurrents in Patriarchal Life

9.8.1 "Through You All Families Will Be Blessed": Missional Mandate (Gen 12:3)

God's inaugural promise framed Abraham's vocation in global terms—"all families of the earth shall be blessed through you"—establishing centrifugal mission thrust long before Sinai. The Hebrew verb *nivr'khu* (Gen 12:3) carries reflexive sense: nations shall entrust themselves to blessing available in Abraham.

Patriarchal narratives depict this mandate materially (famine relief), spiritually (prayer), and diplomatically (treaties). Each foreign interaction becomes micro-fulfillment: Pharaoh's court learns Yahweh's power, Abimelech's household is healed, Melchizedek receives tithe and offers blessing. The promise reappears as leitmotif—repeated to Isaac (Gen 26:4) and Jacob (Gen 28:14)—embedding mission across generations. Paul later interprets it as gospel announced beforehand to Abraham (Gal 3:8). Abraham's open-tent policy exemplified proactive welcome; caravans found rest and heard stories of the Most High. His camp's mixed multitude—native and imported servants—foreshadowed church mosaics of Jew and Gentile. The mandate required internal holiness to sustain external witness; blessing nations necessitated covenant distinctness. Abraham's altars served as public theology, inviting observers to encounter Yahweh without coercion. Thus Genesis seeds a missionary imagination that spans scripture, culminating in Jesus's Great Commission. Understanding Abraham's missional mandate reframes patriarch not merely as tribal founder but as evangelistic prototype.

9.8.2 Intercessory Roles: Praying for Sodom, Healing Abimelech's Household

Abraham's advocacy before God for Sodom (Gen 18:23–32) illustrates missional intercession: pleading for righteousness amid corruption. His argument advanced justice tempered by mercy, modeling prayer that wrestles with divine holiness for the sake of the lost. The dialogue teaches proportion—persistence tempered with reverence—and sets benchmark for prophetic ministry. Later prophets—Moses after golden calf, Jeremiah for Judah—echo Abraham's stance. Likewise, Abraham's prayer that healed Abimelech's closed wombs (Gen 20:17) shows that covenant people mediate life to outsiders. The episode prefigures Elijah's rain-ending prayer and Peter's healing ministry in Acts. Intercession moved beyond words: Abraham's rescue of Lot embodied prayer put to action. These stories integrate spiritual and practical mission—advocacy plus intervention. Intercessory identity prepared Israel's priestly vocation to bless nations (Ex 19:6). For modern readers, Abraham models global prayer burden, urging believers to stand in gap for cities under moral fire. His prayers exhibit gospel posture: desire for repentance, not retribution. Intercession thus operates as silent missionary force, shaping destinies of peoples before watching heaven.

9.8.3 Ethical Wealth-Sharing: Tithes, Alms, and Famine Relief

Abraham's economic practices conveyed blessing: he tithed to Melchizedek (Gen 14:20), declined war spoils that might bind him to Sodom (Gen 14:23), and later endowed sons of Keturah with gifts before sending them eastward (Gen 25:6). These actions model wealth as instrument of witness rather than self-indulgence. Tithing channeled gratitude into support of priestly ministry, establishing prototype for Israel's Levite sustenance. Refusal of Sodom's gifts preserved testimony that God alone enriches His servants, freeing Abraham to give without ulterior motives. During regional famines, Abraham likely shared stored grain with neighboring clans; Genesis hints at mutual aid networks among Amorite allies. Ethical wealth-sharing continues through Joseph, who stores Egypt's grain to feed nations (Gen 41:57). New-Testament echoes appear in Paul's Jerusalem relief offering (2 Cor 9). Abraham's pattern challenges affluent believers to leverage assets for common good, signaling kingdom values. Almsgiving, when rooted in covenant generosity, opens hearts to God's character, fulfilling missionary mandate. Ethical stewardship rebukes consumerist cultures and invites inquiries into source of hope. Wealth-sharing therefore operates as tangible gospel, declaring that blessing never terminates on the blessed. The patriarch's financial ethics complete portrait of mission where proclamation, prayer, and generosity converge.

9.9 Covenant Signs in a Foreign World— Circumcision, Altars, and Oaths

9.9.1 Marking the Body: Identity and Witness among Outsiders (Gen 17:9-14)

When God required circumcision on the eighth day, He etched His covenant into living flesh, turning every male body in Abraham's camp into a testimony that could not be hidden beneath garments or forgotten like a misplaced charm. Foreign servants purchased with silver received the sign alongside freeborn sons, declaring that covenant grace embraced ethnically diverse households before Sinai codified inclusivity. In bustling oases or Philistine garrisons, the distinctive scar provoked questions that opened doors for witness: "Why submit young boys to this cutting?" The answer rehearsed Yahweh's promise—offspring innumerable, nations blessed, land secured—which in turn distinguished Abraham's faith from Canaanite rituals that sought fertility through sympathetic magic. Circumcision functioned as counter-cultural protest against phallic cults of Baal Peor, redirecting attention from erotic power to divine fidelity. The act carried social cost: warriors healing from circumcision were vulnerable, as Shechem's men discovered in Dinah's story (Gen 34), yet Abraham trusted that God who commanded the cut would protect convalescing defenders. Each new generation experienced covenant pain before memory, teaching that belonging begins with surrender. Even women, though not circumcised, felt the sign's ripple—wives nursed sons through recovery, midwives timed births to ensure timely rite, and matriarchs narrated Isaac's own circumcision as laughter-soaked proof of promise (Gen 21:4-6). In Egypt centuries later, Moses nearly forfeited his mission until Zipporah's flint knife renewed the sign (Ex 4:24-26), revealing that lapse in visible identity endangers spiritual calling. Paul later reinterpreted the mark, urging a "circumcision of the heart" for Gentiles (Rom 2:28-29), yet never trivializing Abraham's obedience; he saw bodily sign and inward reality as concentric circles of the same covenant witness. Thus, wherever Abraham traveled, scarred flesh silently proclaimed allegiance, reminding foreigners that the Most High lays claim to every life part, even the hidden.

9.9.2 Portable Altars: From Shechem to Bethel as Public Theology (Gen 12:7-8; 13:3-4)

Abraham's journey reads like a string of cairns—stone altars rising beside terebinths, on wind-lashed ridges, and near shady oases— each one converting contested ground into liturgical classroom. At Shechem he built the first, pivoting from Canaanite shrines that honored El-Berith to a rough pile declaring Yahweh as true landowner. Moving south, he pitched his tent between Ai and Bethel, raising another altar where smoke ascended within sight of pagan observers who burned incense to Asherah in groves below. These portable sanctuaries required no taxed populace or royal decree; they borrowed local stones, sanctified by covenant story and sacrifice. Offering animals from his own herds, Abraham demonstrated stewardship rather than exploitation of creation—a subtle sermon to cultures that sacrificed children at city walls (Deut 12:31). Each altar memorialized a fresh revelation—promise of descendants, assurance after Lot's departure, covenant cut in smoking firepot vision—so geography and theology fused into a living map. Visitors who followed caravan trails could trace divine faithfulness by counting soot-blackened rocks. Later, Jacob would rebuild at Bethel, layering generation upon generation of testimony (Gen 35:7). Elijah, centuries after, invoked this patriarchal pattern on Mount Carmel, repairing twelve-stone altar to confront Baal prophets (1 Kings 18:30-32). Altars thus functioned as mobile seminary, teaching hospitality hosts and caravan guests that worship thrives without monumental temples. Even in Philistine Gerar, where building permanent shrines might provoke suspicion, Abraham planted a tamarisk and invoked El Olam (Gen 21:33),

270

illustrating that trees and stones can preach. Modern pilgrims walk these sites, sensing how ordinary terrain becomes threshold when gratitude piles stone upon stone.

9.9.3 Hand-Raised Oaths: Swearing by Yahweh before Pagan Kings (Gen 14:22-23)

Abraham's diplomacy consistently culminated in lifted hands—visible gestures anchoring invisible commitments. To Sodom's king he swore, "I have lifted my hand to the LORD, God Most High," refusing even a sandal strap lest gratitude stray from Yahweh to human patronage. That declaration, delivered in open valley amid war spoil glitter, reframed victory economy: wealth must never blur the miracle of divine rescue. At Beersheba's well, he and Abimelech exchanged livestock while invoking deity as witness; the oath reconciled shepherd quarrels and inscribed covenant justice onto desert aquifers (Gen 21:31). Hand-raised language migrated into Mosaic jurisprudence—false swearers faced divine wrath (Lev 19:12)—and into psalmic worship where uplifted palms signaled trust (Ps 63:4). Even pagan kings learned to respect the gesture: after Pharaoh's household suffered plagues, any subsequent Hebrew vow carried weight in royal memory. The practice modeled transparent negotiation, contrasting secret sorcery of Near-Eastern courts that relied on omens and hidden knives. By rooting agreements in Yahweh's name, Abraham exported theological ethics into international law, a precursor to prophets who later demanded truthful oaths for societal stability (Jer 4:2). New-covenant teaching elevates yes-and-no simplicity, yet echoes patriarchal integrity: let word be bond because Father in heaven hears (Matt 5:34-37). Thus, every raised hand in Abraham's story verticalized horizontal contracts, stitching divine authority into mundane affairs and tutoring nations in accountability before the living God.

These covenant signs—scar, stone, and sworn palm—became reference points for later prophets who retold patriarchal narratives to confront empires and comfort exiles.

9.10 Echoes in the Prophets—Retelling Patriarchal Internationalism

9.10.1 Isaiah's Nations Streaming to Zion: Abrahamic Fulfillment (Isa 2:2-4; 51:1-2)

Isaiah beckons hearers to "look to Abraham your father... for he was one when I called him," using the patriarch as template for divine multiplication (Isa 51:2). The prophet's vision of nations ascending Zion's slopes with swords reforged into plowshares (Isa 2:4) expands Abraham's tent to cosmic proportions. He taps Salem's priest-king imagery—Jerusalem as peace epicenter—to imagine foreign peoples seeking Torah, not tribute. The oracle reverses Kedorlaomer's rapacious coalition: now Gentiles gather not to plunder but to learn covenant ethics. Isaiah recycles altar themes; holy mountain becomes permanent altar attracting Ethiopians who present gifts (Isa 18:7). Even Egypt, once plague-stricken, receives healing and worships alongside Assyria (Isa 19:23-25). Isaiah's rhetorical "highway" from Egypt to Assyria converts war corridors into pilgrimage routes, echoing Abraham's earlier trail between Nile and Euphrates. The prophet roots universal hope in specific ancestry, ensuring inclusivity does not erase election. By invoking Abraham, Isaiah assures traumatized Judah that small remnant can again seed global blessing. His message comforts exiles by proving that geographic displacement cannot thwart promise trajectory established in patriarchal wanderings.

9.10.2 Jeremiah's Oracles against Foreign Kings: Covenant Ethics Applied (Jer 46–49)

Jeremiah stands at Jerusalem's crumbling gates pronouncing doom on Egypt, Moab, Ammon, Edom, Damascus—names that trace back to Lot and Ishmael. His oracles leverage familial bonds: descendants who scorn covenant mercy reap ancestral warnings. Against proud Moab he recalls Lot's cave origins, denouncing complacency aged "from youth" like undisturbed wine (Jer 48:11). Ammon's claim on Israelite land is rebutted with genealogy—"Has Israel no sons?" (Jer 49:1). Egypt, earlier refuge for Abraham and later oppressor of his seed, will feel sword of Nebuchadnezzar (Jer 46:13-26). Yet Jeremiah also promises restoration—Egypt will be inhabited again (Jer 46:26)—mirroring Abraham's pattern of judgment-tempered mercy. The prophet's geography of judgment underscores that covenant ethics, first displayed in Abraham's oaths and altars, govern international accountability. Jeremiah, like Abraham rescuing Lot, advocates for oppressed; he pleads with Edom to abandon pride lest they become insignificant (Jer 49:15). Thus patriarchal narratives furnish Jeremiah's rhetorical arsenal, translating ancient interactions into contemporary foreign policy critique.

9.10.3 Ezekiel's Salem Vision: Priest-King Ideal Reimagined (Ezek 40–48)

Ezekiel's temple vision culminates with a river flowing east, healing desert and Dead Sea, inviting fishermen to cast nets where Lot's wife once turned to salt (Ezek 47:8-10). The prophet assigns tribal allotments horizontally across promised land, granting foreigners inheritance by adoption (Ezek 47:22-23) and thereby fulfilling Abrahamic inclusion. At the center stands a prince who eats bread before the Lord—a faint echo of Melchizedek's Eucharistic gesture. Ezekiel merges royal and priestly roles, anticipating Messiah who administers justice and leads worship. The city receives a new covenant name, "THE LORD IS THERE" (Ezek 48:35), echoing Abraham's *El Olam* invocation at Beersheba. Measuring rods delineate sacred space as meticulously as Abraham's weighed silver

273

defined Machpelah—legal precision ensuring lasting peace. Ezekiel's vision transforms patriarchal prototypes into eschatological blueprint where internationalism, holiness, and land converge harmoniously.

Prophetic retellings seeded hopes that flowered into diverse religious memories—Jewish, Christian, and Islamic—each tracing lines back to Abraham's foreign interactions.

Conclusion The tapestry of foreign engagements shows that Abraham's tent pegs are never driven into isolated soil; they are hammered into a world of rival emperors, righteous outsiders, and watching neighbors. Each episode—whether a priest's bread and wine, a king's uneasy restitution, or an emperor's defeated coalition—adds another thread to God's revelation that His covenant is both particular and expansive. By the chapter's end, Abraham stands as more than a clan leader; he is a diplomatic envoy, an intercessor for cities under judgment, and the prototype of a people called to carry blessing beyond their borders. These wider interactions foreshadow a priest-king who will embody all offices perfectly and a kingdom where every tribe finds its place. As the narrative hands the promise to Isaac, we carry forward the conviction that faith is authenticated not only at family altars but also in the public squares of a diverse and restless world.

Chapter 10 – Echoes in the Hebrew Scriptures: Posthumous Legacy

Though Abraham himself passed from the scene, his footsteps continued to press deeply into Israel's story, resonating in altars rebuilt by his heirs, in promises whispered at Sinai, and in the very architecture of the Promised Land. As Israel wandered through deserts, crossed rivers, and fought for footholds, patriarchal recollections furnished the framework for identity and hope. His name—invoked beside Isaac and Jacob—became a rallying cry at every altar, a benchmark in every genealogical list, and a touchstone in prophetic laments and declarations. From the stones piled at Bethel to the silver weighed in Hebron, each echo of Abraham's life gave texture to Israel's laws, worship, and national boundaries. In this chapter, we trace how the Father of Faith, though long gone, continued to speak through covenant signs, ancestral remembrances, and the liturgies that shaped a people destined to carry his blessing into every age.

10.1 From Mourning to Memory—Immediate Repercussions after Machpelah

10.1.1 Communal Lament in Hebron: Rituals for a Patriarch's Passing

When Abraham died at a "good old age" and was gathered to his people, the news rippled through Hebron like the strike of a mourning bell (Gen 25:8). The Hittite community and nomadic clans that had settled around Machpelah convened for public lament, echoing Canaanite and Mesopotamian traditions of collective mourning conducted at city gates. Women clad in sackcloth and ashes circled the cave's entrance, wailing songs of remembrance that recounted Abraham's hospitality under the Oaks of Mamre and his faithful dialogues with kings. Men cut their garments in grief, though Mosaic law would later limit such self-mutilation (Lev 19:28). The assembly brought oil to anoint Abraham's tent, symbolizing honor even in loss, while incense burned at the new altar erected above the cave's roof. Priestly singers—likely Levite servants inherited from Isaac—led responsive chants: "O God Most High, You who made heaven and earth, remember Your servant" (citing Gen 14:19). Storytellers recounted his travels from Ur to Canaan, each stop marked with altar and well, reminding attendees that covenant memory lived in land and liturgy alike. The mourning rituals blended tribal customs with nascent Yahwistic elements: no metallic instruments were used, in deference to later prohibitions (1 Sam 15:23). After seven days, the community concluded with a final procession to the field of Ephron, where Abraham had negotiated ownership, underscoring that even death cannot void a just acquisition (Gen 23:16). Tear-stained stones from the cave courtyard were carved into small memorial pillars, each inscribed with Abraham's name, ensuring pilgrims would recall his legacy long after oral laments faded. In these rituals, Hebron became covenant mausoleum and teaching center, where Patrickian memory shaped collective identity. The communal lament set pattern for Israel's later funeral customs—mourning tents, dirges, and memorial feasts—as ways to honor those who walked in faith's footsteps. Through these first sorrowful ceremonies, Abraham's passage became living liturgy, imprinting his life into land and communal soul.

10.1.2 Isaac's Succession: Transfer-of-Blessing Narratives (Gen 25 : 5–11)

Abraham's bequest—"All that I have" to Isaac, plus gifts to sons of concubines sent east—formalized transfer of covenant prominence (Gen 25:5–6). This division underscored primogeniture's transformation: Isaac alone inherited the promise, reversing cultural norms of firstborn advantage found in Canaanite inheritance customs. The narrative emphasizes divine economy: wealth need not be equally shared when covenant seed must remain unbroken. Isaac's acceptance of the birthright without recorded dispute contrasts sharply with Jacob and Esau's later rivalry, signaling spiritual maturity in succession. Genesis notes Abraham's burial "by his son Isaac" (Gen 25:9), cementing filial devotion and continuity of faith. Isaac's role emerges through brief note of weeping and conducting funeral rites "for his father," a template later mirrored by Jacob for Joseph (Gen 50:1–3). The successful transition avoided civil strife common in ancient Near East, where half-siblings often contested patrimony. Isaac's household thus became sole steward of patriarchal altars and wells, inheriting both physical sites and theological vocation. His role set standard for Israelite kings—David and Solomon—who traced legitimacy through proper succession rather than military coup. The succinct succession story foreshadows Israel's later dynastic prayers to "establish the throne of Your servant" (2 Sam 7:16). By securing Isaac's undivided inheritance, God kept covenant promise on track, preventing lineage fragmentation. Readers observe how divine sovereignty shapes family structures to preserve redemptive purposes. Isaac's unchallenged succession exemplifies the blessing's singular focus, a motif Pauline epistles later underscore (Gal 3:16). Thus, immediate aftermath of Machpelah illustrates both human piety and divine design in handing forward the promise torch.

10.1.3 Keturah's Branches and the Dispersion of Gifts to the East (Gen 25 : 1–4, 6)

Following Sarah's death, Abraham married Keturah, bearing six sons—Zimran, Jokshan, Medan, Midian, Ishbak, and Shuah—whose tribal lines spread eastward into Arabian deserts (Gen 25:1–4). The gifts he sent "to the sons of his concubines" before Isaac's succession included livestock, silver, and personal servants, ensuring they could establish independent settlements (Gen 25:6). These distributions correspond to Mesopotamian traditions where patriarchal estates were apportioned to secondary heirs to prevent future disputes. The dispersion facilitated Abraham's wider legacy: through Keturah's offspring emerged Midianite clans whose priestly expertise later aided Moses (Ex 2:15). Jokshan's sons Sheba and Dedan founded incense trade centers that biblical prophets would reference (Ezek 27:22), extending Abrahamic blessing into commercial corridors. Zimran's progeny likely migrated northeast toward Elamite frontiers, illustrating covenant seed's reach beyond Canaan. Abraham's deliberate grant to Keturah's sons echoes his earlier bequest to Ishmael (Gen 17:20), balancing familial compassion with covenant priority. The eastward diaspora became foundation for emerging nations—some later adversaries, others unexpected allies—echoing covenant's universal yet particular pattern. Ishbak and Shuah's descendants assimilated local customs, contributing camel-herding and metalworking skills to burgeoning desert economies. This strategic gifting prevented disenfranchised rebellion, promoting stability across Abrahamic territories. The narrative records the departure "to the country eastward," language mirrored in ancient treaties specifying buffer zones. By distributing gifts provisionally rather than granting land title, Abraham maintained central covenant land for Isaac's line, aligning with future Israelite land laws (Num 36:7). These posthumous arrangements demonstrate prudent estate planning infused with theological foresight: Abraham's family networks would carry his spiritual DNA far beyond the Jordan. The dispersion of gifts to the east thus sets stage for Mosaic encounters with Midianites and for prophetic oracles concerning desert tribes, ensuring patriarch's impact endured across multiple fronts.

With Isaac and Keturah's sons firmly settled, the covenant narrative refocuses on Isaac and Jacob, each experiencing divine reaffirmations that echo Abraham's initial call.

10.2 Covenant Continuity—Reaffirmations to Isaac and Jacob

10.2.1 Beersheba Vision: "I Am the God of Your Father Abraham" (Gen 26 : 23–25)

During a famine, Isaac withdrew to Gerar where God appeared to him by night, echoing the Abrahamic promise: "Fear not, for I am with you… I am the God of Abraham" (Gen 26:24). This direct revelation reassured Isaac that covenant presence transcends generations and geographic shifts. He built an altar, called on Yahweh's name, and dug a well—actions mirroring his father's worship at Shechem and Mamre. The well was named "Shibah," reinforcing tripartite ritual: altar, invocation, and water source— physical symbols of divine faithfulness. Philistine neighbors, witnessing Isaac's prosperity despite previous conflicts, recognized covenant favor and signed treaty oaths under seven ewe lambs, reflecting submission to Yahweh rather than local deities. The vision's reassurance provided Isaac with confidence to maintain altars amid hostile surroundings, shaping his pastoral leadership. Isaac's altar-setting under moonlit skies suggests continuity of worship rhythms passed from Abraham. This episode intertwines land possession with divine presence, affirming that covenant truth abides where memory of Abraham's God remains alive. The Beersheba vision thus becomes local religion's pivot, transforming wells into spiritual markers. Future Israelite tradition would cite this event when legitimizing priestly duties at Shiloh, Bethel, and later Jerusalem. The repeating formula—"I will multiply your descendants… because Abraham obeyed my voice"—underscored conditional promise tied to faithfulness. Isaac's public worship and treaty model supply blueprint for subsequent covenant renewals in Joshua's era. Through Beersheba, the torch of promise passed unbroken from father to son, illuminating path for Jacob's dream.

10.2.2 Ladder at Bethel: Stones, Vows, and Patriarchal Parallels (Gen 28 : 13–15)

Fleeing Esau's wrath, Jacob slept with a stone for pillow at Luz, dreaming of a ladder reaching heaven's gate, crowned by angels ascending and descending (Gen 28:12). Yahweh's voice assured him: "I am with you… I will not leave you," echoing promises first given to Abraham (Gen 12:1; 26:24). Jacob awoke, awestruck, anointed the stone with oil, and called the place "Bethel" (house of God). He erected the pillar—like Abraham's altars—declaring, "This stone shall be God's house," weaving personal encounter into familial theology. His vow—to give tenth of all he received if God preserved him—mirrors tithe to Melchizedek, linking ladder vision to priest-king counsel (Gen 14:20). Bethel's ladder imagery prefigures temple steps and later David's aspirations for house built for Yahweh (2 Sam 7). Jacob bound himself through oath, raising hand and naming Bethel as "gate of heaven," integrating open-air theophany into covenant architecture. The vision's promise of land, offspring, and universal blessing echoes Abrahamic covenant but personalizes it for Jacob's journey. Jacob's public altar gave Israel future pilgrimage site, reactivated centuries later by Jeroboam and worship reformation errors. Bethel's sacred stones became milestones in tribal memory, marking intersection of divine

280

initiative and human response. Jacob's vow catalyzed his transformation from trickster into Israel—"he who strives with God"—incorporating patriarchal parallels into his identity. Thus, Bethel functions as generational covenant hinge, reinforcing continuity of promise across father-son succession. The ladder motif underscores that covenant unfolding requires both vertical divine outreach and horizontal human ascent. As Isaac's reaffirmation at Beersheba secured land promise, Jacob's Bethel vision anchored relational promise, preparing tribal genealogies woven with celestial access.

10.2.3 Name Change to Israel: Wrestling as Legacy Embodiment (Gen 32 : 24–30)

On the eve of meeting Esau, Jacob wrestled with a divine figure until dawn, refusing to release his opponent until he received blessing—a profoundly corporeal enactment of covenant struggle (Gen 32:24–26). The mysterious adversary re-named him "Israel," "he struggles with God," affirming Abraham's seed must wrest purposefully in faith. Jacob's limp—resulting from hip injury—became lifelong testament to divine encounter, akin to circumcision scar marking covenant membership. His insistence on blessing parallels Abraham's tenacious prayers for Sodom's remnant, underlining intercessory lineage. The name Israel punctuates later tribal identity: Jacob's twelve sons named people who would persist in wrestling with holiness amid battles and exiles. Patriarchs thereafter bore Jacob's new name in divine spoken oaths and angelic visions (Hos 12:4-5). The wrestling episode bridges Bethel's vision and Peniel—"face of God"—where Jacob declared "I have seen God face to face, and yet my life is preserved" (Gen 32:30). This personal transformation proves covenant continuity not merely through words but through embodied struggle. Israelites would recall Jacob's wrestling in annual festivals of atonement, meditating on divine-human engagement. The narrative teaches that inherited promises require active engagement—faith is not passive heritage

281

but dynamic wrestle. Jacob's new name thus embodies Abrahamic legacy in human form, transmitting covenant identity through lived experience. The wrestling motif reappears in Hosea's imagery of Israel as wife struggling with God's love. Thus, covenant continuity for Isaac and Jacob manifests in vision, vow, and wrestling—three narrative pulses connecting patriarchs across ages.

From individual reaffirmations, the focus expands to how Jacob's twelve sons collectively shape tribal identity, inscribed in blessing poems and camp formations.

10.3 Tribal Identity—Twelve Sons, Twelve Stones, Twelve Gates

10.3.1 Birth-Seat Rivalries: Leah, Rachel, and the Matriarchal Mandate

Leah and Rachel's competition for Jacob's affection produced twelve sons and one daughter, each birthladen with matriarchal commentary—Reuben as "unstable" (Gen 29:32), Simeon and Levi as "instruments of violence" (Gen 29:33–34), Judah as "praise" (Gen 29:35). The sibling rivalry underscores how matriarchal struggles shaped Israel's foundational tribes, each linked to Persian-era treaty holograms of family dynamics inscribed on tribal banners. Bilhah and Zilpah, Rachel's and Leah's handmaids, bear additional sons— Dan, Naphtali, Gad, Asher—evidencing surrogate motherhood as accepted practice in ancient Near East. Each mother named her child with theological intent: Zebulun as "honored," Issachar as "reward," embedding women's voices in covenant poetry. Rivalries over seating—who nursed at whose knee—affected tribal hierarchies later reflected in census orders (Num 1). The matriarchs' negotiating of servant gifts and bridal wages foreshadowed tribal land allocations. Their labor in tent weaving and goat-herding provided resource base for each tribe's initial cohesion. Naomi's later displacement in Moab echoes matriarchal vulnerability when sons

282

die, reminding Israel of ancestral grief. Women's agency in bearing and naming children underscores that tribal identity arises as much through maternal devotion as paternal blessing. The narrative honors this matriarchal mandate by preserving these birth stories in canon. Future Midrashim would celebrate these women as prototypes of faith under adversity. The birth-seat rivalries thus become generational template for Israel's unity amid diversity. Through their wombs, twelve stones would later mark tribal gates, each daughter-tribe pairing representing matriarchal legacies. The matriarchal narrative affirms that covenant seed sprouts from complex soil of love, jealousy, and divine promise.

10.3.2 Blessings of Jacob: Patriarchal Poetics and Prophetic Trajectories (Gen 49)

On his deathbed, Jacob invoked poetic blessings over each son— Reuben's instability, Simeon and Levi's swords, Judah's scepter, Benjamin's ravenous nature—crafting prophetic trajectories that shaped Israel's destiny (Gen 49:1–27). These benedictions functioned like oracle-poetry, aligning family traits with future tribal roles: Judah's rule, Zebulun's naval commerce, Issachar's scholarship. The blessing of Judah as "lion's cub" prefigures Davidic monarchy and Messianic hope (Heb 7:14). Joseph's sons, through Ephraim's predominance, symbolized covenant continuation despite birth order reversal, illustrating divine election's sovereign choice. Dan's "snake" metaphor informed his later idolatrous tendencies (Judg 18), while Gad's "raider" identity shaped his half-tribe's eastern military frontier role. Patriarchal poetics provided Israel's chroniclers with thematic scaffolding for historical books—Joshua's tribal allotments echo Jacob's words. Kings and prophets later appealed to these words when urging tribes to repent according to ancestral calling. The poetic structure— parallel couplets, chiasm, and wordplay—mirrors Hebrew wisdom literature's stylistic norms. Archaeological finds of Hebron burial site discovered ostraca referencing Jacob's "blessings," indicating

283

early cultic memory. Jacob's benedictions thus became theological blueprint for national self-understanding, writing character sketches that tribes internalized across generations. This convergence of poetry and prophecy ensured tribal identities aligned with covenant imperatives while accommodating historical nuance. Jacob's blessings, rooted in matriarchal beginnings, complete tribal identity architecture, readying Israel for wilderness encampment geometry.

10.3.3 Encampment Geometry: Bannered Tribes around the Tent of Meeting (Num 2)

As Israel marshaled for Sinai, the census revealed twenty-two thousand fighting men per tribe (Num 2), each positioned around the Tabernacle with tribal banners matching Jacob's benedictions: Judah's lion standard to the east, Reuben's ox emblem to the south, Ephraim's man-child insignia to the west, Dan's eagle symbol to the north. This encampment geometry materialized kinship poetry into spatial order, embedding tribal roles into sacred architecture. Each tribe's proximity to Tabernacle signified covenant relationship—Levi's clans encircled the holy structure as priestly guardians. The banners functioned as mobile landmarks, guiding herdsmen's flocks and camp servants in daily worship routes. Tribal flag designs incorporated color symbolism—scarlet for blood atonement, blue for heavenly connection, purple for royal promise. The orderly arrangement prevented inter-tribal skirmishes, mirroring Abraham's peacemaking ethos at Mamre. The encampment reinforced that unity arises from diversity: each tribe distinct yet centered on covenant presence. Annual festivals saw tribes process in designated quadrants, reviewing roles assigned by patriarchal blessings. Cartographic reconstructions of Sinai camps align with later descriptions of "four corners of the earth," highlighting universal mission (Ezek 7:2). The encampment's design imbued geography with theological narrative, reviving memory of Abraham's tent while projecting national identity. Moses later instructed that when the ark advanced, only Judah's standard led, honoring Abraham's fourth son's future kingship. Thus, tribal banners and camp layout demonstrate posthumous legacy of patriarch: covenant pilgrimage transformed into corporate worship structure. The encampment geometry transitions from personal covenant journey to communal pilgrimage, setting stage for Exodus resonances.

As Israel moved from Sinai toward Canaan, the Exodus patterns—God's deliverance, covenant rites, and sacrificial signs—resounded Abraham's preliminary agreements with the Most High.

10.4 Exodus Resonances—Deliverance Patterns Rooted in Abraham

10.4.1 Burning Bush Vocabulary: "God of Abraham, Isaac, and Jacob" (Ex 3 : 6)

When Moses encountered the burning bush, God introduced Himself as "the God of your father, the God of Abraham, the God of Isaac, and the God of Jacob," anchoring Israel's liberation in patriarchal relationship (Ex 3:6). This formula invoked God's covenant history, reassuring Moses that past promises guaranteed present deliverance. The repetition over three generations underscored faithfulness across time, validating that Israel's bondage in Egypt did not annul Abrahamic covenants. The use of ancestral names marked theological continuity: God's interactions with Moses mirrored earlier dialogues with Abram's tent. The burning bush's holy ground echoed Abraham's altars, establishing personal encounter as locus of mission. Moses' hesitation to accept the call reflects Abraham's own reluctant departure from Haran, suggesting parallel narratives of divine commissioning. Israel's exodus, then, functions as corporate fulfillment of Gen 15:13–14, where descendants would be oppressed and later emerge with great possessions. The patriarchal invocation also framed the plagues as extension of divine supremacy first demonstrated in Pharaoh's court. By hearkening to Abraham's faith, Moses embodied covenant continuity, leading new generation

285

out of foreign servitude. This introductory pericope shaped Exodus liturgy—Deuteronomy later commanded Israelites to remember deliverance "so that you may fear the Lord your God all the days" (Deut 6:13). Thus, burning bush vocabulary draws direct line from Abrahamic interactions to national salvation, knitting individual faith into communal identity. The passage transitions into deliverance sequences that mirror patriarchal rescue patterns.

10.4.2 Blood, Plagues, and Passover: Covenant Fulfilment of Gen 15 : 13–14

God's prophecy to Abraham—"your offspring will be strangers... and I will bring them out with great possessions" (Gen 15:13–14)— found specific enactment in the Passover rituals. The lamb's blood on doorposts parallels Abraham's sacrifice beneath oaks, marking households as venerable spaces protected from judgment. The sequence of plagues echoes divine interventions in Pharaoh's court under Abraham (Gen 12:17) and Abimelech (Gen 20:17), reaffirming God's pattern of warning, plague, and release. The tenth plague, slaying firstborn, institutes a new covenant sign analogous to circumcision: visible, generational, and tied to obedience. Passover unleavened bread speaks of urgent departure, reminiscent of Abraham's tent-fold at divine summons. Exodus's deliverance feast fulfills the promise that oppressors would let Israel go "with great wealth" (Ex 12:36). Gifts from Egyptians—jewelry and silver—mirror Abraham's spoils returned with Lot (Gen 14:23). The dystopian experiences of Israel's sojourning echo Hagar's wilderness trial (Gen 21:17), but culminate in national exodus. Passover's annual observance ensures that every Israelite household recalls Abraham's distant hope and Moses's decisive leadership. The festival's liturgy ties children's questions to patriarchal recollections, instructing families to recite foundational stories. Thus, blood and plagues create a covenant bridge from Abraham's initial promise to Sinai's law—interweaving deliverance with sacrificial remembrance. This pattern demonstrates that institutional

286

rites can root deeply in ancestral narrative, ensuring communal memory across generations.

10.4.3 Sinai Covenant as Marital Vow: Bride Price Once Promised in Genesis 17

The giving of Torah at Sinai carried nuptial language—"You shall be to me a treasured possession... a kingdom of priests and a holy nation" (Ex 19:5–6)—echoing Genesis 17's marital framework where God betrothed Abraham in sign of circumcision (Gen 17:2–4). The vow-like structure presents Israel as bride, with laws as marriage articles binding two parties. The "blood of the covenant" sprinkled on people (Ex 24:8) recalls Abraham's sacrificial rituals in the cup of Abrahamic fellowship (Gen 15:9–10). The festival of Weeks (Shavuot) commemorates Torah reception, paralleling Festal feasts established under Abraham for remembrance (Gen 21:8). Legal stipulations—on justice, mercy, and neighbor love—draw from Abraham's ethical examples in foreign courts. The Sinai treaty's ceremony of building altar, reading text, and offering sacrifices follows Hittite vassal treaty model, yet centers Yahweh's sovereign grace toward a committed bride. The covenant's covenant renaming of Israel—Ephraim, Manasseh—reflects God's naming of Abram and Sarai. Marital imagery underscores intimacy: God likens Israel to spouse he bore and redeemed (Hosea 2:19). Understanding Sinai covenant as continuation of Abrahamic vow enriches reading of Torah as loving-law rather than oppressive code. This connection closes loop from Genesis promises to Exodus fulfillment, demonstrating unity of Scripture's covenant theology. Sinai's marital vows lead naturally to wilderness waypoints where patriarchal signs reappear.

From Sinai's marital covenant, Israel again wanders through wilderness, retracing patriarchal waypoints where wells and altars guide their journey toward settlement.

287

10.5 Wilderness Waypoints—Re-Digging Patriarchal Wells

10.5.1 Paran and Beer-lahai-roi: Hagar's Springs Revisited by Israel

When Israel encamped in the wilderness of Paran, the memory of Hagar's flight to Beer-lahai-roi resonated as they contended for water at Rephidim (Ex 17:1–7). Moses struck the rock at Horeb, echoing Hagar's divine provision under a different name but the same God who "saw me" in the desert (Gen 16:13). Paran's arid expanse forced scout parties to recall that Abraham's servant had sought wells in Haran, while Hagar had discovered an unexpected spring where Ishmael's survival depended on it. The law given at Sinai even protected wells: "You shall not move your neighbor's landmark" (Deut 19:14) and "You shall not withhold the wages of poor and needy" (Deut 24:14), extending covenant justice to water rights. As Israel moved toward Kadesh-barnea, they passed sites associated with patriarchal sojourns, reinforcing that wilderness waypoints belonged to their story. Later, the Rephidim rock would be called "Massah" and "Meribah," naming the place of testing and quarreling, yet linking it back to foundational well struggles. Joshua's itineraries would designate Beer-lahai-roi region for the tribe of Simeon (Josh 19:8), institutionalizing Hagar's spring into Israelite geography. The identification of these springs in post-exilic records shows sustained collective memory—water sources that once saved a fugitive now served an entire nation. Midrashic traditions even locate Hagar's well near Elim's twelve springs (Ex 15:27), suggesting that Israel's oasis thirty-six pools connected to Abraham's family history. Pilgrimage routes later marked these spots with stones inscribed: "Remember Abraham's God here." The re-digging and re-naming of wells signified covenant continuity, transforming Hagar's private miracle into public salvation landmarks. Thus, Paran and Beer-lahai-roi become dual waypoints where patriarchal exile meets national pilgrimage, unified under Yahweh's unchanging care.

10.5.2 Manna Beside Terebinths: Echoes of Mamre's Hospitality

In the wilderness, Israel found quail and manna by oaks of Mamre-like groves (Ex 16:13), evoking Abram's invitation to the LORD under Mamre's terebinths (Gen 13:18). The manna's daily gathering—two quarts per person—mirrors the communal meals Abram shared when Philistines and Egyptians witnessed his altar worship. Israel's morning collection was precisely measured, teaching dependence on God's provision rather than human storehouses. Beneath tent-like canopies of acacia and oak, families recalled how Abram welcomed strangers with curds and milk beside similar trees. The term *lechem ha-shem* ("bread of heaven") underscored that physical sustenance came from the same source as covenant promises. Later liturgical poets would describe manna as "hidden manna," connecting Exodus feasts to Abraham's secret altars in Canaan. Wisdom literature cites manna's taste like "honey cakes" (Ps 81:16), recalling Abraham's attributes of hospitality and generosity. The pattern of daily gathering and Sabbath double-portion echoes Abraham's rhythms of altar-building and rest under sacred trees. Israel's dependence on manna by terebinths reinforced that covenant blessing transcends territory and time: what once sustained guests under Mamre now nourished a people journeying to David's throne. The manna tradition shaped wilderness worship: stone tables adjacent to camp altars became tables of the presence, patterned after Abraham's open-air hospitality. Thus, manna beside terebinths transforms patriarchal hospitality into national identity: a rhythm of gratitude, dependence, and shared story beneath silent witnesses of God's provision.

10.5.3 Pillar of Cloud, Pillar of Fire: Expanding the Torch and Smoking Pot Imagery

The smoking pot and flaming torch that passed between the pieces of Abraham's covenant sacrifice (Gen 15:17) find grander expression in Israel's journey: a pillar of cloud by day and pillar of fire by night (Ex 13:21–22). The singular torch symbolizing God's presence at Machpelah becomes a guiding beacon for millions crossing wilderness expanses. This dynamic phenomenon revealed divine commitment: the same God who pledged Abraham descendants as numerous as stars now led Israel with visible glory. Camped at Sinai, Moses saw cloud descend like incense, reminiscent of altar smoke at Hebron's cave. The fire pillar lighted paths into unknown territory, just as Abraham journeyed by faith into the land not yet owned. The dual pillars communicated guidance and protection: cloud concealing Israel from Egyptian chariots, fire deterring nocturnal predators. Prophets later equated God's Spirit as burning lamp within hearts (Zech 4:2–6), drawing on pillar imagery. The wilderness tabernacle's menorah cemented torch symbolism, echoing cloud's canopy motif above the Holy Place. Psalms recall the pillar when exalting God as "a lamp to my feet" (Ps 119:105), merging personal guidance with communal leadership. The torch and smoking pot thus evolve from private covenant signs into corporate theophany, ensuring that Abrahamic markers inform Israel's collective worship. Their journey under these pillars anticipates church's procession from baptismal font to altar, participating in God's unending pilgrimage with His people.

Having experienced wilderness waypoints suffused with patriarchal echoes, Israel prepared to enter Canaan, where conquest and land tenure extended Machpelah's legal precedent across tribal allocations.

10.6 Conquest and Land Tenure—Legal Title Deeds Extended

10.6.1 Machpelah's Clause in Joshua's Allocation: Hebron Given to Caleb (Josh 14 : 13–15)

In the division of Canaan, the hill country of Hebron—including Machpelah where Abraham was buried—fell to Caleb as reward for faithfulness, invoking Joshua's oath: "to you and your children I give Hebron" (Josh 14:13). This grant cited patriarchal ownership as basis for tribal entitlement, formalizing Abraham's purchase in national tenure law. Caleb inherited not by force but through covenant fidelity, reflecting Abraham's trust in divine promise despite his advanced age when Isaac was born. The narrative emphasizes that legal claims hinge upon ancestral precedent: "just as the LORD said to Moses... so Joshua gave him Hebron" (Josh 14:14). Caleb built cities in the region, integrating past pilgrimage sites into his clan's patrimony. Ephraim's allotment refrained from encroaching on Hebron's borders, respecting Abraham's cave cave deed. Judges later record Hebron as royal refuge for David, confirming its strategic and symbolic significance. Post-exilic chroniclers reiterated this history in genealogy lists, linking returning families to Caleb's name. Thus, Machpelah's clause becomes archetype for Israelite land distribution: a covenant-legal model framed by patriarchal rights. The explicit citation of Abraham's transaction validates written records and communal memory as authoritative in territorial claims.

10.6.2 Covenant Boundary Formula: "From the River of Egypt to the Great River" (Ex 23 : 31; Deut 11 : 24)

God's promise to Abraham included land "from the river of Egypt to the great river, the Euphrates" (Gen 15:18), a formula echoed in Exodus 23:31 and Deuteronomy 11:24 as Israel's maximum borders. These covenants specified geographic limits that encompassed the territories of Canaanite, Philistine, Moabite, and Babylonian domains. The boundary formula framed Israel's military strategy during conquest—cities like Jericho and Hazor were targeted to secure eastern and western flanks. Priests carrying the ark led crossings at Jordan, symbolizing divine boundary-crossing authority. Prophets lamented Israel's overreach when they imposed tribute taxes beyond promised lines (Amos 1:12). Post-exilic sermons called for hope that one day the rivers would once again mark fulfilled promises (Jer 12:14–15). Rabbinic maps engraved this formula into synagogue mosaics, reminding diasporic Jews of ancestral borders. The boundary text functions as both historical guide and eschatological blueprint, anticipating future restoration when the earth yields fruit under Messiah's reign (Joel 3:18). Abraham's initial land grant thus provides theological compass for Israel's identity amid shifting empires.

10.6.3 Cities of Refuge: Mercy Ethics Traced to Abrahamic Intercession (Num 35 : 9–34)

The ordinance establishing six Cities of Refuge for unintentional manslayers (Num 35:9–34) echoes Abraham's intercession for Sodom, where pleading mercy led to sparing righteous few. These sanctuary cities—Kedesh, Shechem, Hebron, Bezer, Ramoth, Golan—function as spaces where guilt is weighed against intent, paralleling Abraham's negotiation for remnant. Levitical law required a fair trial and levirate-style family provision, ensuring that accidental killers found protection under covenant law. Hebron's dual role as refuge city and patriarchal tomb superimposes intercession ethic on ancestral soil. Murder-trial regulations, including retrial before council of elders, mirror Abram's appeals before Yahweh for Sodom's fate. Provision of bread and water in these cities links back to Abraham's hospitality under terebinths and Melchizedek's bread and wine. The fatal avenger's barred access reflects Abraham's boundary decisions at Beersheba, where juridical lines preserved covenant purity. Cities of Refuge embody mercy balanced with justice, a theme integral to Abrahamic legacy. In Judges and Kings, asylum narratives recall these guidelines, affirming that mercy extends beyond tribal affiliation. Rabbi-Moses Maimonides later listed these cities among commandments "positive and negative," cementing their origin in patriarchal intercession patterns. Thus, mercy ethics in land tenure law trace their DNA back to Abraham's pleading for preservation of the righteous remnant.

As Israel transitioned from tribal commonwealth to monarchy, David's reign at Hebron and Solomon's temple dedication reflected patriarchal parallels, reaffirming that throne and priesthood stem from Abrahamic origins.

10.7 Monarchy Mirrors—Davidic Narratives and Patriarchal Parallels

10.7.1 Hebron Kingship: David's Seven-Year Rule on Abraham's Turf (2 Sam 2 : 1–4; 5 : 4–5)

After Saul's decline, David was anointed king over Judah at Hebron, the city of Abraham's sojourn and sepulcher (2 Sam 2:1–4). His seven-year–and–six-month reign there mirrored Abraham's initial rule in Canaan before expanding to Mamre. David restored Machpelah's monuments, describing his residence as "God's inheritance" and modeling stewardship of ancestral sites. He established altars on eastern hills, blending Abrahamic worship patterns with emerging royal rituals. The city's strategic location atop the Judean ridge provided security and control over trade routes, much as Abraham had valued highlands for tent hidden-ness. David's ties to Hebron honored tribal unity; clans long loyal to Judah recognized covenant leadership emanating from patriarchal ground. His anointing ceremony beneath Tekoah's terebinths revived Abram's method of seeking divine guidance under trees. David's military victories expanded inherited promise boundaries, yet he always deferred to oracle-priest Nathan, whose Melchizedek references kept royal authority under divine priestly check. Hebron's inclusion in David's narrative underscores that monarchy emerged organically from patriarchal covenant, not as foreign imposition. His joyful Psalm 133, rejoicing in brotherly unity at Hebron, echoes Abraham's mediation with Lot. Thus, David's Hebron kingship functions as thematic extension of Abraham's geopolitical and spiritual legacy.

10.7.2 Melchizedek Echo in Psalm 110: Priest-King Typology Renewed (Ps 110 : 1–4)

Psalm 110 opens with Yahweh's decree to David: "Sit at my right hand... until I make your enemies a footstool" (Ps 110:1), then shifts to "You are a priest forever after the order of Melchizedek" (Ps 110:4). This fusion of royal and priestly office identifies David's line with Salem's ancient priest-king, reaffirming Abraham-Melchizedek encounter as enduring archetype. Temple liturgies invoked both dimensions—offering sacrifices at priests' hands while enthroning Davidic king on throne. The psalm's liturgical use on festival days framed royal coronations as divine investitures akin to Abram's covenant ceremonies. Second Temple Judaism produced messianic expectations centered on this dual office, anticipating One who would mediate and reign supremely. Early Christians applied Ps 110 to Jesus, reading Him as ultimate Melchizedek heir and fulfillment of Davidic promise (Heb 5:6). The Psalm's enduring place in Jewish, Christian, and even Islamic psalmody testifies to its foundational echo of patriarchal typology. Its inclusion in Qumran hymns further demonstrates cross-sect resonance of priest-king ideal. Thus, Psalm 110 renews and amplifies Abrahamic typology for monarchic and messianic dimensions, reinforcing that covenant promise converges in royal priesthood.

10.7.3 Solomon's Prayer of Dedication: "God of My Father" as Covenant Anchor (1 Kin 8 : 23–25)

At the dedication of Solomon's temple, the king invoked Abraham, Isaac, and Jacob: "O Lord, God of Israel, there is no God like You... keep what You have promised to Your servant David" (1 Kin 8:23). He appealed to the "ark of Your covenant" resting in the Holy of Holies—a development from Abraham's portable altars to permanent sanctuary. Solomon's prayer cited patriarchal hope for land security, offspring prosperity, and temple worship (1 Kin 8:25), intertwining Davidic request with Abrahamic geography. The temple's cedar beams and gold overlay represented material fulfillment of genealogical decorations promised to Abraham's descendants. Solomon's liturgy incorporated sacrificial tithe regulations derived from Abraham's tithe to Melchizedek, transforming private giving into national offering. Pilgrims from "all nations under heaven" witnessed the prayers, echoing Genesis 12:3's global blessing rhythm. The prayer balanced petition—"may Your eyes be open" (1 Kin 8:29)—with thanksgiving for "Your goodness in giving Your servant David a wise son" (1 Kin 8:20). By calling God "my father," Solomon connected Davidic and Abrahamic paternity. His dedication rite formalized the United Monarchy's role as caretaker of patriarchal legacy. The temple's symbolism—ark above mercy seat—resonated with the smoking pot and torch imagery of Genesis 15:17, now housed in a fixed shrine. Thus, Solomon's prayer anchors covenant history in worship space, ensuring that Abraham's promise persists in national theology. The monarchical mirror completes circle from wandering tents to settled temple, readying Israel for prophetic reprise.

As monarchy flourished, prophets revisited Abraham's stories to frame new ethical calls and consolations for exilic and post-exilic communities.

10.8 Prophetic Reprise—Abraham in Ethical Oracles and Consolations

10.8.1 Isaiah's Quarry Metaphor: "Look to Abraham Your Father" (Isa 51 : 1–2)

In exilic Isaiah, the prophet urges Israel to "look to Abraham" and "listen to the one who called you from the womb," employing quarry-image language—"I called him alone, and blessed him and made him many" (Isa 51:2). The metaphor of quarrying rock emphasizes divine initiative: Abraham was singled out from primordial chaos, just as Israel emerges from exile by God's digging hand. Isaiah contrasts desert wilderness before Abraham with impending renewal where "righteousness shall go before him" (Isa 46:13). The call to gaze back serves therapeutic function—exiles regain faith by remembering patriarch's faithful responses under trial. This exhortation parallels Abraham's gaze at stars during promise sign (Gen 15:5), turning physical looking into spiritual trust. Isaiah's quarry trope also evokes stone altars that Abraham built, reinforcing worship as transformative work. The section weaves legal calls for social justice—"loose the chains of injustice" (Isa 58:6)—with patriarchal example of hospitality, bridging personal memory and national ethics. By invoking Abraham, Isaiah legitimizes critiques of idolatry in Jerusalem, holding covenant people to the standard of their forefather. The prophet's sermon thus becomes both warning and consolation, affirming God's unbroken faithfulness from Ur to Babylon.

10.8.2 Ezekiel's Land Restorations: Covenant Oaths and Everlasting Peace (Ezek 34 :23–24; 37 :26–28)

Ezekiel foretells a day when God will set "one shepherd" over Israel—"My servant David"—and "I will make with them an everlasting covenant" (Ezek 34:23–24), echoing Abraham's "everlasting God" title at Beersheba (Gen 21:33). His vision of dry bones reviving into living army (Ezek 37) parallels deliverance promises made to Abraham's seed in Gen 15:18. The prophet's land-restoration oracles—cities rebuilt, fields sown, temple restored—mirror patriarchal acquisitions and altars reshaped for worship. Ezekiel commands binding of ancient oath stones—"I have sworn to them that I will give them the land" (Ezek 37:25)—reinforcing Abraham's sign of sacred oath as boundary marker. The imagery of peace trees—cedars and cypresses—growing in covenant land recall Abraham's tamarisk planting and hospitality canopies. Prophetic consolations blend legal renewal with poetic recapitulation of promise trajectories. Ezekiel's "God-with-them" refrain (Ezek 48:35) resonates with Abraham's "I will be God to you and to your offspring" (Gen 17:7). Restoration theology thus loops back to patriarchal assurances, demonstrating ancient oaths' perpetual validity. Ezekiel's futuristic temple, with its sacrificial altars and gates named after tribes, intersects with tribal geometry established under Abraham. The prophet's synthesis of legal, poetic, and visionary genres underscores covenant continuity from patriarch to remnant. Ezekiel's consolatory oracles ensure that Abrahamic legacy grounds hope amid communal dislocation.

10.8.3 Micah's Remnant Theology: Promise to Jacob, Steadfast Love to Abraham (Mic 2 :12–13; 7 :18–20)

Micah ends his book with triumphant vision: "I will surely assemble all of you, Jacob; I will gather the remnant of Israel; I will place them together as the sheep of Bozrah, like a flock in its pasture" (Mic 2:12–13), echoing Jacob's "flock" imagery and Abraham's promise of numerous descendants. Micah celebrates Yahweh's steadfast love—*hesed*—"Who pardons iniquity... who keeps steadfast love for thousands" (Mic 7:18–20), recalling Abraham's intercession for Sodom and divine mercy on Hagar's line. The prophet's remnant motif resonates with Abraham's negotiation down to ten righteous, framing communal preservation as continuously tethered to patriarchal advocacy. Micah's call for justice, kindness, and humility (Mic 6:8) channels Abraham's hospitality, mercy, and walking before God (Gen 18:19). The final doxology cites forgiveness "to the thousandth generation," amplifying Genesis's promise to Abraham of blessing "for ever" (Gen 17:7). Micah thus weaves patriarchal theology into his oracles, offering both ethical critique and assurance of restoration. His use of shepherd and flock metaphors ties back to Abraham's pastoral beginnings. The remnant theology underscores that covenant identity persists in small faithful bodies, just as ten righteous could have spared a city. Micah's prophetic reprise reaffirms Abraham's enduring role as father of faith whose legacy informs justice and mercy in every age.

Having surveyed how prophets retold Abraham's story to challenge and console Israel, we turn to wisdom literature, where sapiential reflections distill patriarchal faith into pithy counsel.

10.9 Wisdom Literature—Sapiential Reflections on Patriarchal Faith

10.9.1 Job's Eastern Heritage: Parallels with Keturah's Sons

Job's narrative situates him among the "sons of the east" (Job 1:3), a phrase that echoes the dispersion of Abraham's concubine-sons to the east (Gen 25:6). Both Job and Keturah's children inhabit desert zones where pastoral wealth and tribal alliances define status. Job's wealth in camels, oxen, and servants mirrors Abraham's provision for Zimran, Jokshan, and Midian, emphasizing common cultural patterns of nomadic affluence. Job's dialogues about divine justice recall Abraham's negotiations over Sodom's fate—both figures wrestle with God's righteousness in extreme circumstances (Job 23:3–7; Gen 18:30–32). Hagar's wilderness cry at Beer-lahai-roi (Gen 16:13) prefigures Job's lament, "My soul is weary of my life" (Job 10:1), revealing that inhospitable lands provoke deep theological reflection. Job's friends come from Teman and Şeba—tribal names associated with Abraham's wider kin—underscoring solidarity among eastern tribes in crises. The wisdom speeches that follow demonstrate how Eastern traditions of oral debate shaped Israelite wisdom corpus. Job's insistence on a mediator (Job 9:33) parallels Abraham's appeals through Melchizedek, linking intercession practices across genres. Both patrilineal and matrilineal inheritance evoke divine blessing that persists amid suffering—Job ends with doubled prosperity (Job 42:10), akin to Abraham's flourishing after Covenant of Pieces. Job's mention of the "sons of Job" and their feasts (Job 1:4) echoes Abrahamic hospitality, though later judged insufficient without righteous living. The pattern of trial and restoration in Job mirrors Isaac's testing at Gerar and subsequent wells re-digging, indicating that patriarchal motifs inform wisdom theology. Job's final view of God's handiwork (Job 42:5–6) resonates with Abraham's star-counting meditation (Gen 15:5)— both conclude that human understanding yields to divine majesty. Thus, Job integrates eastern heritage and patriarchal faith into sapiential framework, showing that Abraham's legacy permeates even non-Israelite wisdom traditions.

10.9.2 Proverbs' Friend of God Motif: Integrity and Generational Blessing

The book of Proverbs twice invokes the "friend of God" label (Prov 22:11; Friend of God appears explicitly only there), reflecting back on Abraham—"the friend of God" (2 Chr 20:7; Is 41:8). Esteemed in wisdom circles as exemplar of faith-integrity, Abraham's life informs Proverbs' ethics: "He who finds a wife finds a good thing, and obtains favor from the LORD" (Prov 18:22) echoes Abraham's acquisition of Sarah and divine favor. Verses on inheritance—"a good man leaves an inheritance to his children's children" (Prov 13:22)—mirror Abraham's meticulous provisioning for Isaac and Keturah's sons. Proverbs 3:5–6 calls readers to "trust in the LORD… and He will direct your paths," a succinct restatement of Abraham's call to leave Haran (Gen 12:1–4). The emphasis on fair weights (Prov 11:1) revives Abraham's refusals of fraudulent gains in Sodom (Gen 14:23). Generational blessing—the "father of many nations" theme—underlies advice on child-rearing (Prov 22:6), prescribing "train up a child in the way he should go," akin to Abraham's teaching Isaac and later Jacob's sons. Integrity rewarded (Prov 28:18) parallels Abraham's deliverance and prosperity despite moral lapses, illustrating divine recompense for uprightness. Proverbs' portrayal of hospitality (Prov 31:20) echoes Abraham's tent-door care for strangers, linking compassion to wisdom. The motif of "walking with the wise" (Prov 13:20) resonates with Abraham's alliances with Melchizedek and Heber the Kenite. Thus, Proverbs weaves Abrahamic character into its corpus, urging readers to emulate patriarchal virtues for communal and familial blessing.

10.9.3 Psalm 105 and 106: Historical Recitals as Covenant Catechism

Psalm 105 recounts Abraham's journey: the sojourn in Canaan (Ps 105:12–15), the divine promise of descendants (Ps 105:8–11), and his rescue of Lot (Ps 105:16–22), serving as lectionary for covenant history. The psalm's liturgical use in Second Temple synagogue embedded patriarchal memory in communal worship, ensuring each generation heard Abraham's faith tested and rewarded. Psalm 106 offers complementary perspective, lamenting Israel's recurrent failures despite Abrahamic example—"they did not remember His hand" (Ps 106:13)—and calls for remembrance of patriarchal mercies. Both psalms function as catechetical recitals: teaching theology through narrative, moving from Abraham to Exodus to wilderness. The phrasing "He established a testimony in Jacob and appointed a law in Israel" (Ps 105:42) bridges Abraham's circumcision covenant (Gen 17) with Mosaic Torah. Psalm 105's portrayal of Joseph in Egypt (Ps 105:16–22) foreshadows Abraham's Egyptian sojourn, framing deliverance theme across patriarchal arcs. The inclusion of Lot's rescue demonstrates Abraham's role as intercessor, offering blueprint for covenant mediator. Psalm 106 returns to Mesopotamian idolatry to reproach

300

Israel, contrasting ancestral fidelity with national infidelity. Liturgically, these psalms bookend festivals: Psalm 105 at Passover, Psalm 106 at Tabernacles, linking patriarchal promises to yearly pilgrimages. Their historical recitals function as covenant catechism—narrative theology setting moral and ritual standards. Through these psalms, Abraham's legacy becomes living liturgy shaping Israel's self-understanding and worship rhythms.

Having seen wisdom and worshipers draw on Abraham's life, we now examine how post-exilic genealogists re-edited ancestral lists to re-root a displaced people.

10.10   Post-Exilic   Genealogies—Chronicler's Theological Edit

10.10.1 Adam-to-Abraham Tableau: Re-rooting a Displaced People (1 Chr 1)

Chronicles 1 opens with Adam and runs through Abraham to post-exilic returnees, intentionally linking Israel's origins to primeval creation. This genealogical tableau re-roots a people uprooted by Babylonian exile, affirming that their identity stretches back to humanity's dawn. By positioning Abraham at the crest of this lineage, the chronicler underscores his role as covenant pivot. The meticulous naming of generations creates cosmic continuity: from Adam's creation to Noah's flood, to Abraham's call, each figure stands as link in unbroken chain. Post-exilic scribes likely arranged these lists to foster communal unity across returning tribes, reminding them of shared ancestry. The inclusion of lesser-known names (e.g. "Abiram" in 1 Chr 1:2) demonstrates breadth of research and canonization of broad traditions. The Chronicler's theology affirms that returning exiles participate in foundational covenants dating back to Abraham's promise. This genealogy counters any sense of civilizational orphanhood, offering lineage credentials for temple service and land claims. The Adam-to-Abraham arrangement also anticipates New Testament genealogies that trace Messiah to creation (Luke 3:38). Thus, Chronicles' opening list becomes theological manifesto: exile cannot sever covenant links that stretch through millennia. The Chronicler's edit ensures Abraham remains central anchor in Israel's restored identity.

10.10.2 Returnee Registries: Land, Temple, and Tribal Re-alignment (Ezra 2; Neh 7)

Ezra 2 and Nehemiah 7 record registries of returning exiles, specifying priests, Levites, temple servants, and laity by ancestral houses. These lists invoke Abrahamic genealogies to validate land allotments and temple roles, echoing covenant tenure models seen in Machpelah's purchase and tribal allocations under Joshua. Returnees had to present certified lineage documents—todim—and evidence of temple service, reflecting patriarchal practices of proof through witness lists at Hebron (Gen 23:18). The lists differentiate "children of Solomon's servants" from priestly families, illustrating continuity of Keturah's descendants integrated into Judah's restoration (Ezra 2:61–63). Land-grant decisions considered ancestral inheritance claims dating to tribal origins in Jacob's blessings. The public reading of these registries during New Moon festivals anchored communal memory in ancestral story. Persian authorities likely endorsed these documents to administer taxes and religious duties. The returnee registries thus functioned as legal and theological instruments, knitting together diverse families—descended from Abraham's seed—into unified worship community. These records signal that covenant identity is genealogical and spatial: tied to temple and land. The Chronicler's emphasis on tribe-by-tribe re-alignment re-established covenant boundaries reminiscent of Abraham's rented burial field. Thus, returnee registries carry forward patriarchal patterns of land and worship continuity.

10.10.3 Ezra-Nehemiah's Prayer Confessions: Re-citing Genesis Promises (Neh 9; Ezra 9–10)

In Nehemiah 9, the assembled people stand in fasting, confessed sins, and read aloud from "the Book of the Law of your servant Moses," recounting God's faithfulness from "the days of Abraham" (Neh 9:7). This prayer recounts patriarchal promises—land promises, multiplying descendants, and rescue from slavery— drawing direct line from Abraham to current restoration. The litany highlights Hagar's and Isaac's stories as precursors to Israel's own deliverance. Ezra 9–10 records confession over intermarriage, invoking Abrahamic separateness—"You did not spare the first man, Hagar" (Ezra 9:13)—to compel covenant purity. The communal vow to put away foreign wives echoes Abraham's boundary-setting warnings against Canaanite marriages (Gen 24:3). Repeated references to Abraham's calling and promises root Israel's failures and restoration in patriarchal narrative. The prayer concludes with covenant renewal sealed by reading Torah and offering sacrifices, paralleling Abraham's sacrificial rituals under covenant oaths. These confessions demonstrate that Genesis promises provide both liturgical content and moral framework for post-exilic reform. The communal voice—"our God, spare us"— echoes Abraham's intercession for Sodom, modeling corporate advocacy. Thus, Ezra-Nehemiah's prayer confessions renew Abrahamic legacy as living resource for repentance and renewal in covenant life.

With genealogies and confessions anchoring post-exilic identity, the chapter now turns to liturgical practices that bring Abrahamic memory into the church's feasts, prayers, and communal rhythms.

10.11 Liturgical Afterlife—Feasts, Prayers, and Communal Memory

10.11.1 Passover Haggadah: Four Cups and the Four-Generation Prophecy

The Passover Haggadah structures the Seder around four cups of wine, echoing divine promises in four patriarchal generational shifts: to Abraham ("I will bring you out"; Ex 6:8), to Isaac ("I will establish My covenant"; Gen 26:3), to Jacob ("I will give ... the land"; Gen 28:13), and to the people of Israel ("I will bring you into the land"; Lev 25:38). This mapping embeds Abraham's promise trajectory into the Seder's narrative arc. Grandmothers sing "Avadim hayinu" ("We were slaves"), connecting Hagar's wilderness deliverance to Israel's bondage in Egypt. The Four Questions reference elements of each patriarch's story—bread instead of leaven; liberation owed to God's oath to Abraham. The cup of blessing (*baruch*) recalls Abraham's hospitality with Melchizedek's bread and wine. Seder plate elements—bitter herbs, charoset, shankbone—illustrate labor and sacrifice continuity from the patriarchs through Exodus. The invitation "All who are hungry, let them come and eat" mirrors Abraham's tent-door invitations (Gen 18:4). Elijah's cup left untouched symbolizes future fulfillment of the Abrahamic blessing reaching all nations (Gen 12:3). Recitation of "Next Year in Jerusalem" concludes the Haggadah, echoing Abraham's hope for presence in the promised land. Thus, the Haggadah transforms patriarchal narrative into communal remembrance and eschatological anticipation.

10.11.2 Daily Amidah Blessing: "Shield of Abraham" in Synagogue Liturgy

In the weekday Amidah prayer, Jews bless God as "Shield of Abraham" (*Magen Avraham*), invoking patriarchal protection in daily life. This appellation—rooted in Genesis 15:1 ("fear not,

Abram, I am your shield")—ensures that every worshipper recalls Abraham's divine defense before battles of faith. The Amidah's progression—from praise to request to thanksgiving—parallels Abraham's pattern of altar prayer: call on God's name, present need, then offer gratitude. The blessing "Shield of Abraham" precedes petitions for survival, drawing confidence from covenant promises. Medieval prayer masters like Rabbi Judah HaLevi composed poetry expanding on this title, celebrating Abraham's endurance against Nimrod's furnace. The shield motif informed kabbalistic meditations on divine protection, framing patriarchal faith as spiritual armor. Contemporary liturgy includes personal intentions (*kavanot*) at this blessing, inviting worshippers to echo Abraham's trust under trial. The Amidah's use across daily services, festivals, and fast days embeds Abrahamic memory into the rhythm of life. Thus, the "Shield of Abraham" blessing carries patriarchal legacy from ancient wells into modern prayer shawls.

10.11.3 Sukkot Tents and Patriarchal Pilgrimage: Re-enacting Nomad Hope

The festival of Sukkot commands Israelites to dwell in booths "so that your generations may know that I made the children of Israel dwell in booths" (Lev 23:42–43), evoking Abraham's tent-dwelling pilgrimage. Temporary sukkot structures constructed of branches mirror nomadic tents Abraham raised across Canaan. Families eat, post, and even sleep in sukkot, recalling patriarchal hospitality and divine provision in transient dwellings. The festival's water-libation ceremonies beneath sanctuary canopy echo the brews at Beersheba's el-olam invocation. Citron and palm-branch processions around the altar reenact pilgrimage circuits taken by Abraham when visiting Shechem, Bethel, and Hebron. Rabbinic tradition links Sukkot to miraculous cloud canopy in wilderness, tying back to Abraham's smoking pot covenant sign. Psalms sung during Sukkot—"Let my prayer come before You like incense" (Ps 141:2)—recall incense offered at Machpelah funeral. Thus, Sukkot becomes living anthropology of Abrahamic sojourn, teaching trust in God's provision beyond permanent houses. The mitzvah to invite "the poor, the orphan, and the widow" into sukkot repeats Abraham's model of generous hospitality (Gen 18:3). Through Sukkot, Israel annually rehearses patriarchal hope in incarnate form, preparing hearts for final pilgrimage into restored land.

Conclusion Abraham's posthumous legacy weaves through Scripture as a continuous refrain: his faith shapes Israel's deliverance songs, anchors its land treaties, and undergirds the monarchy's claim to divine favor. Even in the exile, his memory offered a lifeline—an assurance that God's promises outlast empires and geographical displacements. As priests and prophets summoned his example to challenge injustice or to comfort the broken, the patriarch's shadow stretched across generations, affirming that covenantal faithfulness does not die with the pioneer but reverberates in the worship, ethics, and identity of all who follow in his stead. In preparing to cross into the New Covenant, we glimpse how Abraham's enduring echoes provide both foundation and launchpad for the coming fulfillment in Christ.

Chapter 11 – Abraham in the New Testament: Apostolic Interpretation

In the New Testament, Abraham emerges not merely as ancient progenitor but as living prototype for gospel proclamation, faith embodiment, and the shape of the church's mission. From the opening verses of the Gospels—where Matthew and Luke anchor Jesus's identity in Abraham—to the pulpit of Acts and the pulpit letters of Paul and Hebrews, the apostles continually return to the patriarch's story as key to understanding Christ's person and work. Abraham's journey of trust, his hospitality to strangers, and his willingness to sacrifice Isaac become theological lenses through which the early church interprets justification, covenant inclusion, and sacrificial love. This chapter traces how New Testament writers appropriate Abraham's life, weaving his promises into the very fabric of Christ's redemptive narrative and the worldwide fellowship it inaugurates.

11.1 Genealogies and Birth Narratives—Anchoring Jesus in the Patriarch

11.1.1 Matthew's Royal Line: Three Fourteens and the David–Abraham Arc

Matthew opens his Gospel with a tightly structured genealogy of fourteen generations from Abraham to David, fourteen from David to the exile, and fourteen from the exile to Christ (Matt 1:17). This numeric symmetry underscores Jesus's royal legitimacy: fourteen being the numeric value of David's name (DVD = 4+6+4). By anchoring the first group at Abraham, Matthew affirms that Jesus inherits the Abrahamic promise of blessing to all nations (Gen 12:3), yet also fulfills the Davidic kingship promise (2 Sam 7:12–16). The genealogy includes unexpected figures—Tamar, Rahab, Ruth, Bathsheba—signaling that God's grace extends beyond ethnic Israel into the wider world, foreshadowing the Gentile mission. Matthew's arrangement highlights key turning points: Abraham's call, David's throne, exile's judgment, and Christ's birth as restoration. Each name functions as covenant milestone, linking Old Testament narrative to the Messiah's arrival. By beginning with Abraham, Matthew locates Jesus within God's redemptive plan that started with one faithful ancestor. The underlying pattern also communicates that God's promises transcend the brokenness evidenced by exile. Matthew's use of fourteen sets a theological grid: Jesus is culmination not only of David's line but of the wider Abrahamic pedigree. Readers are invited to see in Jesus the continuation and perfecting of patriarchal faith. The genealogy thus becomes a proclamation: the promised Seed has come in royal splendor. By bridging Abrahamic promise to Christ's nativity, Matthew signals that the kingdom inaugurated in Jesus fulfills God's covenant across generations. This royal line then flows into the narrative scenes of the nativity, where scriptural fulfillments multiply. The genealogical frame ensures that every reader meets Jesus first as renewed fruit of Abraham's faith.

11.1.2 Luke's Priestly Line: Adam-to-God Inclusivity through Abraham

Luke situates Jesus's ancestry in a backward sweep from Joseph all the way to Adam and to God (Luke 3:23–38), yet he carefully inserts Abraham at the center of the list, reaffirming the patriarch's pivotal role in God's family. Where Matthew emphasizes royal descent through David, Luke highlights priestly and universal descent, connecting Jesus to every human being via Adam and to the covenant community via Abraham. Each generational pair links Old Testament figures to the New: "the son of Enos, the son of Seth, the son of Adam, the son of God." By placing Abraham at the midpoint, Luke balances Jewish particularity with Gentile inclusivity: Jesus is both Jewish Messiah and Savior of all. The genealogy affirms that salvation flows through the Abrahamic axis yet radiates outward to encompass all humanity. Luke's arrangement reflects his concern for marginalized peoples—Samaritans, Samaritans, women—and underscores the universal scope of Christ's mission. The listing of Terah, Nahor, Serug, and Nahor before Abraham emphasizes the gradual emergence of covenant faith in family history. Luke's narrative then transitions to the annunciations, where Gabriel quotes Genesis 17: "You will be called the Son of the Most High," echoing Abrahamic tree of promise. The priestly nuance is evident as Luke likens Zechariah's temple service to Abraham's altar-building. Through Luke's line, Jesus becomes both the Last Adam and ultimate heir of Abraham's promise. This dual identity equips the reader to understand Jesus's ministry among Gentiles and Jews alike. The genealogy thus establishes theological groundwork for the Gospel's universal proclamation. By connecting Adam's original blessing to Abraham's seed promise, Luke frames Jesus as fulfillment of both cosmic and covenant hopes.

11.1.3 Nativity Canticles: Mary and Zechariah Echo the Promise to Abraham

Luke weaves two canticles—Mary's Magnificat (Luke 1:46–55) and Zechariah's Benedictus (Luke 1:68–79)—that resound with Abrahamic promise language. Mary sings of God raising up a mighty Savior from the house of David but first remembering "the mercy promised to our fathers, to Abraham and to his offspring forever" (Luke 1:54–55). Her words echo Septuagint renderings of Genesis 17: "I will confirm My covenant... to Abraham and his seed forever." Zechariah, filled with the Holy Spirit, proclaims God "has raised up a horn of salvation for us in the house of His servant David" (Luke 1:69) and speaks of God visiting His people to "give knowledge of salvation to His people in the forgiveness of their sins" (Luke 1:77), resonating with covenant themes Abraham first received. Both canticles invoke deliverance from enemies, feeding the hungry, and lifting the humble—virtues Abraham embodied in his hospitality. Mary's emphasis on both physical and spiritual nourishment parallels promises of land and seed, now transfigured into Messiah's deliverance. The canticles function liturgically in Christmas and Advent worship, reminding congregations of covenant continuity. Their use of covenant vocabulary links Old and New Testament theologies seamlessly. Mary and Zechariah become living echoes of Abrahamic faith, proclaiming mercy and fulfillment in the child yet unborn. These hymns situate Jesus's birth within God's grand narrative, where patriarchal promises find their climactic expression. The nativity canticles thus serve as the early church's doxological response to the long-awaited fulfillment of Abraham's hope.

Having established Jesus's identity through patriarchal genealogy and canticles, we turn to Gospel narratives where Jesus Himself invokes Abraham to define true sonship and eternal destiny.

11.2 Gospel Dialogues—Jesus Appeals to "Father Abraham"

11.2.1 John 8:39–58: True Sonship versus Biological Descent

In John 8, Jesus confronts Jewish opponents who claim Abraham as their father, yet He distinguishes true children of Abraham by faith and obedience rather than mere physical descent (John 8:39). When challenged, Jesus declares that Abraham rejoiced at His day, anticipating sight of Messiah (John 8:56), thus asserting His pre-existence and divine identity. The Jewish interlocutors misunderstand, seeking to kill Him for blasphemy; Jesus responds that "before Abraham was, I am" (John 8:58), echoing Yahweh's self-designation in Exodus 3:14. By this, Jesus claims participation in Abraham's calling before Isaac's birth, yet transcends time as the "I AM." His argument shows that true Abrahamic lineage is rooted in receiving God's word and believing in His Son. The dialogical setting—temple courts—parallels Abraham's public dialogues with kings, transforming patriarchal witness into prophetic proclamation. Jesus's opponents, though children of Abraham by blood, fail to comprehend the promise's spiritual dimension. Jesus thus redefines "Abraham's seed" in light of faith in Him, aligning with Paul's midrash in Galatians 3. This interchange underscores Gospel theme: continuity with Abraham requires embrace of Christ's revelation. The dramatic claim "I AM" confronted covenant ancestors' understandings, revealing that Jesus fulfills and surpasses patriarchal identity. The passage invites readers to examine their own claims to Abrahamic heritage—based on biology or belief. By appealing to Father Abraham, Jesus legitimizes His mission within the covenant story while unveiling His divine essence. This dialogue transitions into parables illustrating consequences of faith versus unbelief among Abraham's nominal children.

11.2.2 Rich Man and Lazarus: Eschatological Comfort in Abraham's Bosom

In Luke 16, Jesus tells of a rich man in torment and a poor beggar, Lazarus, "carried by the angels into Abraham's bosom" (Luke 16:22). The phrase "Abraham's bosom" becomes metaphor for intermediate heavenly paradise, signifying intimate fellowship with the patriarch. This imagery contrasts starkly with the rich man's suffering, underscoring that earthly wealth does not guarantee divine favor. Placed at Abraham's side, Lazarus partakes in Abrahamic blessings—comfort, rest, and assurance—first promised in Genesis 15. The parable's reversal motif recalls God's lifting of the lowly and bringing down the proud (Luke 1:52), connecting to Abraham's altars of mercy and rescue narratives. The rich man's plea to send Lazarus to warn his family receives Abrahamic counter-logic: revelation comes through Scripture and prophets, not miraculous signs (Luke 16:29–31), again affirming Abraham as model receiver of God's word. Abraham's bosom thus becomes locus of messianic consolation, a teaching used in early church catechesis on the afterlife. Rabbinic literature mentions "Abraham's Bosom" as seat of the righteous, indicating this parable's resonance with existing traditions. The parable calls listeners to action: honor covenant ethics by caring for needy, lest they find themselves excluded from Abrahamic fellowship. Through this story, Jesus uses patriarchal imagery to define eschatological outcomes, reinforcing Abraham's ongoing role as covenant father. The narrative transition leads to further teachings on discipleship costs and reward in the kingdom.

11.2.3 Zacchaeus and the Lost: "He Too Is a Son of Abraham"

When Jesus dines at Zacchaeus's house in Jericho, the crowd grumbles, "He has gone in to be the guest of a man who is a sinner" (Luke 19:7). Jesus responds, "Today salvation has come to this house... for he too is a son of Abraham" (Luke 19:9–10), extending Abrahamic identity to repentant outcasts. Zacchaeus's gesture of restitution—giving half his goods to the poor and repaying fourfold those he defrauded—echoes Abraham's ethical wealth-sharing and refusal of ill-gotten spoils (Gen 14:23–24). By calling Zacchaeus "son of Abraham," Jesus affirms that covenant inclusion rests on faith and transformation, not heritage or social standing. The scene mirrors Genesis narratives of divine hospitality and moral reversal, as Abraham welcomed strangers and interceded for cities. Zacchaeus's joy at salvation evokes Abraham's laughter at Isaac's birth (Gen 21:6). Jesus's choice to stay at Zacchaeus's home demonstrates that authentic covenant fellowship requires table companionship across cultural divides. The transformation of a wealthy tax-collector into a generous host illustrates the fullness of Abrahamic blessing—riches not for personal hoarding but for communal restoration. This encounter underscores mission to "seek and save the lost" as continuation of Abraham's pioneering witness to God's mercy. Zacchaeus's story transitions the narrative from personal encounter to broader call for discipleship characterized by radical generosity. In Jesus's affirmation, Abraham's promise of blessing to all families finds fresh expression in outreach to sinners. The story thus bridges patriarchal hospitality to New Testament missional practice, preparing ground for apostolic preaching in Acts.

Having witnessed Jesus invoke Abraham to define true sonship and promise fulfillment, we turn to Acts, where the apostles employ patriarchal proof to underpin their missionary sermons.

11.3 Acts of the Apostles—Patriarchal Proof in Mission Sermons

11.3.1 Peter at Solomon's Portico: Inheritors of Covenant Blessing (Acts 3)

After healing a lame man at the temple gate called Beautiful, Peter addresses onlookers at Solomon's Portico: "The God of Abraham, the God of Isaac, and the God of Jacob… has glorified His servant

Jesus" (Acts 3:13). By invoking the tri-patriarchal formula, Peter roots Jesus's resurrection in covenant history, presenting it as divine validation of Messiahship foretold to Abraham. Solomon's Portico—named after the royal builder—provides poetic symmetry: the dynasty founded on David (son of Abraham's seed) now glorifies the greater Son. Peter's sermon reminds Jews that promises made to Abraham—land, seed, blessing—culminate in the risen Christ, urging repentance for continued spiritual inheritance. His appeal to Scripture highlights prophecy expectations ("God raised up His servant"; Acts 3:18) grounded in Genesis narratives. The portico setting, a public colonnade, mirrors Abraham's public altar spaces, making worship accessible to all. Peter's address unites healing, testimony, and covenant affirmation in one proclamation. He challenges elders and scribes: if you restore the rejected Cornerstone, you renew covenant fidelity (Acts 4:11). Peter's reliance on Abraham's God underscores continuity: the same God who parted seas and ratified covenants now raises Jesus. Subsequent debates with Sadducees (Acts 4:1–22) hinge on the authority of Abrahamic promise to sustain apostolic mission. The sermon sets template for Gentile mission: faith in Jesus as covenant focus rather than heritage. Peter's witness at Solomon's Portico exemplifies apostolic strategy of contextualizing gospel within patriarchal memory. The narrative then transitions to Stephen's defense, where Abraham's pilgrimage becomes interpretive lens for Israel's journey.

11.3.2 Stephen's Defense: Abraham's Pilgrimage as Typology of Exodus (Acts 7)

In his speech before the Sanhedrin, Stephen recites Abraham's calling out of Ur, his settlement in Canaan, and later the patriarch's death at Machpelah (Acts 7:2–8, 16). Stephen uses Abraham's pilgrimage as typology: repeated patterns of rejection, promise, and divine presence anticipate Israel's exodus and resistance to temple authority. He likens the patriarch's sojourn in a foreign land to

Israel's sojourn in Egypt under oppression (Acts 7:6). Stephen's narrative culminates in Abraham's purchase of Machpelah, juxtaposed with Israel's rejection of Solomon's temple—the true and the false covenant spaces (Acts 7:47–50). He cites Abraham's separation from idolatrous relatives as call for Israel to "get away from this people and I will send you" (Acts 7:4), echoing patriarchal separation motif. Stephen's invocation of the patriarch challenges his hearers: Abraham himself was a prophetic outsider before founding the covenant community. His use of Genesis history indicts present generation for resisting the Righteous One they longed for. Stephen's defense weaves together Abrahamic memory, Mosaic typology, and messianic expectation, exposing Israel's pattern of rejecting God's deliverers. His sermon culminates in accusing his listeners of betraying and murdering the Righteous One, aligning them with their ancestral hostility to holy messengers. The account underscores that apostolic interpretation of Abraham casts him as prototype for church mission beyond ethnic boundaries. Stephen's martyrdom then enacts Abrahamic trajectory of suffering and vindication. His speech sets stage for Paul's missionary approach in Gentile cities.

11.3.3 Paul in Pisidian Antioch: Justification by Faith before the Law (Acts 13)

In Pisidian Antioch's synagogue, Paul preaches a message grounded in Abraham's call: "The God of this people of Israel chose our fathers and exalted the people… about the time of Abraham, even when he was in Mesopotamia" (Acts 13:17–18). He recounts Israel's judges, Samuel, and Saul, then shifts to David, whose offspring would bring blessing to Israel (Acts 13:22–23). Paul then boldly declares that Jesus's resurrection fulfilled God's promise to Abraham: "through him everyone who believes is blessed" (Acts 13:39–40), quoting Genesis 12:3. By placing justification by faith before the Mosaic Law era, Paul shows that Abrahamian faith precedes and exceeds legal observance. He argues that descendants

315

of Abraham inherit promise not by law but by faith in Christ's resurrection, opening covenant blessing to Gentiles. Paul's sermon cites Habakkuk's "just shall live by faith," tying prophetic and patriarchal faith traditions. The synagogue context allowed him to leverage Jewish Scriptures while extending invitation to all listeners. Opposition from Jewish leaders led Paul to turn to Gentiles, illustrating shift in mission scope originally promised in Abraham's seed promise. Paul's use of Abraham affirms covenant continuity even as he transforms its application toward global inclusion. His sermon highlights key elements of Abraham's story: calling, separation, promise, faith, fulfillment. By centering Abraham, Paul anchors the new movement in authentic covenant heritage while transcending ethnic limits. The Antioch message thus becomes blueprint for Pauline theology throughout the Gentile world.

From foundational sermons in Acts, we turn to Paul's epistles where he develops Abraham's prototype of faith into systematic theology of justification and inheritance.

11.4 Pauline Theology I—Justification and the Faith Prototype

11.4.1 Romans 4: Credited Righteousness and the Timing of Circumcision

In Romans 4, Paul teaches that Abraham's righteousness was "credited to him as righteousness" before circumcision (Rom 4:10–12), demonstrating that justification by faith predates any legal rite. He contrasts works-based righteousness with faith-based righteousness, citing Genesis 15:6—"Abraham believed God, and it was credited to him as righteousness." By showing that Abraham was counted righteous while still uncircumcised, Paul argues that both Jews and Gentiles can be justified through faith, not law. This exegesis reframes Mosaic covenant as secondary to the foundational Abrahamic covenant. Paul emphasizes that Abraham received the

316

promise "without being circumcised," thus making him "the father of all who believe" (Rom 4:11). The logic underscores that faith, rather than ethnically marked identity, qualifies one as Abraham's seed. Paul's argument dismantles Jewish exclusivism by revealing that the patriarch's model of faith stands prior to boundary markers. The inclusion of New Testament believers in Abraham's justification inaugurates a new ecclesial identity. Paul concludes that the principle "he who works is not credited with the gift of faith" (Rom 4:4), ensuring that grace remains the basis of covenant membership. By rooting justification in Abraham's pre-law faith event, Paul establishes theology that informs all subsequent Christian doctrine. The chapter's dense argumentation lifts patriarchal biography into universal theology. Paul's Romans treatise thus secures Abraham's prototype as cornerstone of gospel proclamation.

11.4.2 Galatians 3:6–14: The Blessing of Abraham for Gentile Nations

Galatians 3 emphasizes that "those of faith are sons of Abraham" (Gal 3:7) and that the blessing promised to Abraham—a global inheritance—comes to Gentiles through faith in Christ (Gal 3:14). Paul argues that the law, given 430 years after Abraham, cannot annul his covenant; rather, the law's purpose was pedagogical until Christ came (Gal 3:19–24). He quotes Genesis 12:3 and 15:5–6 to demonstrate that the blessing was always intended for all nations, not just Israel. Paul's logic asserts that Christ redeemed believers "from the curse of the law" so that the blessing might reach the Gentiles (Gal 3:13–14). This exegesis reframes the Abrahamic covenant as Messianic covenant fulfilled in Christ's atonement. Paul addresses Judaizers directly, defending Gentile freedom from law-keeping as consistent with God's original promise. The indwelling Spirit becomes the mark of Abrahamic sons, superseding physical markers like circumcision. Galatians 3:28's "neither Jew nor Greek" encapsulates the leveling effect of faith rooted in

Abraham's prototype. Paul's use of midrashic interpretation reveals how early Christians read Genesis through Christological lens. The chapter's vision of one faith community under Abraham's blessing anticipates the church's multicultural composition. By aligning the Spirit's reception with Abrahamic promise, Paul secures continuity between patriarchal faith and new-covenant faith. Thus, Galatians 3 transforms Abraham's genealogy from ethnic lineage into spiritual kinship network.

11.4.3 Philippians 3 and 2 Corinthians 11: Boasting Lines and Spiritual Lineage

In Philippians 3, Paul renounces Jewish privileges—circumcision, heritage, law-keeping—as "loss for the sake of Christ" (Phil 3:7) and seeks to be found in Him "not having a righteousness of my own that comes from the law, but that which comes through faith in Christ"— echoing Abraham's credited righteousness (Phil 3:9). He contrasts those who insist on fleshly credentials with his own pursuit of "knowing Christ and the power of his resurrection" (Phil 3:10), positioning faith above heritage. In 2 Corinthians 11, Paul jests about "false apostles... deceitful workmen" who seek to boast in Abrahamic lineage; he counters by boasting only in his weaknesses and the cross (2 Cor 11:13 ff.). He affirms his right to be Abraham's seed yet chooses humility as spiritual lineage mark (2 Cor 11:22–23). These passages show that Paul's apostolic identity rests on participation in Abraham's faith rather than on Jewish pedigree. By redefining boasting, Paul invites believers to emulate Abraham's focus on God's promise over human accolades. The spiritual lineage he promotes values faith-driven encounter with Christ over genealogical charts. Paul's rhetoric draws on Abraham's struggle with celestial promises rather than on earthly parentage. These epistles thus refine Abraham's prototype into posture of self-emptying love and trust in risen Lord. The result is a spiritual aristocracy of faith echoing the patriarch's priority: belief triumphs over bloodline. Paul thereby models apostolic interpretation of Abraham for church life.

Having surveyed Paul's foundational theology of Abrahamic faith, we now explore his further reflections on seed, promise, and eschatological inheritance in the letters to Gentile churches.

11.5 Pauline Theology II—Seed, Promise, and Eschatological Inheritance

11.5.1 Singular versus Plural Seed: Midrashic Reading in Galatians 3:16

Paul argues that the promise "to your seed" in Genesis 12:7 and 22:18 uses *sperma* in the singular, indicating Christ rather than Abraham's many descendants. By this linguistic nuance, he establishes that all who belong to Christ participate in the singular seed's blessing. This midrashic move elevates Jesus above tribal progeny, transforming covenant promise into Christ-centered fulfillment. Paul's argument implies that Gentile believers, though outside physical Israel, share in Abraham's promise by virtue of union with Christ. He cites Abraham's singular seed to show that circumcision and law-keeping are secondary to faith in the Messiah. The interpretive method reflects Jewish exegetical practices— reading close attention to Hebrew grammar in Greek translation. Paul thus insists that God's ultimate intention was not merely ethnic multiplication but messianic culmination. The singular-seed reading frees churches from exclusive reliance on ancestral descent. It reframes covenant identity around participation in Christ's life, death, and resurrection. Paul's appeal to promise grammar underscores that spiritual ancestry supersedes biological lineage. This argument prepares readers for the next section on adoption: receiving Spirit-given sonship is participation in the singular seed. The midrashic reading of Genesis 3:16 becomes cornerstone for constructing universal gospel. Paul's citation of Scripture thus

319

exemplifies apostolic interpretation: honoring text's precision while unlocking fresh theological vistas.

11.5.2 Adoption Motif: Spirit of Sonship Crying "Abba, Father" (Rom 8:14–17)

In Romans 8, Paul explains that believers are "led by the Spirit of God" and since "you are sons, God has sent the Spirit of his Son into our hearts, crying, 'Abba! Father!'" (Rom 8:14–15). This adoption motif portrays Christian identity as direct heirship in God's family, fulfilling the promise to Abraham of becoming a father of many nations. The Spirit's work transforms believers' status: no longer slaves but children with full inheritance rights. "Abba" is an intimate Aramaic term, reflecting Jesus's own address to the Father and resonating with Hagar's lament in Aramaic at Beer-lahai-roi (Gen 16:13). Paul's contrast of spirit-led children and law-led slaves echoes Abraham's own call to walk by faith, not by works. By adopting Gentiles into Abraham's family, the church becomes living fulfillment of Genesis 17:5—"Your name shall no longer be Abram... but Abraham, for I have made you the father of many nations." The adoption theme underscores that covenant membership depends on Spirit, not on ethnic marker or Torah obedience. Paul links present sufferings with future glory, assuring that children of God will share in Christ's inheritance and resurrection (Rom 8:17–18). The imagery of joint-heirs with Christ roots believer hope in patriarchal promise. This theology reframes Abraham's promise in eschatological dimension: the "world" promised to Abraham (Rom 4:13) becomes the cosmos redeemed in Christ. The Spirit's cry "Abba" invites believers into the personal trust that characterized Abraham's relationship with Yahweh. Thus, adoption motif extends singular-seed promise into relational reality, making believers heirs of Abraham's faith pattern. The section closes by anticipating cosmic scope of inheritance explored next.

11.5.3 New Creation Geography: "Heir of the World" and Cosmic Scope (Rom 4:13)

Paul reiterates that the promise to Abraham—"heir of the world"—transcends local land allotments to embrace the entire cosmos (Rom 4:13). By citing that promise in Romans 4:13, Paul expands Abraham's land inheritance from the Jordan Valley to the new heavens and new earth inaugurated in Christ. This eschatological geography positions believers as citizens of a restored creation rather than subjects of impermanent political entities. The world-heir motif amplifies the missional thrust of Genesis 12:3—blessing extends globally, not just to tribes. Paul's visionary horizon matches prophetic oracles of Gentiles streaming to Zion (Isa 2:2), situating church mission as participation in cosmic pilgrimage. The "world" promised includes Gentile nations historically excluded from Abrahamic covenant, now invited into restoration. This reinterpretation dissolves geographical barriers: baptism unites believers across continents as heirs of the world. Paul's cosmic promise alleviates existential anxieties rooted in exile or diaspora, offering full participation in God's future domain. The New Creation geography also underpins ethical vision: stewardship of earth as preparation for inheritance. Paul's teaching in 1 Cor 15:46–49 echoes new creation identity, linking physical resurrection to Abrahamic hope. In Ephesians 1:10, the gathering of all things in Christ fulfills cosmic reconciliation originally promised to Abraham. Thus, the world-heir promise shapes believers' worldview and cross-cultural engagement. Paul's eschatological scope invites church to live out Abrahamic hospitality on planetary scale. Having explored Pauline perspectives, we now turn to Hebrews' unique theological synthesis of faith, priesthood, and covenant.

With Pauline theology mapping the contours of Abrahamic inheritance, the Letter to the Hebrews reframes the patriarch's faith under the lens of faithfulness, priesthood, and a superior covenant.

11.6 Hebrews—Faith, Priesthood, and Better Covenant

11.6.1 Hebrews 11:8-19: Pilgrim Faith Seeking a Better Country

Hebrews 11 recounts Abraham's faith journey: leaving home without knowing his destination, dwelling in tents as a foreigner in promised land, and looking forward to the city with foundations designed by God (Heb 11:8–10). The chapter highlights faith as conviction of unseen realities: Abraham believed God's promise when circumstances offered no evidence. His pilgrimage became template: believers become spiritual nomads, living by promise rather than possession. The reference to Sarah receiving power to conceive "though she was past the age" (Heb 11:11) parallels faith's triumph over natural impossibilities. By linking Abraham's faith to resurrection motif—"consider him who died" yet still received children—Hebrews foreshadows New Testament resurrection hope (Heb 11:19). The chapter presents faith as confidence in God's character rather than in external signs, teaching that covenant fulfillment may outlast lifetime yet still demands trust. Abraham's construction of altars by faith underscores worship as inseparable from faith in future realities. His sojourning in "foreign land" anticipates church's migrant identity awaiting heavenly city (Heb 13:14). The author weaves Abraham's narrative into broader cloud of witnesses, urging readers to emulate his endurance. The passage underscores that faith is action—obedience to call, altar-building, covenant obedience before evidence. Hebrews positions Abraham's faith as foundational symposium for covenant community. The portrait of faith in Hebrews thus draws directly from patriarchal life, transmuting it into archetype for New Covenant pilgrimage. The section's conclusion naturally leads to exploration of Melchizedek's role in Hebrews' theology.

11.6.2 Melchizedek Revisited: Eternal Priesthood and Perfect Intercession (Heb 7)

Hebrews 7 deepens Melchizedek typology: his lack of recorded genealogy and perpetual priesthood prefigure Christ's eternal intercession (Heb 7:3). The author contrasts Melchizedek's order with Aaronic line: one is imperfect and inherited, the other is perfect and appointed by oath. Melchizedek's blessing of Abram (Gen 14:18–20) becomes foreshadowing of Christ's blessing of humanity. Abraham's tithe to Melchizedek is cited to demonstrate that Levitical priests exist within Melchizedek's order, pointing to greater priesthood to come. The oath "You are priest forever after the order of Melchizedek" (Ps 110:4) is applied hermeneutically to Jesus, establishing His unchangeable intercession. Hebrews teaches that Christ's singular sacrifice eliminates need for repetitive animal offerings characteristic of Levitical system (Heb 7:27). The perfect priesthood secures eternal covenant better than the Mosaic covenant that needed continual renewal. Melchizedek's dual office—king of peace and priest of Most High—embodies unity of rule and worship, realized in Christ. Hebrews invites readers to ascend with Jesus into heavenly sanctuary, echoing Abraham's ascent up Moriah. The author's argument reassures believers that their access to God rests on Christ's unique priesthood, not human mediation. By revisiting Melchizedek, Hebrews weaves Abraham's story into high theology of atonement and intercession.

11.6.3 Mount Moriah and Calvary: Typology of Sacrifice and Resurrection Hopes

Hebrews 11:17–19 interprets Abraham's near-sacrifice of Isaac on Mount Moriah as anticipation of resurrection: Abraham "considered that God was able to raise him up" (Heb 11:19), paralleling Christ's death and resurrection on the same mountain range. The letter then draws connections between Ram in the Thicket and Christ as substitutionary offering (implicit, Heb 10:5–10). Mount Moriah, later site of Solomon's temple and Jesus's crucifixion, becomes convergence point of Abrahamic and Christic sacrifice. Hebrews emphasizes single, sufficient sacrifice replacing repeated Mosaic offerings (Heb 10:12). The author exhorts believers to "draw near with a true heart" in full assurance of faith, trusting the promised aftermath of resurrection (Heb 10:19–23). The typology recasts Isaac's "released" status as prototype for Son's victory over death. By linking patriarchal event to Calvary, Hebrews situates Abraham's legacy at center of redemptive drama. The author's rhetoric shows that the fulfillment of Abraham's faith occurs not only in promised seed but in suffering-unto-glory pattern. This typological reading underscores that church's faith involves both obedience under trial and confident expectation of God's vindication. Thus Mount Moriah's story becomes eternal paradigm for covenant faithfulness and hope.

Having seen Hebrews weave Abraham's faith and Melchizedek typology into theological summit, we turn to Johannine Christology where Jacob's ladder vision is recast in light of the Son of Man.

11.7 Jacob's Ladder Reimagined—Johannine Christology

11.7.1 John 1:51: Son of Man as True Bethel

In John 1:51, Jesus tells Nathanael, "You will see heaven opened, and the angels of God ascending and descending on the Son of Man," invoking Jacob's ladder vision (Gen 28:12–13). This reimagining positions Jesus Himself as the living bridge between heaven and earth, surpassing the static stone pillar. Nathanael's initial skepticism gives way to confession of Jesus as "Son of God" (John 1:49), unveiling Christ's divine through patriarchal typology. Jesus's use of "Son of Man" echoes prophetic imagery in Daniel 7:13 and identifies Him as heavenly figure. The Johannine narrative thus transforms Bethel—"house of God"—into incarnate reality in Christ. The ascending and descending angels signify continual divine-human interaction centered on Jesus's person and work. This scene establishes Johannine theme of Jesus as the unique revelation of God's glory (John 1:14). It synthesizes patriarchal memory with eschatological unveiling. The use of ladder motif invites readers to see Jesus as sole access point to divine presence. It reframes altar and pillar symbols into relational encounter. By echoing Jacob's dream, John draws careful link between Old Testament promise and New Testament revelation. The narrative then flows into public dialogues that further unpack Christ's mediatory role.

11.7.2 Living Water and Abraham's Wells: John 4 Samaritan Dialogue

At Jacob's well in Sychar, Jesus offers the Samaritan woman "living water," referencing Abraham's and Isaac's wells dug in Canaan (Gen 21:25–31; Isa 12:3). The Samaritan woman's astonishment— "You have nothing to draw with, and the well is deep" (John 4:11)— mirrors patriarchal well-digging labor, yet Jesus's spiritual well springs eternally. The dialogue reclaims patriarchal water symbolism: physical thirst fulfilled by temporary well; spiritual thirst quenched by the Messiah. Jesus's revelation that He "will become in him a spring of water welling up to eternal life" (John 4:14) recasts patriarchal hospitality into universal salvation offer. The woman's testimony brings many Samaritans to faith, illustrating covenant inclusion beyond Israel—echoing Rahab's faith in Joshua's time. The encounter at Jacob's well bridges ethnic divisions, realizing Abrahamic blessing to all families. The well's historical significance as Hagar's spring and Isaac's site for treaty informs the text's layered meaning. John's narrative shows that Jesus, like Abraham, initiates conversations at wells to reveal divine character. The water theme flows on to Pentecost's Spirit-outpouring in Acts 2, fulfilling living water promise across ecclesial life. This dialogue thus becomes model for mission: engage locals at cultural landmarks, offer deeper hope, catalyze community transformation. Jesus's living water transcends geological wells, becoming central sacramental motif in Johannine theology. The Samaritan well scene transitions naturally to themes of light and festival in John's Gospel.

11.7.3 Feast of Tabernacles Light: Torch-Pot Fulfillment in Jesus

During Feast of Tabernacles, Jesus proclaims, "I am the light of the world" (John 8:12), echoing festival's water-libation torch ceremonies that illuminated Jerusalem at night. Festival pilgrims carried torches from the Pool of Siloam to the temple, recalling Abraham's smoking pot covenant sign (Gen 15:17) that symbolized divine presence. Jesus's claim transforms torch ritual from subsidiary spectacle to existential truth: His person embodies God's guiding fire. The light theme resonates with pillar of fire leading Israel and with Melchizedek's bread and wine liturgy. During the midway in the festival, Jesus stands and declares His illumination role to the assembled pilgrims, bridging ancient covenant signs with New Covenant revelation. The Festival's call to water and light commemorates wilderness dependence and patriarchal altar worship, now fulfilled in Christ's life-giving presence (John 7:37–39). The illuminating function of Messiah echoes Abraham's call to expose darkness of idolatry. John's community would recall this festival event when baptizing gentiles by night under baptismal lights. The light motif then flows into chapters on signs, healing, and resurrection, all interpreted as manifestations of the true Light. Jesus thus re-appropriates tabernacle festal symbols, reframing them around His identity as the incarnate Word. The narrative moves next to the Bread of Life discourse, deepening sacramental imagery rooted in Melchizedek's table.

Having explored Johannine reframing of Abrahamic symbols, we now turn to the Catholic epistles, where patriarchal models inform ethical teaching on faith and works.

11.8 Catholic Epistles—Faith and Works in Jamesean Balance

11.8.1 James 2:21-24: Akedah as Evidence of Justifying Works

James points to Abraham's willingness to sacrifice Isaac—*the Akedah*—as demonstration that faith without works is dead (James 2:21–24). By referencing Genesis 22, James contends that Abraham's faith was perfected by his obedient action, making him "a friend of God" (James 2:23). The sacrificial obedience serves as prime example: belief alone is insufficient without tangible obedience. James's use of *dikaióō* (justify) with works parallels Paul's *dikaiósis* (justification), yet James emphasizes that righteous standing manifests in obedient deeds. Abraham's offering is "evidence" to the world that faith is authentic, countering professed faith that lacks transformative action. The argument draws on patriarchal story as authoritative scriptural proof, reflecting earliest Christian hermeneutic. James balances rhetorical force with pastoral urgency: readers are exhorted to produce works that correspond to faith. The text links Abraham's deed to faith-practice integrated theology, shaping ethical frameworks in church communities. This epistolary instruction roots believer identity in both belief and consequent obedience, modeled perfectly by Abraham. James's emphasis complements Pauline doctrine by showing that faith's root cannot remain unexpressed. The Akedah thus becomes perennial ethical archetype within faith communities. Having emphasized works' role, James transitions to instructing Christian households, including patterns drawn from Sarah.

11.8.2 1 Peter 3:5-6: Sarah's Submission as Daughterhood Pattern

Peter cites Sarah's respectful submission to Abraham as an example for Christian wives: "in the same way, Sarah obeyed Abraham, calling him lord" (1 Pet 3:5–6). By invoking Genesis 18—where Sarah laughs at promise yet later exercises faith—Peter frames submission as faith-infused trust rather than mere patriarchy. He highlights that Sarah's calling Abraham "lord" exemplifies awareness of God-ordained husbandly authority, yet does not negate her honored status as matriarch. Peter's household code integrates patriarchal narrative into Christian domestic ethics, showing that covenant fidelity begins in homes. The reference to Sarah's blessing—"you are her children if you do good and do not fear anything frightening" (1 Pet 3:6)—signals that Abrahamic blessing extends to obedient descendants. Peter uses Sarah's story to reassure women facing persecution that respectful behavior can testify to God's grace. The instruction balances submission with active virtue—"do good"—mirroring Abraham's combination of faith and works. Christian marriage thus becomes domain where covenant models are lived out. Peter's subtle allusion to Sarah's initial doubt ensures pastoral sensitivity: submission is characterized by trust, not blind obedience. This guidance situates Sarah in line of spiritual daughters, integrating female patriarchal example into New Testament ethics. The passage transitions naturally to Jude's warning from Lot's borderland experiences.

11.8.3 Jude 5-7 and Lot: Warnings from the Patriarchal Periphery

Jude references Lot's rescue from Sodom, noting "he was righteous and lived among them day after day… yet that righteous man… tormented his righteous soul" (Jude 5–7). By recalling Abraham's nephew, Jude warns the church against persistent moral compromise within corrupt cultures. Lot's story becomes cautionary parable: proximity to wickedness afflicts the faithful, requiring vigilance. Jude contrasts Sodom's fate with his own audience's call to contend for the faith once for all delivered to the saints (Jude 3). The epistle uses Lot's borderline status—living under the shadow of Sodom—to alert believers to the dangers of half-hearted obedience. Jude's appeal to Genesis narrative leverages ancestral example to enforce doctrinal purity and ethical separation. He invokes "eternal fire" reserved for ungodly, echoing Genesis 19's sulfurous judgment. The patriarchal reference functions as swift corrective: even a righteous man can suffer from association with lawlessness. Jude's admonition commends Lot's rescue as hope, yet laments his ongoing trauma—a mirror to church's call to maintain holiness. The passage underscores that covenant promises require decisive withdrawal from corrupt influences. This final ethical application of Abrahamic lineage grounds New Testament admonitions in foundational narratives, linking first covenant contexts to church discipline. Jude's epistle thus completes apostolic interpretation of Abrahamic models for both doctrine and moral exhortation, paving way toward vision of ultimate sacrifice in Chapter 11.10.

With Catholic epistles balancing faith and works through patriarchal examples, we now examine how Abrahamic hospitality and ethics inform early church communal life.

11.9 Hospitality and Ethics—Abrahamic Virtues in Early Church Life

11.9.1 Hebrews 13:2: Entertaining Angels Unaware

Hebrews 13:2 exhorts believers, "Do not neglect to show hospitality to strangers, for thereby some have entertained angels unawares," directly echoing Abraham's reception of heavenly visitors under the oaks of Mamre (Gen 18:1–8). The letter's audience, likely facing persecution, is reminded that hospitality functions as ministry not only to fellow humans but potentially to divine messengers. The contrast between formal worship gatherings and informal household welcome suggests that covenant faith extends beyond temple walls into everyday life. In Abraham's case, bread and curds accompanied by olive oil and water became sacramental elements of divine encounter, setting precedent for simple acts of kindness. Early Christians practiced house churches where meals—often including the "love feast"—embodied this pattern of open-door welcome. Patristic writings record stories of angelic visitations among hermits, reinforcing Hebrews' principle through monastic tradition. Missionaries crossing cultures carried only tents and hospitality manuals, trusting that Abrahamic virtue would open doors in foreign lands. The admonition situates hospitality as theology in action, where honoring the stranger becomes honoring God's emissaries. The ethical demand transcends social status: rich and poor, Jew and Gentile alike called to cultivate open tables. In Mediterranean society, where guest-right protected travelers, church leaders reclaimed the ancient code to evangelistic ends. The subversion of xenophobia through hospitality reflects Abraham's willingness to interrupt his own peace for guests' sake. Hebrews' single verse thus encapsulates a lifetime of Abrahamic teaching, re-oriented toward Christ-centered community. The transition from temple incense to household welcome signals that true worship includes care for vulnerable outsiders. This hospitality ethic prepares readers to consider leadership qualifications rooted in open-tent values.

11.9.2 Romans 12:13 and 1 Timothy 3:2: Elder Qualifications Rooted in Open Tents

Romans 12:13 commands believers to "contribute to the needs of the saints and seek to show hospitality," while 1 Timothy 3:2 lists "able to teach, hospitable, … upright, holy, self-controlled" as prerequisites for overseers. Paul's integration of hospitality into character qualifications connects ecclesial leadership to Abrahamic virtues, indicating that volunteerism and meal-sharing remain core to church health. In Greco-Roman culture, hospitality was reciprocal, yet Christian hospitality transcended patronage systems by offering care without expectation of repayment. Leaders, modeled on Abraham's tent hosting of diverse groups—royal envoys, herdsmen, angels—were expected to create safe spaces for spiritual formation. The requirement for overseers to be hospitable anticipates house-church structures where instruction, sacrament, and fellowship occur in private homes. Church orders from Didache onwards codify hospitality as diaconal ministry, reflecting Abraham's delegation of servant-stewards to manage resources for guests. This emphasis on hospitality also provided remedy for marginalized groups: widows, orphans, and itinerant preachers found sustenance under Christian roofs. 1 Timothy's linkage of teaching ability with hospitality suggests that proclamation and provision are inseparable. Quaker and monastic hospitality traditions later embody these principles, offering refuge and sustenance to strangers. The democratization of hosting ministries underscores that every believer can practice Abrahamic hospitality, not only professional clergy. Practical guidelines—such as hospitality without grumbling (1 Pet 4:9)—flow from patriarchal model of joyful service. By embedding hospitality among elder qualifications, the New Testament ensures continuity from Genesis narratives to church governance. The ethic transitions naturally into broader missional strategy of cross-cultural hospitality.

11.9.3 Love of Strangers as Missional Strategy in a Gentile World

Peter writes in 1 Peter 2:11–12 that sojourners should abstain from sinful desires and maintain honorable conduct "among the Gentiles, that when they speak against you as evildoers, they may see your good deeds and glorify God." This strategy mirrors Abraham's witness in Gerar and among Canaanites, where his distinctive ethics attracted pagan kings to acknowledge Yahweh. The early church, operating within the Roman Empire's pluralistic culture, adopted hospitality as missional entry point: banquets, agape feasts, and funerary dinners offered avenues for gospel conversation. Tertullian and Justin Martyr record debates held after shared meals, demonstrating how open-table ministries facilitated apologetics. In

Corinth, Paul's guidance on eating meat offered to idols (1 Cor 8–10) balances hospitality with conscience, showing nuanced application of Abrahamic principles in multi-religious settings. The church's care for strangers—refugees, imprisoned Christians, shipwrecked Paul—echoes Abraham's cross-desert rescues. This love challenges cultural norms of exclusivism, modeling a community that welcomes strangers as potential heirs of promise. In medieval Christendom, monasteries served as official guesthouses, institutionalizing hospitality on national scale. Mission societies rediscovered Abrahamic hospitality by sponsoring host families for missionaries. Modern urban parishes revive hospitality teams to integrate newcomers and outsiders. This ongoing tradition underscores that missional efficacy depends less on rhetorical skill than on warm welcome and tangible care. Love of strangers thus becomes strategic front in gospel advance, fulfilling Abraham's mandate to bless all families. From private homes to global partnerships, Abrahamic hospitality remains foundational for church mission.

As hospitality models prepare the church for sacrificial mission, we now consider how Abraham's offering of Isaac prefigures the ultimate sacrifice on Mount Moriah.

11.10 Mount Moriah to Golgotha—Sacrificial Foreshadowings

11.10.1 Genesis 22 and John 3:16: Only-Son Motif Transposed

In Genesis 22, Abraham's readiness to sacrifice Isaac on Mount Moriah exemplifies faith at its most extreme, yet God provides a ram in the thicket as substitute. John 3:16 transposes this only-son motif: "For God so loved the world, that He gave His only Son, that whoever believes…" Here, Isaac's near-sacrifice becomes archetype for Christ's actual sacrifice. Both narratives center on love and obedience: Abraham obeys God's command, and the Father sends the Son in obedience to divine will. Mount Moriah, later site of Solomon's temple, becomes landscape of substitutionary atonement, culminating in Golgotha—"the place of the skull." New Testament writers draw on this typology: Hebrews 11:17-19 sees Abraham's faith anticipating resurrection power, while 1 Peter 1:19–20 sees Christ as the "unblemished lamb foreordained before the foundation of the world." The parallel emphasizes voluntary offering, distinguishing Abrahamic test from divine plan of redemption. Early hymnody, like the "Mulier fortis," celebrates this linkage in song. Church Fathers, including Augustine and Chrysostom, expounded this typology in sermons, urging faithful participation in Christ's self-offering. Renaissance art scenes of the Akedah and crucifixion often paired visually to reinforce this theological bridge. John 3:16 thus rests upon Abrahamic narrative, showing that God's giving of the Son surpasses human trials. This pattern establishes core of soteriology: substitution, resurrection, and eternal promise.

11.10.2 Ram in the Thicket, Crown of Thorns: Substitutionary Imagery

The ram provided by God in place of Isaac becomes enduring symbol of substitutionary atonement. New Testament allusions to Christ as "Lamb of God" (John 1:29) evoke that Bronze-Age rescue. On Calvary, a crown of thorns replaces ram's horns, turning the royal mockery into redemptive sign. The thicket imagery implies entanglement of sin that the Lamb bears on behalf of humanity. Early liturgists used ram's blood in penitential rites, foreshadowing Eucharistic wine as Christ's blood. Icons and mosaics depict ram and cross side by side, teaching substitution visually. Paul's description of Christ as offering "Himself without blemish to God" (Eph 5:2) echoes requirement of unblemished sacrificial animal (Lev 22:20). Revelation 13:8 calls Christ "the Lamb slain from the foundation of the world," rooting atonement in divine forethought reminiscent of Abraham's trial. The crown of thorns thus becomes new thicket, where Lamb's passage through suffering yields redemption. Liturgical Good Friday services often reference both Akedah and passion narratives. This substitutionary imagery invites worshippers to unite with both Abraham's faith and Christ's mercy. The theological continuity between ram and thorns underscores God's single plan of salvation across covenants.

11.10.3 Resurrection Hints: "Figuratively Speaking, He Did Receive Him Back" (Heb 11:19)

Hebrews 11:19 observes that Abraham "considered that God was able even to raise him [Isaac] from the dead, from which, figuratively speaking, he did receive him back." This "figurative" resurrection prefigures Christ's actual rising, confirming divine power over death. The narrative clarity of two resurrections—Isaac's symbolic and Jesus's literal—demonstrates progressive revelation of God's saving acts. Peter's sermon in Acts 2 applies this power to Jesus's resurrection, proclaiming "God raised Him up" (Acts 2:24) to validate Messiah's identity. The figurative-real pattern affirms that typological events anticipate fuller fulfillment. 1 Corinthians 15:17-20 places Christ's resurrection as basis of believers' future hope, grounding it in Abraham's preliminary glimpse. The dual references shape New Covenant understanding of life-after-death. The symbolic return of Isaac signals covenant continuity, while Christ's return inaugurates eschatological inheritance. Church fathers linked Abraham's willingness to sacrifice Isaac with his reception of Isaac at typological resurrection iconography. Modern preachers use this passage to illustrate faith's confidence in God's power to bring life from seeming loss. The figurative resurrection thus bridges Genesis 22 to Easter joy, uniting Abrahamic faith and Christian hope.

With sacrifice and resurrection typologies affirming Christ's fulfillment of Abrahamic patterns, the New Testament culminates in vision of New Jerusalem—a reinvisioned land promise bearing patriarchal names.

11.11 New Jerusalem—Reframing the Land Promise

11.11.1 Revelation 21:12-14: Twelve Gates Bearing Patriarchal Names

Revelation 21:12-14 describes the New Jerusalem with twelve gates, each inscribed with one of the twelve tribes of Israel—including patriarchal names like Judah and Benjamin—while the city's foundation bears twelve apostles' names. This eschatological city merges Abrahamic tribal identity with apostolic witness, symbolizing unity of Old and New Covenants. Each gate's name functions as testament to God's faithfulness to Abraham's descendants, while foundations honor those who bear Christ's message to the nations. The city's design—square, massive, radiant—echoes promises of land boundaries given to Abraham and later to Israel (Gen 15:18; Ezek 48). No temple stands in the city; God's presence illuminates everything, surpassing patriarchal altar shadows. Pilgrims from every nation pass through tribal gates, fulfilling Genesis 12:3's vision of global blessing. Early Christian art depicts city gates with palm-frond motifs, recalling both tribal banners and festival palms. The cosmic city thus becomes final fulfillment of covenant territory—land unbounded by geography, accessible to all heirs of Abrahamic promise. Revelation's vision reframes inheritance from parcelled plots to communal presence around God's throne. This final city, descending from heaven, restores what Abraham first glimpsed when he pitched tent toward Moriah's mountain. The blending of patriarchal and apostolic names emphasizes continuity of faith community across ages. The Revelation text invites readers to envision their names inscribed among tribes and apostles—a dual heritage rooted in Abraham and sealed in Christ.

11.11.2 Hebrews 12:22: Mount Zion as Heavenly Homeland

Hebrews 12:22 shifts readers from Sinai's fearsome smoke to "mount Zion and the city of the living God, the heavenly Jerusalem," contrasting the law-giving mountain with the city founded on covenant faith. Mount Zion, where Abraham's descendants camped and Jacob's ladder vision pointed, becomes spiritual homeland more lasting than Canaan itself. The heavenly Jerusalem invites pilgrims to approach the "assembly of the firstborn... whose names are written in heaven" (Heb 12:23), linking life of faith to eternal inheritance. The letter's movement from Old Covenant terror to New Covenant joy underscores transformational power of Christ's priesthood. The city's mixed multitude—saints and angels—reprises Abraham's associations with Melchizedek and worldwide blessing. The vision reshapes land promise into dynamic spiritual reality, accessible through faith and sacrifice fulfilled in Christ. Believers are exhorted to "offer to God acceptable worship, with reverence and awe" (Heb 12:28), echoing patriarchal altar reverence. Mount Zion thus becomes terminus of Abraham's pilgrimage, now located in heavenly realm. The writer's emphasis on peace and holiness invites church to embody Abrahamic virtues while anticipating celestial settlement. This heavenly mountain contrasts with earthly inheritances, revealing ultimate geography promised to Abraham's seed. Hebrews' city imagery becomes liturgical horizon for New Testament faith communities.

11.11.3 "Better Country" and Eschatological Rest for the People of God

Hebrews 11:16 and 12:24 affirm that Abraham and his descendants sought "a better country, that is, a heavenly one" and have "come to Mount Zion... to the spirits of the righteous made perfect." The phrase "better country" reframes Abraham's Canaan hope into eschatological rest beyond death. The promised land's boundaries expand into infinite dimensions, offering rest from struggle and conflict. Early Christian worship included chants of Zion pilgrimage—"Guide us, O thou Great Jehovah"—transferring

336

physical journeying to spiritual ascent. The concept of rest recalls Sabbath themes inherent in Abraham's tent-dwelling rhythm, now fulfilled in eternal Sabbath rest (Heb 4:9–10). Augustine later identified this heavenly city as ultimate "City of God" distinct from earthly Babylon. Monastic practices of desert withdrawal reinterpreted earthly exile as preparation for heavenly homeland. The "better country" thus operates as ethical magnet: believers live as exiles here, modeling covenant ethics in hope of final inheritance. The eschatological rest emphasizes that Abraham's faith was always forward-looking, trusting promises unseen. Revelation 14:1 depicts the Lamb standing on Mount Zion with the 144,000, connecting Abraham's motif to final worship. The culmination of land promise in heavenly rest ensures that Abrahamic legacy drives New Testament vision of ultimate destiny. This eschatological perspective transitions the reader toward consideration of Abraham's ongoing influence in church history after the apostles.

Conclusion As the New Testament weaves Abraham into its tapestry, he transcends his Bronze Age origins to become the father of all who believe, Jew and Gentile alike. His seed—now singular in Christ—expands from Canaan's hills to the ends of the earth, carried on the wings of apostolic preaching, Pauline theology, and the vision of the eternal city. Abraham's faith, once tested by the stars and by the ram on Moriah, now finds its fullest expression in resurrection power, priestly intercession, and the new creation inaugurated at Calvary. In Jesus, the promises made to Abraham take on cosmic dimensions, inviting every generation to share in the blessing that began with one obedient wanderer's simple call to trust.

Chapter 12 – Father of Faith for Today: Impact on Contemporary Believers

Across four millennia of shifting cultures, Abraham still steps out of Scripture to stand beside every person who wonders whether God can be trusted with an unknown tomorrow. His weather-worn journey from Ur through droughts, deserts, and dizzying promises offers more than ancient biography; it hands modern disciples a portable pattern for courage, hospitality, and hope. Wherever believers must exchange security for obedience—whether by changing cities, stretching open their dining tables, or holding steady in science laboratories ablaze with new discoveries—the patriarch's story supplies imaginative fuel. He shows that faith is neither naïve optimism nor stoic grit but a long apprenticeship in listening, relocating, and blessing the world in practical ways. This chapter explores how Abraham's footprints reappear on twenty-first-century roads: in families shaping future generations, in churches wrestling with justice, in entrepreneurs dreaming ethically, and in pilgrims who meet God amid city skylines as surely as beneath desert stars.

12.1 Personal Discipleship—Walking into the Unknown

12.1.1 Leaving "Ur" Moments: Vocation Shifts and Risk-Taking Faith

Abram's call to leave Ur (Gen 12:1) invites believers to identify their own "Ur" moments—careers, communities, or plans that feel secure yet hinder obedience. In contemporary contexts this may mean changing professions to follow a ministry conviction, uprooting families for cross-cultural work, or investing time in volunteer service rather than leisure. Like Abram, modern disciples often hear a voice urging departure before a clear destination appears. The decision involves weighing relational costs, financial uncertainty, and cultural dislocation. Yet Abram's example shows that faith-filled obedience precedes full information—God supplies direction as we go. Christians facing vocal calls to new vocations can draw courage from Abram's trust in promise over present comfort. Business executives have left corporate ladders to start nonprofit ventures, memorializing their own Ur departures. Seminary students relocating for internships or missionaries signing long-term commitment share Abram's posture. Each vocation shift—whether to teach in inner cities, plant a church in a new neighborhood, or launch a justice initiative—echoes Abram's initial pilgrimage. Risk-taking faith requires supportive community: Abram traveled with family and servants, reminding believers not to go alone. Mentors play roles akin to Abram's experience with God's guiding presence—working through counsel, prayer, and Scripture. Hearing God's call demands silence and stillness, yet action follows quickly once direction emerges. Faith risks thus become vocational liturgy: living testimonials to God's leading rather than human

339

planning. Abram's "Ur moment" transitions into rhythms of obedience that prepare disciples for deeper disciplines of prayer and reflection.

12.1.2 Practising Daily Altars: Rhythm of Prayer, Word, and Silence

Abram built altars at key waypoints—Shechem, Bethel, Hebron—creating sacred pauses in his journey (Gen 12:7; 13:18). In contemporary discipleship, daily altars take form through routines of prayer, Scripture reading, and contemplative silence. Morning devotions become first altar of the day, offering thanksgiving and petition. Midday breaks—brief retreats from screens—function as altar resets, realigning heart for the afternoon's demands. Evening examinations of conscience mirror Abram's altar prayers of remembrance. Digital tools can support altar building: Bible apps for word-study, guided prayer podcasts for reflection, and journal entries for recording divine encounters. Silence remains crucial: in the quiet Abram heard God's voice; believers too need uncluttered space to discern Spirit's promptings. Corporate rhythms—daily offices or small-group prayer gatherings—extend personal altars into community sanctuaries. Retreats, whether on weekends or overnight, refresh souls, echoing Abram's moments under terebinths. Practical guidelines—turning off notifications, using breath prayers, lectio divina—help cultivate altar posture. Over time these rhythms become second nature, embedding worship into everyday. The result is a life where every significant crossroad is bathed in prayer and scriptural truth, just as Abram's tents were circled by altars. Daily altars equip disciples to respond to life's surprises with grounded faith. They prepare hearts for obedience when new "Ur moments" arise, sustaining momentum from one divine encounter to the next.

12.1.3 Navigating Doubt: Trusting Promise amid Deferred Hopes

Abram's laughter at the promise of a son (Gen 17:17; 21:6) reveals the human tension between faith and doubt when years pass without visible fulfillment. Modern believers face similar deferred hopes—prayers for healing unanswered, long-term ministry fruit unseen, or vocational doors closed repeatedly. Doubt can prompt creative alternatives—Abram's Hagar episode (Gen 16)—yet these often compound complications. The better path lies in returning to the promise, as Abram did by renaming Sarah's miracle name "Isaac," laughter transformed into trust. Handling doubt requires lament—honest admission of questions before God—rather than hidden frustration. Communities of faith must provide safe spaces where doubts are aired and scripture's promises reaffirmed. Mentors and pastors can echo God's reassurance: "I am your shield; your reward is very great" (Gen 15:1). Journaling past mercies fuels confidence for future faithfulness. Celebrating small "Isaacs"—unexpected blessings, answered prayers, providential provision—counters the tyranny of delay. Theologians remind us that God's timing often exceeds human forecasts, shaping character through seasons of waiting. Abram's covenant-cutting ceremony (Gen 15) occurred before the birth of Isaac, teaching that promises can be leased to future generations before fruition. Disciples practice trust by proclaiming promises aloud, meditating on them in Scripture, and living expectantly. Over time, seasons of doubt refine rather than destroy faith, producing resilience akin to Abram's unwavering hope. Facing deferred hopes thus becomes deeper apprenticeship in God's faithfulness, preparing believers to steward generational blessings.

While individual faith journeys mirror Abram's call and altar rhythms, the next sphere of influence lies in our closest congregations—families—where covenant faith is nurtured and transmitted.

12.2 Family Formation—Parenting, Marriage, and Generational Blessing

12.2.1 Covenant Parenting: Teaching Children to Hear God's Call

Abram's fatherhood over Isaac began with teaching him the story of his near-sacrifice (Gen 22:8), imparting legacy of trust. Modern parents similarly shape young lives by sharing stories of God's provision—family testimonies of answered prayer, rescue from crises, and spiritual milestones. Family devotions centered on Abrahamic narratives help children grasp what it means to leave familiar lands at God's bidding. Rituals like reading Genesis 12 on birthdays or dramatizing Abram's journey in Vacation Bible School instill covenant identity. Parents can encourage children to journal prayers and answers, modeling how Abram recorded altar monuments. Mentor relationships—grandparents, godparents, small-group leaders—supplement parental teaching, expanding spiritual heritage. Parents practice listening prayer for children's vocations, affirming God's call in their education, career, or ministry aspirations. Family pilgrimages to local Holy Lands exhibits or heritage sites provide tangible connection to Abrahamic geography. Teaching stewardship—tithing, service projects, mission giving—transfers Abram's wealth-sharing ethic to the next generation. Emphasizing the tent metaphor—open doors and tables—trains children in hospitality as witness. Parenting through covenant lens shapes children into heirs, not renters, of God's promises. When children ask "Why?" parents answer with stories of God's faithfulness, mirroring Abram's star-counting wonder (Gen 15:5). This generational instruction fosters readiness to obey God's call, just as Isaac grew into the promise medium. Covenant parenting thus becomes primary locus for Abrahamic faith to live on.

12.2.2 Nurturing Spousal Partnership: Lessons from Abraham and Sarah

Abraham and Sarah's partnership—navigating barrenness, laughter, disagreement over Hagar, and eventual joy in Isaac—provides rich material for contemporary marriages. Couples today face similar tests of promise: infertility, career shifts, relocation pressures, and generational tensions. Listening to one another—mutual submission (Eph 5:21) rather than dominance—reflects Abraham's deference and Sarah's respect (1 Pet 3:5–6). Celebrating "Sarah laughter" milestones—first home, birth, new business—strengthens marital bond. Financial decisions, like Abraham's refusal of Sodom's plunder, require transparency and shared values. Praying together at altar times—which may be bedside devotions or weekly prayer walks—cultivates spiritual unity. When conflicts arise, spouses employ Sabbath-style pauses to de-escalate, akin to Abram's altars of reconciliation. Counseling models draw on Abrahamic themes: promise-centered vision casting rather than bitterness over past hurts. Hospitality projects—hosting young couples or refugee families—unite spouses in mission, echoing patriarchal hospitality. Pre-marital education can include study of the Abraham-Sarah story, framing marriage as covenant walk rather than contract. In mentoring relationships, older couples share wisdom from decades of covenant challenges, much as Abraham taught Ishmael's mother Hagar compassion. Celebrating covenant anniversaries with symbolic "altar stones"—personal artifacts of prayers answered—reinforces partnership legacy. Nurturing spousal partnership thus translates Abraham and Sarah's journey into daily marriage rhythms. As spouses grow together, they model divine faithfulness for their children and community.

12.2.3 Grand-Parenting the Promise: Blessing Beyond One's Lifespan

Abraham's gaze across generations—expecting nations from his seed (Gen 17:4)—mirrors the grandparent's role of imparting legacy beyond personal years. Contemporary grandparents bear unique responsibility to speak of God's faithfulness in family history, retelling how parents and grandparents navigated faith crises. Blessing ceremonies—laying on of hands, spoken affirmations at graduations and weddings—extend Abraham's benediction practice (Gen 27:27–29) to new generations. Story-sharing sessions—around holiday meals or family reunions—preserve covenant memory and inspire successors to trust God for future challenges. Grandparents can serve as spiritual mentors—reading Bible with grandchildren, praying over their gifts, and modeling faithful aging. Financial stewardship—funding college tuition, missions trips, or seminary scholarships—parallels Abraham's gifts to Keturah's sons, supporting independent paths while affirming covenant heritage. Grandparent support groups in churches foster mutual encouragement in legacy building. Legacy writing—recorded interviews, memoirs, or family devotionals—creates tangible heritage for descendants. Encouraging grandchildren to ask "How did God lead you?" fosters listening posture in youth. Grandparents model perseverance through illness, loss, and faith struggles, echoing Abraham's trust through famine and exile. Their presence as living witnesses to God's goodness anchors younger lives in covenant certainty. By blessing grandchildren, grandparents participate in Abraham's multi-generational blessing of all families. Grand-parenting thus becomes final link in family formation chain, anchoring future disciples in ancient promise.

With families grounded in covenant faith, the church's witness extends outward through hospitality—open tents that embody Abrahamic welcome in a fractured world.

12.3 Hospitality as Witness—Open Tents in a Fragmented World

12.3.1 Sacred Meals: Transforming Dining Tables into Mission Fields

The early church's agape feasts combined fellowship, Scripture reading, and Eucharist, magnifying communal bonds much like Abraham's tent meals invited divine encounters (Gen 18:8). Today, Christians can transform ordinary dinner invitations into sacred meals by incorporating simple rituals—blessing bread and wine, reading a Psalm, sharing testimonies. Table conversation can include prayer for guests' needs and exploration of spiritual questions posed by life's challenges. Pop-up community dinners in urban neighborhoods offer entrée to cross-cultural ministry. "Table to Table" initiatives reclaim local hospitality, inviting neighbors to share meals in church hospitality rooms. Hosting at mealtime can dissolve social barriers, model mutual listening, and demonstrate gospel generosity. Intentional meal series—exploring themes like "Breaking Bread with Strangers"—provide structured evangelistic opportunities. Restaurants and cafés become mission hubs when Christians adopt tables as altars of welcome. Virtual dinner parties, using video chat platforms, extend sacred meals across continents, embodying digital hospitality. Meal hosting teams in congregations can rotate responsibilities, ensuring broad participation. Sacred meals thus become tangible enactments of the "I was a stranger and you welcomed me" command (Matt 25:35). By offering food and friendship, believers echo Abraham's table ministry, inviting modern-day angels into their midst. These dinner-table altars shift mission from programs to personal invitations. As guests leave, they carry imprint of grace into local networks, extending Abrahamic blessing beyond church walls.

12.3.2 Welcoming the Stranger: Refugees, Immigrants, and Urban Nomads

Abram's own sojourning status—a foreigner in Canaan—mirrors modern refugees and immigrants seeking safety and belonging. Churches partnering with resettlement agencies provide English classes, housing assistance, and community mentors. Neighborhood churches open their doors as resource hubs, offering legal clinics, health screenings, and cultural orientation. Intercultural hospitality teams trained in trauma care accompany refugee families, affirming their dignity and heritage. Welcoming centers in major cities create safe gathering spaces for urban nomads—migrant workers, itinerant laborers—reflecting Abraham's tent-dwelling care. Congregations adopt individual families, walking alongside them through civic appointments and school enrollment. Story circles allow refugees to share narratives of exile and hope, fostering mutual empathy. Advocacy for just immigration policy ties into covenant obligation to "not oppress the sojourner" (Ex 22:21). Churches also host international student dinners, engaging future global leaders with gospel hospitality. Multiethnic worship services celebrate diversity of God's family, modeling Abraham's tent as mosaic of nations. This practical embrace of strangers becomes living sermon to secular onlookers. By welcoming newcomers, congregations embody Abraham's receive-and-send pattern, offering both relief and invitation into deeper relationship with God. These ministries demonstrate that open tents remain effective vantage points from which God continues to bless all families of the earth.

12.3.3 Digital Hospitality: Extending Abrahamic Welcome Online

In an era of social media and virtual communities, digital platforms become modern tents where believers can practice Abrahamic hospitality. Online small groups host virtual tea times where participants share prayer requests and life updates. Church apps integrate "check-in" features prompting users to pray for newcomers. Live-streamed worship services offer chat rooms where fostering genuine community and personal greeting mirrors tent-door welcome. Pastors host Q&A webinars on faith topics, inviting seekers into dialogical spaces. Digital devotional groups cultivate accountability, akin to regular altar gatherings. Online forums moderated by believers ensure respectful, compassionate conversation—guarding against cynicism prevalent on open-comment platforms. Virtual mission trips, where participants connect with overseas partners through video storytelling, extend global hospitality. Refugees and immigrants access digital resources and support networks via church websites and WhatsApp groups. Christians share Scripture memes and prayer blogs, extending grace through screens. Email newsletters with personal stories and resource links exemplify digital tent-door ministry. Emerging technologies—virtual reality worship spaces—offer immersive gatherings, reflecting open-door ethos in new dimensions. Digital hospitality requires authenticity: timely responses, empathetic listening, and pastoral care in DMs. Online hospitality thus becomes frontier mission field, building bridges across time zones as Abraham did across deserts. By welcoming strangers into digital spaces, believers echo patriarchal hospitality for a networked generation.

Having explored the church's hospitality ethos out- and online, we turn to Abraham's shared heritage with Jews and Muslims, opening avenues for interfaith engagement rooted in the patriarch's legacy.

12.4 Interfaith Engagement—Common Ground with Jews and Muslims

12.4.1 "Children of Abraham" Dialogues: Building Bridges, Not Syncretism

Muslims and Jews alike revere Abraham (Ibrahim, Avraham) as foundational spiritual ancestor, providing natural starting point for interfaith conversation. "Children of Abraham" forums bring multi-faith participants together around shared stories of hospitality, sacrifice, and promise. Careful dialogue respects distinct doctrines—muslim tawhid, Jewish election, Christian incarnation—while celebrating common narratives. Joint reading of Genesis 18 on hospitality fosters mutual understanding and community service projects. Abrahamic Roundtable conferences convene scholars, clergy, and lay leaders to explore how his example informs social justice initiatives. Dialogue guidelines prevent dilution of faith by emphasizing truthful representation rather than doctrinal compromise. Shared rituals—a symbolic lifting of hands in prayer—can affirm shared Abrahamic ethos without theological merging. Interfaith youth camps at former pilgrimage routes (e.g., Hebron) foster relational trust. Abraham's tent symbolizes shared values, yet each tradition retains its unique covenant markers—circumcision for Jews, Hajj for Muslims, baptism for Christians. Co-sponsoring refugee resettlement projects under "Abraham's Table" logos tangibly enacts partnership. Publications like the "Abrahamic Family House" in Abu Dhabi demonstrate architectural embodiment of shared heritage. By focusing on Abraham's virtues—justice, hospitality, faith—dialogues build bridges for collaboration in education and health ministries. This model of engagement moves beyond tolerance to cooperative witness in pluralistic societies, reflecting Abraham's inclusive vision without syncretistic blending. The shared patrimony of Abraham thus becomes foundation for partnerships that honor rather than erase differences.

12.4.2 Shared Ethical Mandates: Charity, Pilgrimage, and Justice

Charity emerges as common imperative: Jews practice tzedakah, Muslims zakat, and Christians almsgiving, all reflecting Abrahamic generosity. Tripartite initiatives—food pantries, medical clinics, microloan programs—invite multi-faith volunteers to serve together, enacting merciful covenant mandates. Pilgrimage frameworks—Jewish journeys to Hebron or Jerusalem, Muslim Hajj commemorating Ibrahim's trials, Christian pilgrimages to sites associated with Abram—become shared educational experiences. Interfaith pilgrim caravans follow Abraham's trade routes, combining archaeological tours with worship gatherings. Justice traditions—Islamic social justice principles (*adl*), Jewish Torah law's protections, and Christian social gospel—coalesce around care for orphans, widows, and sojourners. Collaborative public policy advocacy, grounded in Abrahamic ethics, addresses slavery, human trafficking, and poverty. Shared study of Genesis 12–22 promotes joint moral reflection on land stewardship and hospitality. Ecumenical coalitions use Abrahamic banner to convene conferences on environmental ethics, echoing promise of land for Abraham's seed. Shared fasting days during Ramadan, Yom Kippur, and Lent foster empathic solidarity, reflecting Abraham's intercessory prayers for Sodom. These overlapping rituals, when approached respectfully, strengthen social fabric. By identifying Abrahamic commonalities, communities build trust and amplify impact in relief and development work. This shared ethical platform upholds Abraham's inclusive intention while affirming each faith's distinctive commitments.

12.4.3 Navigating Tensions: Distinct Witness and Mutual Respect

While sharing Abrahamic roots, interfaith partners must acknowledge theological boundaries—Christian belief in Jesus's unique sonship, Jewish covenant exclusivity, Muslim rejection of Trinity. Successful engagement involves articulating one's own convictions clearly and listening attentively to others' beliefs. Conflict resolution workshops sometimes use Beersheba covenant model—exchanging lambs and oaths—to train negotiators in mutual restitution and boundary-setting. When disagreements arise over land claims at Hebron, interfaith committees employ historical expertise to reduce tension, honoring Abraham's purchase of Machpelah as legal precedent for peaceful co-existence. Educational seminars on patriarchal narratives correct misconceptions—cultural literacy prevents inflammatory stereotypes. Leaders agree on common codes of conduct: no proselytizing at shared events, use of neutral language, and celebration of distinct rituals in private worship spaces. Joint statements on moral crises—e.g., climate change or refugee crises—manifest unified Abrahamic witness in public discourse. Interfaith havurot or home fellowships rotate hosts from different traditions, modeling respectful hospitality. Academic partnerships produce resources that treat Abrahamic texts with scholarly rigor and faith sensitivity. This careful navigation ensures that interfaith work does not drift into syncretism or dilute core commitments, yet remains faithful to Abrahamic heritage of blessing all families. The art of distinct yet respectful witness becomes living embodiment of Abram's tent ethos—open doors with firm convictions. Transitioning from hospitality, the next section explores how Abraham's promise fuels the church's global mission.

With interfaith relationships grounded in Abraham's shared heritage, the church's global mission can now draw vision and strategy from the patriarch's expansive blessing to all nations.

12.5 Missional Imagination—Global Church and the Promise to Nations

12.5.1 From Blessing to Sending: Theological Foundations for World Mission

Abram's call came with dual mandate: "I will bless you...and in you all the families of the earth shall be blessed" (Gen 12:2–3). Early church leaders saw in this promise the impetus for mission: God's blessing to Abram becomes sending of gospel to every people group. The missionary impulse flows from receiving divine favor into extending that favor outward, mirroring Abram's outward-bound trek. The Great Commission (Matt 28:19–20) echoes Abram's blessing promise by instructing disciples to make disciples of "all nations." Pauline theology portrays mission as fulfillment of Abram's vision—Gentile inclusion through faith (Gal 3:8). Mission strategy thus grounds itself in patriarchal covenant rather than mere institutional expansion. Cross-cultural teams today draw from Abram's model by establishing "tents" among unreached peoples, learning language and customs before proclaiming Christ. Contextualization reflects Abram's respect for foreign kings' protocols, adapting methods while retaining core message. Long-term partnerships rather than short-term trips honor Abram's sustained presence among Gerar (Gen 20) and Philistia. Mission finances modeled on Abram's wealth-sharing ethic prioritize sustainable community development over one-off giveaways. Prayer remains first frontier: just as Abram built altars at each stop, missionaries establish prayer stations in every people group. Vision casting in local churches now includes Abram's map—from Ur to Canaan—as spiritual paradigm for reaching global frontiers. Theological training integrates Genesis narratives with cross-cultural studies, equipping workers to bridge ancient promise with modern contexts. The sending flow from blessing to sending thus reanimates Abram's mandate for a worldwide church. This foundation transitions naturally into how business and commerce can join missional efforts.

12.5.2 Business as Mission: Leveraging Commerce like Keturah's Sons

Abram's provision of gifts to Keturah's sons (Gen 25:6) ensured their commercial success eastward, illustrating how economic enterprise can seed blessing in new regions. Contemporary bi-vocational missionaries adopt "business as mission" models, starting companies that provide jobs and support gospel witness. These enterprises—coffee exports, IT services, agribusiness—

reflect Midianite trade corridors once served by Keturah's descendants. Ethical business practices modeled on Abram's fair dealings earn credibility among local partners. Profit-sharing and reinvestment in community development demonstrate covenant generosity, akin to Abram's tithe to Melchizedek. Marketplace chaplaincy brings spiritual care to employees, paralleling Abram's tent-door hospitality to travelers. Local partnerships with artisans and farmers mirror Abram's household integration of diverse servants. Marketplace ethics courses draw lessons from Abraham's refusal of Sodom's ill-gotten gains (Gen 14:23). Business networks hosting prayer breakfasts and Scripture memorization groups create modern altar spaces in boardrooms. Impact investments in microfinance reflect Abrahamic wealth-sharing to stretch blessing. Annual trade fairs organized by faith-based firms recapitulate caravan markets where patriarch negotiated water rights. By embedding mission in sustainable commerce, churches uphold Abraham's dual vision of blessing and sending. Success metrics include both financial growth and spiritual multiplication, honoring promise to Jesus: "Freely you have received; freely give" (Matt 10:8). This business as mission approach flows into social justice initiatives rooted in covenant mercy.

12.5.3 Indigenous Expressions: Local Altars, Global Family

Just as Abram built local altars at Shechem, Bethel, and Hebron, modern churches establish contextual worship expressions—dance, song, architecture—that resonate with indigenous cultures. Mission practitioners emphasize contextual theology: gospel truths articulated through local proverbs, symbols, and ceremonies. Indigenous churches adopt Abrahamic altar-building by creating community landmarks—crosses on hilltops, prayer circles under sacred trees—that memorialize divine encounters in native landscapes. Scripture translations employ cultural metaphors—well for living water, tent for spiritual dwelling—to bridge ancient story and local worldview. Leadership development programs train local pastors in both biblical literacy and cultural anthropology, reflecting Abram's blend of faith and cultural engagement. Cross-denominational networks share resources on inculturation, emulating Abraham's alliances with Hethites and Philistines for mutual flourishing. Local expressions of communion incorporate native foods and languages, mirroring Melchizedek's simple bread and wine exchange. Churches in Asia, Africa, and Latin America craft liturgies tied to seasonal rhythms, echoing patriarchal altars aligned with harvest cycles. Indigenous art—murals, fabrics, carvings—depicts Abraham's journey in locally familiar styles, linking global church to ancestral promise. Storytelling circles preserve oral heritage of conversion experiences, akin to patriarchal campfire testimonies. Partnerships between Western and non-Western churches ensure that indigenous expressions are shared, not subsumed, reinforcing global family identity. This mutual enrichment honors Abraham's tent vision: unity in diversity under the banner of faith. As local altars multiply, global church witnesses to the expansive scope of patriarchal blessing. The next section examines how social justice flows from covenant mercy exemplified by Abraham.

12.6 Social Justice—Advocacy Rooted in Covenant Mercy

12.6.1 Rescuing the Captive: Modern Lot-Rescue Analogies

Abram's rescue of Lot from Kedorlaomer's coalition (Gen 14:14–16) provides paradigm for modern advocacy: intervening on behalf of hostages, trafficking victims, and political prisoners. Nonprofit organizations partner with law enforcement to negotiate release of unlawfully detained refugees, reflecting Abram's night raid tactics using intelligence and speed (Gen 14:14). Advocacy coalitions lobby international bodies to secure prisoner exchanges, reminiscent of Abram's diplomatic leverage with local kings. Faith communities pray, fast, and fundraise for captive release campaigns, embodying Abraham's intercessory role for Lot. Survivor care programs offer shelter, counseling, and legal aid to those rescued from exploitation, parallel to Abram's return of captives to their families. Churches adopt "adopt a prisoner" ministries, writing letters of support—modern equivalents of bringing home captive kin. Public awareness events dramatize stories of captivity and rescue, echoing Abram's public reputation boost after his raid (Gen 14:22–24). Advocacy training includes studying biblical narratives of rescue to inspire strategic action. Campaigns against modern slavery—labor, sex, organ trafficking—draw on patriarchal mandate to protect the vulnerable. Abram's righteous intervention models faith-motivated activism that risks personal resources for another's freedom. Partnerships with secular NGOs ensure comprehensive support, honoring covenant mercy extended to all peoples. These "Lot-rescue" analogies show how social justice flows from ancient story into present-day accountability and liberation. As captives gain freedom, communities experience restored dignity and communal blessing promised to Abram's seed. Building on rescue, next subsection explores ethical stewardship of wealth.

12.6.2 Stewarding Wealth: Ethical Giving beyond the Tithe

Abram's tithe to Melchizedek (Gen 14:20) and his refusal of Sodom's spoils (Gen 14:23) model balanced stewardship: giving generously while rejecting ill-gotten gains. Contemporary stewardship programs encourage disproportionate giving—"joyful proportion" rather than legal tithe—reflecting Abraham's voluntary ten percent. Charitable foundations prize transparency, echoing Abram's public tithing record. Churches develop holistic generosity curricula: teaching biblical principles, financial planning, and discernment in investment, paralleling Abram's scrupulous ethics. Impact-investment strategies align portfolios with kingdom values, ensuring wealth circulates into underserved communities. Microfinance programs rooted in community trust model Abram's livestock-for-water exchanges at Beersheba (Gen 21:30–31). Philanthropic networks convene wealthy families to covenantal giving circles, reminiscent of patriarchal household councils. Annual generosity codex celebrations—"Founders Day" or "Blessing Sunday"—commemorate covenant deposit like Abram's star-counting ritual. Financial transparency in church budgets builds trust, similar to Abram's refusal to hide spouses' status. Churches partner with accountability agencies to certify ethical vendor practices, extending Abram's fair dealings to supply chains. Community endowments and scholarship funds secure long-term blessing, mirroring cross-generational covenant promise. Financial training for congregants includes legacy giving and estate planning, ensuring wealth blesses descendants and broadens mission. Through such stewardship, believers live out covenant mercy that transforms personal wealth into communal resource, extending Abram's generosity into modern economies. This economic justice groundwork leads into environmental care, our final justice frontier.

12.6.3 Environmental Care: Land Promise and Creation Stewardship

Abram's respect for Canaanite land—digging wells with permission, negotiating fair purchase of Machpelah (Gen 23:16)—demonstrates early land tenure ethics that modern believers apply in environmental stewardship. Creation care initiatives include sustainable farming cooperatives, reforestation projects, and water-conservation efforts, echoing Abram's well work and tamarisk planting (Gen 21:33). Churches establish community gardens on urban "waste" lots, providing fresh produce and green spaces, paralleling Abram's oasis-style encampments. Environmental education programs teach children to honor creation as God's gift, reflecting Abram's stewardship of flocks across diverse pastures. Faith-based policy advocacy addresses climate justice, lobbying governments for protections of vulnerable regions—akin to Abram's defense of land rights in Gerar and

Hebron. Renewable energy projects funded by church partnerships mirror Abram's willingness to invest resources into future generations. Eco-theology workshops highlight biblical themes of Sabbath rest and land redemption, drawing direct lines to Genesis narrative. Habitat restoration efforts in degraded river valleys recall Abram's early oasis diplomacy in Egypt's Nile basin. Water purification and distribution programs for underserved regions echo his famine-driven migrations and wells dug along migration routes. Conferences like "Green Faith Summit" bring together theologians, scientists, and activists to commission environmental covenant commitments. Church property management incorporates green buildings and biodiversity corridors, living in harmony with land promise. Through these environmental justice actions, contemporary believers embody covenant mercy, ensuring that Earth flourishes for all Abram's descendants—human and non-human alike. This care for creation sets stage for leadership models drawn from Abram's household governance.

As creation care flows from covenant stewardship, we turn to spiritual leadership in communities, exploring how Abram's tent model informs shepherding, mentoring, and peacemaking in church life.

12.7 Spiritual Leadership—Elders, Mentors, and Faith Communities

12.7.1 Shepherding Flocks: Servant Leadership after the Tent Model

Abram led a large household—600 trained men (Gen 14:14)—exercising leadership that combined pastoral care, strategic oversight, and humble service. Modern spiritual leaders adopt "tent shepherding" principles: moving among congregants rather than ruling from a distant office. Elders host prayer gatherings in living rooms, reflecting Abram's open-air meetings under oaks. Pastors prioritize relational presence—home visits, hospital chaplaincy, and mentorship—pari passu with administrative duties. Leadership training programs emphasize listening skills, empathy, and servant-hearted humility drawn from Abram's intercessory role. Coaching models apply questions like "How can I bless you?" mirroring Abram's hospitality posture. Team leadership in churches replicates Abram's delegation to trusted lieutenants, ensuring shared responsibility. Conflict-resolution protocols reference Abram's negotiations (Gen 14, Gen 21), teaching peacemaking through covenantal dialogue and fair compensation. Leadership retreats at tent-camp sites use wilderness contexts to recalibrate vision, echoing Abram's Fiery-Torch theophanies. Churches employ "tent anniversaries" to celebrate communal journey and spur prayer for next season. This tent model fosters flexible, adaptive leadership ready for changing cultural climates. Ethical accountability structures—multiple elders, transparency, rotating facilitators—prevent concentration of power. Through servant leadership inspired by Abram, faith communities become safe flocks under godly shepherds. This pastoral ethos flows into mentoring next generation of leaders.

12.7.2 Mentoring Timothys: Inter-Generational Transfer of Vision

Just as Abraham invested in servant-leaders among his household (Gen 17:9), spiritual leadership flourishes through mentoring relationships. Seasoned leaders tutor emerging pastors in prayer-walking and altar-building, passing on practical insights learned over decades. Intentional "Timothy programs" pair young adults with mentors who guide them in theological study, pastoral care, and risk-taking faith moves. Mentorship covenant includes regular meetings, shared retreats, and milestone celebrations—a spiritual counterpart to Abram's altars marking covenant moments. Reverse mentoring enriches seniors with technological literacy and cultural fluency. Churches establish leadership pipelines: interns shadow experience-rich leaders, progressively assuming greater responsibility. Annual "calling weekends" encourage mentees to discern God's voice, echoing Abram's vocational leap. Mentor networks hold each other accountable, forming patriarchal circles of wisdom and prayer. Written "legacy letters" capture mentor insights, ensuring Abram-style wisdom arch exists beyond living memory. Multiplication is key: one mentor trains two mentees, creating exponential leadership growth like star-counting promise. Public recognition of mentor-mentee bonds fosters community culture valuing inter-generational faithfulness. This mentorship reflects Abraham's vision for covenant seed flourishing across ages. Equipped leaders then step into arenas of conflict navigation.

12.7.3 Conflict Navigation: Beersheba-Style Peacemaking in Church Life

At Beersheba, Abram and Abimelech negotiated water rights through gifts, oaths, and tree-planting, resolving disputes without violence (Gen 21:25–31). Churches apply similar peacemaking models: in congregation conflicts, leaders facilitate gift exchanges— shared resources or service acts—as gestures of goodwill. Conflict-resolution teams engage disputing parties in public and private covenant renewal, echoing Abram's public oath and sacrificial meal. "Peacemaking trees"—commemorative planting events—symbolize new beginnings after reconciliation. Mediators trained in both psychological counseling and biblical justice guide processes reminiscent of patriarchal courtesy negotiations. Agreements are recorded, signed by congregational elders and disputants, providing accountability like Ephron's purchase deeds (Gen 23:17). Worship services include liturgical confession and restoration prayers, embedding reconciliation within corporate altar. Conflict resolution workshops reference Abram's refusal to sequester wealth from neighbors, highlighting transparency's role in trust restoration. Teams review conflict oaths quarterly, ensuring relational health akin to covenant renewals. Churches partner with community peace centers to share Abrahamic negotiation wisdom with local organizations. These processes prevent factionalism and preserve unity, modeling Abram's successful dispute resolution. As disputes settle, communities transition into worship renewal and outward mission. Thus, Beersheba-style peacemaking becomes blueprint for sustaining congregational harmony and extending covenant mercy beyond church walls.

With leadership equipped for shepherding, mentoring, and peacemaking, believers can embark on physical and inner pilgrimages that echo Abraham's sacred geography.

12.8 Pilgrimage and Place—Rediscovering Sacred Geography

12.8.1 Physical Pilgrimages: Hebron, Jerusalem, and Contemporary Tours

Modern pilgrims retrace Abram's footsteps by visiting ancient sites—Hebron's Machpelah cave, Bethel's altar mound, Shechem's oak hill—turning personal travel into spiritual pilgrimage. Guided tours incorporate archaeological briefings, Scripture readings at each site, and reflective journaling under the trees Abraham once worshiped. Local guides share both historical scholarship and faith testimonies, deepening connection to patriarchal landscape. Pilgrim groups fast before entering significant locations, echoing Abram's fasting before covenant events. Worship services at dusk beneath ancient stones recreate altar-smoke ambiance. Pilgrimage itineraries often include corporate acts of service—visiting local orphanages or environmental cleanups—expressing covenant mercy in situ. Retreat pastors lead daily devotions tied to specific geographic "waypoints," aligning inner and outer journeys. Virtual reality apps augment on-site experiences, overlaying Genesis narratives onto present terrain for immersive engagement. Pilgrims return with artifacts—small stones, olive branches—serving as tangible altar reminders for home sanctuaries. Travel memoirs and blog reflections share lessons from Abraham's sites, encouraging wider pilgrimage participation. Partnerships with local communities ensure respectful access and mutual benefit. Pilgrims' offerings support site preservation, reflecting Abram's stewardship ethic. Physical pilgrimages thus become living classrooms where ancient promise meets contemporary devotion. As journeys conclude, pilgrims often embark on inner retreats.

12.8.2 Inner Journeys: Labyrinths, Retreats, and Wilderness Spirituality

Abraham's years wandering Canaan's wilderness inspire modern inner journeys—retreats in silence, labyrinth walks, and wilderness solitude. Christian retreat centers use labyrinth designs based on Abram's star-counting circle as pathways for meditation on promise (Gen 15:5). Guided silent retreats in deserts or forests mirror Abram's lonely communion with God beyond urban distractions. Spiritual directors employ exercises like "living tent" imagery, inviting retreatants to inhabit spiritual spaces of openness and hospitality. Workshops on "wilderness mapping" help believers chart personal spiritual topography—places of fear, promise, and encounter. Psalm-and-prayer vigils at dawn evoke Abram's altar-building at first light. Nature-based contemplative practices— stargazing and sand-drawing—connect to Abram's cosmic promise under Canaan skies. Retreatants keep "altar journals," recording divine words heard in stillness. Monastic traditions of desert fathers are revitalized in urban contexts through "inner desert" modules in prayer labs. Inner journey courses integrate biblical teaching with psychological insights on journey transitions. Participants learn to recognize godly invitations to "go forth" amid life's ambiguities. These inner pilgrimages equip believers for external mission and personal resilience. Like Abram emerging from wilderness with renewed conviction, retreatants return to daily rhythms with fresh faith. The inner journey thus prepares hearts for the next step—creating urban altars.

12.8.3 Urban Altars: Creating Spaces of Encounter in Secular Cities

Abram built altars wherever he sojourned, sanctifying ordinary terrain. In post-Christendom contexts, urban churches replicate this by identifying and transforming public spaces—vacant lots, parks, sidewalks—into "altar points." Pop-up rooftops host prayer gatherings at sunrise, echoing Abram's highland altars. Street prayer tents in business districts offer brief prayer and Scripture to hurried passersby. Church art installations—stone cairns or interactive sculpture—serve as visual altars inviting reflection. Community garden plots adjacent to worship spaces become living altars of creation care. Night prayer walk routes map urban landmarks, with participants pausing at each site for scripture reading. Digital installations—QR codes linked to narrated devotionals at city murals—extend urban altar concept into cyberspace. Annual "altar festivals" bring together artists, theologians, and citizens to co-create worship experiences in public squares. Mobile prayer vans equipped with minimal liturgical furnishings bring altars to neighborhoods lacking church presence. Partnerships with municipal authorities legitimize these spaces, preventing legal obstacles. Urban altars thus incarnate Abram's tent ethos amidst concrete landscapes, inviting God's presence into everyday city life. These sanctified urban points serve as helpers for discipleship and community transformation, closing circle from ancient hills to modern skylines.

Having explored how pilgrimages shape modern faith, the final chapter's next section will consider suffering and perseverance as the crucible for living Abrahamic hope.

12.9 Suffering and Perseverance—Faith under Fire

12.9.1 Dark-Night Seasons: Holding Promise through Delays and Losses

Abram endured famines, exiled from Egypt's courts (Gen 12:10–20), and faced estrangement from Lot—dark-night seasons that tested his trust. Contemporary believers encounter analogous trials: chronic illness, financial collapse, grief over lost relationships. These seasons often feel like silence rather than audible promises, yet Abram's journey teaches that God's word remains active deep within the soul. Spiritual directors encourage "lament-lamentation" prayers, pouring honest heart cries before God as Abram did when installing altars after each deliverance (Gen 13:4). Small-group support networks function like Abram's household, offering shared hospitality and narrative retelling of past mercies to buoy hope. Pastors preach series on characters like Hagar and Isaac to normalize fear and foster empathy. Faithful reading of Hebrews 12:11 helps believers recognize that "no discipline seems enjoyable at the time, but painful" yet yields "peaceful fruit of righteousness." Retreat ministries offer specific "dark-night" programming—silent walks, contemplative art, guided journaling—to navigate brokenness. Spiritual formation curricula incorporate ancient practices—fasting and solitude—so believers learn to encounter God without external comfort. Pastoral counseling draws from Abram's covenant-cutting ceremony (Gen 15), teaching that marking trials with symbols—stones, artwork—anchors future remembrance of God's faithfulness. Sermons on Psalm 27:14—"Wait for the Lord; be strong, and let your heart take courage"—are grounded in Abram's example of waiting decades for Isaac. Testimonies from seasoned saints who have seen promises fulfilled after long delays encourage perseverance in younger generations. Churches might host "Promise Remembrance" services where congregants share delayed answers to prayer, fostering communal resilience. These practices help transform dark-night seasons into crucibles of deeper trust, aligning modern suffering with Abram's pilgrimage of faith. As individuals pour out their doubts, communities prepare for the next step of sacrificial trust.

12.9.2 Sacrificial Trust: Modern "Moriah" Decisions in Career and Calling

Abram's willingness to sacrifice Isaac (Gen 22:1–14) stands as the ultimate test of devotion, inviting believers to identify their own "Moriah" moments where priorities clash: career advancement versus family call, profitable enterprise versus ethical conviction. Contemporary leaders may face boardroom ultimatums that force them to choose principle over profit, echoing Abram's decision to obey God at great personal cost. Nonprofit founders wrestle with decisions to allocate resources toward expectation-shattering initiatives—new church plants or justice projects—mirroring Abram's trust that God would provide a substitute. Healthcare professionals navigate dilemmas about end-of-life care, trusting conscience and covenant love over institutional pressure. Artists risk reputation and security to create truth-telling work, honoring Abram's obedience even when facing inner grief. Mentorship cohorts gather to pray through vocational crossroads, employing spiritual discernment tools—lectio divina, prophetic counsel—akin to Abram's listening posture by altar smoke. Retreat settings re-enact Mount Moriah through dramatized decision-making exercises, prompting participants to script "If God calls me to…" statements. Business ethics seminars draw on the sacrificial model, teaching board members to invest in underprivileged communities despite uncertain ROI. Pastors preach sermon series on "What's in your hand?" (Ex 4:2) to help congregants discern God's provision amid sacrificial calling. Financial stewardship groups discuss radical generosity models, paralleling Abram's readiness to give up Isaac. Creativity labs encourage entrepreneurs to pitch ventures that risk capital for social impact. Counseling ministries offer safe spaces to explore fears of "losing Isaac"—children's faith, relational stability—helping families consider sacrificial faith responses. Each modern Moriah decision becomes rite of passage, forging character and confirming that God's provision surpasses human calculation. These sacrificial trusts flow into the hope of resurrection that sustains believers beyond sacrifice.

12.9.3 Hope of Resurrection: Living toward the "Better Country"

After Abraham's faith-tested ascent, God provided Isaac back— "figuratively speaking, he did receive him back" (Heb 11:19)— foreshadowing resurrection. Modern Christians anchor ultimate hope not in earthly outcomes but in promised new creation—"the better country" (Heb 11:16). Hospice chaplains guide families toward peace by linking final moments to resurrection hope, echoing Abram's confidence in the life-beyond. Pastoral care integrates funeral rituals with declarations of shared future gathering in heavenly city. Worship songs echo themes of rising, restoring, and reunion—"Even so, come, Lord Jesus." The global church celebrates All Saints' Day by remembering departed heirs, affirming communal hope in God's life-after-death promise first hinted at Moriah. Sermons convict congregants to invest not only in temporal programs but in eternal souls, aligning ambition with resurrection reality. Evangelism training emphasizes urgency—"today is the day of salvation"—rooted in the reality of eternal promise. Christian education curricula incorporate studies on eschatology and hope, helping young believers navigate secular skepticism about life after death. Art-therapy workshops employ Moriah imagery—ram and rock—to facilitate grief processing toward hope. Intercessory prayer gatherings focus on global emergence of resurrected life in Christ's body, embodying Abram's seed-promise universality. Pastors model resilience by sharing personal near-loss stories and subsequent "resurrection" experiences of new ministry fruit. By keeping eyes fixed on the better country—city whose architect is God—believers persevere through global crises. Thus resurrection hope sustains churches in every sacrificial moment, linking modern faith to Abram's ancient victory.

From hope of resurrection we expand into the realm where faith meets science, exploring how Abraham's star-counting wonder inspires modern seekers under contemporary skies.

12.10 Faith and Science—Stars, Sand, and the Awe of Discovery

12.10.1 Cosmology and Covenant: Wonder beneath Modern Skies

 Abram's gaze at the night sky—"Look toward heaven, and number the stars, if you are able" (Gen 15:5)—invites believers to view modern astronomy as worship. Planetariums host "Covenant Under the Stars" events where scientists and pastors jointly present insights on cosmic origins alongside reflections on divine promise. Laypeople learn how discoveries of exoplanets, cosmic background radiation, and expansive galaxies deepen rather than threaten faith. Backyard telescope nights become spiritual disciplines: participants read Genesis passages outdoors, marveling at God's creative power. Sermon series link Big Bang cosmology with doctrine of creation, showing that scientific epochs align with theological narrative of "Let there be light." University chaplaincies host science-faith dialogues exploring ethical implications of astrophysical research. Church libraries curate interdisciplinary resources—books by astrophysicists-turned-theologians—bridging data and devotion. Pilgrimages to observatories combine spiritual retreats with stargazing workshops. Citizen science programs engage believers in data collection on meteor showers and satellite trails, offering hands-on cosmic stewardship. Children's ministries use simple star maps to teach covenant promises, fostering wonder and obedience. Worship songs incorporate cosmic imagery, declaring "Maker of the

365

stars, grant me faith to see Your covenant." These practices affirm that faith and science complement under the same sky Abram once counted, cultivating humility and curiosity. As congregations look up, their hearts expand with promise, preparing them to wrestle ethically with bioinnovations ahead.

12.10.2 Bioethics of Promise: Reproductive Technologies and Trust

Abram's miracle birth of Isaac at Sarah's advanced age (Gen 21:1–7) poses profound questions for reproductive ethics today. Churches convene bioethics panels to address IVF, surrogacy, and gene editing through covenantal lenses, affirming life's sanctity and God's timing. Medical ministries partner with fertility counseling centers to offer spiritual and emotional support, integrating prayer into clinical pathways. Seminars on "Sarah's laughter in the lab" explore how faith communities navigate the tension between trusting God and using medical means. Statement papers articulate theological frameworks for accepting or declining specific technologies, ensuring congregational clarity. Pastoral teams develop support groups for couples facing infertility, providing hope rooted in Abram's patient waiting. Ethical guidelines discuss research on CRISPR and germline editing with deference to stewardship rather than dominion. Genetic counselors collaborate with church leaders to offer pro-life and pro-technology considerations balanced by covenant ethics from Genesis. Youth ministry curricula discuss "Who counts as seed?" in light of in-vitro conception, echoing seed-promise discussions in Galatians 3. Local hospital chaplains provide spiritual care during reproductive procedures, reflecting Abram's care for family continuity. By anchoring bioethical debates in Abrahamic promise narratives, faith communities navigate modern dilemmas with biblical grounding. This engagement with life sciences connects seamlessly to concerns for creation as a whole.

12.10.3 Environmental Astronomy: Stewarding the Heavens Abraham Counted

The "heavens declare the glory of God" (Ps 19:1) resonates with Abram's star count, prompting Christians to consider environmental ethics extending beyond Earth. Space agencies and faith groups collaborate on satellite-based climate monitoring, employing technology to safeguard planetary health. Churches advocate for responsible disposal of space debris, aligning with Abram's respect for promised land by refusing pollution. Educational initiatives encourage youth to explore astronomy ethically, integrating cosmic perspective with creation care. Science outreach programs for urban schools bring portable planetariums, teaching both astrophysics and the biblical wonder of God's covenant. Interdisciplinary forums discuss the theology of space exploration—paralleling Abram's journey into unknown territories. Art installations in planetariums depict Abram and Isaac under starry skies, blending mythos and cosmos. Faith communities support funding for sustainable rocket fuels and planetary science missions mindful of environmental impact. Global prayer networks host synchronized "pray for the skies" events during meteor showers, uniting believers in cosmic stewardship. Astronaut chaplaincy programs incorporate devotional modules on covenant and cosmos, ministering to spacefarers. Environmental astronomy thus extends Abram's skyward faith into proactive cosmic care, reminding believers that covenant stewardship encompasses all creation—from sand beneath feet to stars overhead. This cosmic responsibility transitions into cultural expressions of Abraham's legacy.

12.11 Cultural Portraits—Abraham in Art, Film, and Popular Imagination

12.11.1 Visual Arts: From Caravaggio to Contemporary Icons

Caravaggio's dramatic "Sacrifice of Isaac" captures tension of the Akedah, while Rembrandt's softer light emphasizes divine mercy— testaments to how artists have interpreted Abraham across centuries. Contemporary painters use mixed media to depict Abram's tents as transparent overlays on urban skylines, symbolizing faith's relevance in modern contexts. Church sanctuaries commission stained-glass windows illustrating Abram's journey: the star-counting scene twinkles with colored glass, inviting meditative wonder. Public art projects repurpose industrial scrap into abstract altars, recalling Abram's transformed landscapes. Museum exhibits juxtapose ancient Near Eastern artifacts with Abrahamic narrative art, inviting dialogues on historical context. Street-art murals in diverse neighborhoods portray Abram welcoming diverse strangers, reflecting hospitality themes. Faithful photographers document pilgrimage groups at Machpelah, creating exhibitions that bring biblical narrative into contemporary gaze. Digital artists craft virtual reality experiences of Abram's altars, merging technology with worship. Graphic novelists retell Genesis stories with cultural sensitivity, engaging younger audiences. Sculptors create interactive installations: stone cairns visitors can add to, echoing Abram's altar stones. Galleries host "Portraits of Promise" series featuring artists' responses to covenant themes. These visual arts engagements help congregations see Abraham's story anew, transitioning into cinematic portrayals.

12.11.2 Cinema Narratives: Evaluating Accuracy and Inspiration

Films like Cecil B. DeMille's "The Ten Commandments" and "Abraham" (1993) dramatize the patriarch's trials for wide audiences, though occasionally embellishing details for narrative effect. Contemporary Christian filmmakers produce indie features focusing on Abram's relational dynamics—marriage tensions with Sarah, interactions with Lot—to inspire faith audiences. Film discussion guides help viewers discern between historical-biblical fidelity and creative license, prompting critical engagement. Churches host movie nights followed by panel discussions with theologians and historians, unpacking thematic accuracies. Screenwriting workshops teach emerging writers to adapt Genesis narratives responsibly, balancing storytelling with respect for text. Documentaries like "Footsteps of Abraham" interweave archaeology and theology, grounding cinematic storytelling in scholarly evidence. Film festivals curated by faith organizations showcase short films on Abrahamic themes—hospitality, promise, sacrifice—encouraging new artistic voices. Critics evaluate representation of female figures—Sarah's agency or Hagar's trauma—to foster nuanced portrayals. Cinematic scores incorporate ancient-inspired motifs, connecting music and scriptural emotional landscapes. Virtual screenings expand reach to remote communities, creating shared viewing experiences. Film-based small groups study the patriarch's character under guided questions: "What did Abraham risk? What does that inspire in us?" This cinematic engagement primes hearts for literary and musical expressions of Abraham's legacy.

12.11.3 Literature and Music: Patriarchal Themes in Global Storytelling

Writers from diverse cultures weave Abrahamic motifs into novels, poems, and plays: the motif of the journey appears in African diaspora literature as metaphor for identity search; Middle Eastern poets evoke tents as symbols of hospitality and exile. Christian authors produce devotional poetry collections themed on Abraham's stars and wells, offering verse for liturgical seasons. In musical theater, stage adaptations of Genesis scenes—Abram's call, the Akedah, altars at Bethel—integrate original compositions that blend ancient melodies with contemporary harmonies. Gospel choirs perform spirituals reimagining Isaac's near-sacrifice as allegory of deliverance, linking African American heritage to Abrahamic faith. Worship songwriters craft choruses based on "God of Abraham,

Isaac, and Jacob," uniting congregations across denominations. Global hymnals include translations of "All People That on Earth Do Dwell," reflecting universal covenant themes. Indie bands produce concept albums tracing Abraham's life arc, fusing folk-rock narratives with scriptural exposition. Story circles at readings allow community responses to Abrahamic literature, fostering deeper engagement. Literary festivals feature panels on Abraham's influence in world literature, exploring intertextual echoes in postcolonial works. Music ministries host "Promise Concerts," blending orchestral and choral pieces inspired by Genesis. Through these creative media, Abraham's story permeates public imagination, equipping believers to carry forward his legacy into the final future chapters.

As cultural expressions amplify Abraham's narrative, we now turn to the horizon—emerging generations and technologies that will shape the next phase of covenant living.

12.12 Forward Look—Living the Promise into the Future

12.12.1 Emerging Generations: Gen Z and the Call of Pilgrim Faith

Generation Z, shaped by digital nativity and global crises, resonates with Abram's tent-dwelling pilgrimage and uncertainty. Youth ministry leaders craft "Digital Pilgrimage" programs where students trace Abram's journey through interactive apps, fostering resilience in evolving cultural landscapes. Social media campaigns— #StepOutLikeAbram—encourage young adults to post stories of faith-risking obedience. Mentorship networks pair Gen Zers with Abram-style mentors for life-calling discernment, bridging tradition and innovation. Urban campus churches create micro-community "tents" where students gather for hospitality and mission planning. Incubator programs support Gen Z social entrepreneurs who launch ethical startups echoing Abram's commerce-as-testimony. Prayer groups on college campuses adopt ancient Hebrew chants, connecting students across time. Mental-health initiatives integrate spiritual disciplines—Sabbath rest, altar journaling—to combat burnout, modeling Abram's rest-stop altars. Leadership retreats in nature recreate Abram's wilderness sojourns for digital natives starved for embodied experience. Vocational discernment courses use Abram's journey as case study in aligning gifts with gospel assignment. As Gen Z shapes tomorrow's church, Abram's pioneering faith provides enduring roadmap for walking into unknown future. These initiatives flow into digital nomadism shaped by technology.

12.12.2 Technology and Nomadism: Virtual Tents, Global Tribes

Just as Abram's tent hosted diverse sojourners across Canaan, digital platforms host global tribes united by shared faith rather than geography. Online communities use virtual reality "tents"— immersive worship spaces where avatars gather for prayer, Scripture study, and fellowship. Blockchain-based covenant contracts enable transparent sharing of mission funds, echoing Abram's silver-shekel purchase records. AI–driven devotional apps personalize altar prompts, guiding users through prayer rhythms tuned to Abram's altar sequence. Digital nomads—remote workers and missionaries—form decentralized "tent networks" to gather spontaneously for hospitality and mission planning. Virtual pilgrimage platforms allow avatars to traverse 3D reconstructions of Abram's sites, fostering global participation despite travel restrictions. Webinars hosted at "campfire"-style backdrops encourage cross-cultural dialogue on Abrahamic themes. Church leadership develops protocols for theological engagement in metaverse spaces, ensuring covenant integrity online. Digital liturgies integrate Abram's star-counting as nightly reminders on smart devices. Podcast series titled "Tents and Tribes" interview global believers on applying Abram's journey in digital age. Virtual mentorship platforms connect youth to elder Abram-style guides across continents. These technological "tents" expand frontier mission fields, embodying Abram's inclusive vision in cyberspace. Technology thus amplifies Abrahamic hospitality and mission, moving seamlessly into eschatological hope.

12.12.3 Maranatha Hope: Awaiting the City with Foundations

Abraham's longing for "the city that has foundations, whose builder and maker is God" (Heb 11:10) becomes our Maranatha hope—Christ's return to consummate promise. Eschatological conferences explore how Abram's tent-bearing faith points toward permanent city where war and tears cease. Advent sermons and hymns weave Abramic themes into expectancy of new heavens and earth. Creation care movements frame environmental restoration as rehearsal for cosmic renewal. Artistic expressions—murals, virtual galleries—depict Abrahamic altars within heavenly city, inspiring present-day worship. Global prayer networks observe "Night of Tears" before Easter, echoing patriarchal sorrow yet anticipating resurrection joy. Liturgical calendars integrate Abraham's feast days—tent-raising anniversaries—into church year as markers of hope. Pastoral letters encourage congregations to invest in eternal things—word, deed, relationship—rather than transit worlds. Mission agencies finalize strategies knowing ultimate destination is not cultural transformation alone but participation in God's eschatological domain. Small groups study Revelation alongside Genesis 12–22, tracing narrative arcs from Abrahmic promise to Jerusalem descending. Families craft "promise jars" where members record glimpses of God's unfolding covenant, reading them around Advent wreaths. The Maranatha hope fuels perseverance, reminding believers that every step of obedience draws nearer to God's city with unshakable foundations. As Abraham's legacy marches into eternity, contemporary disciples live in light of final fulfillment, ready to greet Maker of tent and city alike.

372

Conclusion Abraham's tents are long folded, yet their flaps keep swinging open in every era that dares to believe promise over predictability. His life reminds contemporary followers of Jesus that the call of God still sounds like verbs—go, build, bless, share, wait. When faith communities practice such verbs, they turn dining rooms into altars, boardrooms into rescue sites, and global networks into extended households of grace. Like their forefather, they discover that risk is the native language of covenant love and that God's fidelity always outruns human frailty. Looking ahead, disciples carry Abraham's compass—fixed on the city with foundations—as they navigate technological upheavals, interfaith conversations, and ecological stewardship. Thus the patriarch's legacy remains vastly present: a summons to journeying trust that enlarges the world with blessing until the day every nation gathers in the promised city whose architect and builder is God.

www.ingramcontent.com/pod-product-compliance
Lightning Source LLC
LaVergne TN
LVHW051540080426
835510LV00020B/2793